T0184059

Lecture Notes in Computer Science   11534

Commenced Publication in 1973
Founding and Former Series Editors:
Gerhard Goos, Juris Hartmanis, and Jan van Leeuwen

More information about this series at http://www.springer.com/series/7411

José Pereira · Laura Ricci (Eds.)

Distributed Applications and Interoperable Systems

19th IFIP WG 6.1 International Conference, DAIS 2019
Held as Part of the 14th International Federated Conference
on Distributed Computing Techniques, DisCoTec 2019
Kongens Lyngby, Denmark, June 17–21, 2019
Proceedings

 Springer

Editors
José Pereira (ID)
INESC TEC and University of Minho
Braga, Portugal

Laura Ricci (ID)
University of Pisa
Pisa, Italy

ISSN 0302-9743   ISSN 1611-3349 (electronic)
Lecture Notes in Computer Science
ISBN 978-3-030-22495-0   ISBN 978-3-030-22496-7 (eBook)
https://doi.org/10.1007/978-3-030-22496-7

LNCS Sublibrary: SL5 – Computer Communication Networks and Telecommunications

This Springer imprint is published by the registered company Springer Nature Switzerland AG
The registered company address is: Gewerbestrasse 11, 6330 Cham, Switzerland

Foreword

The 14th International Federated Conference on Distributed Computing Techniques (DisCoTec) took place in Kongens Lyngby, Denmark, during June 17–21, 2019. It was organized by the Department of Applied Mathematics and Computer Science at the Technical University of Denmark.

The DisCoTec series is one of the major events sponsored by the International Federation for Information Processing (IFIP). It comprised three conferences:

- COORDINATION, the IFIP WG 6.1 21st International Conference on Coordination Models and Languages
- DAIS, the IFIP WG 6.1 19th International Conference on Distributed Applications and Interoperable Systems
- FORTE, the IFIP WG 6.1 39th International Conference on Formal Techniques for Distributed Objects, Components and Systems

Together, these conferences cover a broad spectrum of distributed computing subjects, ranging from theoretical foundations and formal description techniques to systems research issues.

In addition to the individual sessions of each conference, the event included several plenary sessions that gathered attendants from the three conferences. This year, the general chair and the DisCoTec Steering Committee joined the three DisCoTec conferences in the selection and nomination of the plenary keynote speakers, whose number was accordingly increased from the traditional three to five. The five keynote speakers and the title of their talks are listed below:

- Prof. David Basin (ETH Zürich, Switzerland) – "Security Protocols: Model Checking Standards"
- Dr. Anne-Marie Kermarrec (Inria Rennes, France) – "Making Sense of Fast Big Data"
- Prof. Marta Kwiatkowska (University of Oxford, UK) – "Versatile Quantitative Modelling: Verification, Synthesis and Data Inference for Cyber-Physical Systems"
- Prof. Silvio Micali (MIT, USA) – "ALGORAND – The Distributed Ledger for the Borderless Economy"
- Prof. Martin Wirsing (LMU, Germany) – "Toward Formally Designing Collective Adaptive Systems"

As is traditional in DisCoTec, an additional joint session with the best papers from each conference was organized. The best papers were:

- "Representing Dependencies in Event Structures" by G. Michele Pinna (Coordination)
- "FOUGERE: User-Centric Location Privacy in Mobile Crowdsourcing Apps" by Lakhdar Meftah, Romain Rouvoy and Isabelle Chrisment (DAIS)

- "Psi-Calculi Revisited: Connectivity and Compositionality" by Johannes Åman Pohjola (FORTE)

Associated with the federated event were also two satellite events that took place:

- ICE, the 12th International Workshop on Interaction and Concurrency Experience
- DisCoRail, the First International Workshop on Distributed Computing in Future Railway Systems

I would like to thank the Program Committee chairs of the different events for their help and cooperation during the preparation of the conference, and the Steering Committee and Advisory Boards of DisCoTec and their conferences for their guidance and support. The organization of DisCoTec 2019 was only possible thanks to the dedicated work of the Organizing Committee, including Francisco "Kiko" Fernández Reyes and Francesco Tiezzi (publicity chairs), Maurice ter Beek, Valerio Schiavoni, and Andrea Vandin (workshop chairs), Ann-Cathrin Dunker (logistics and finances), as well as all the students and colleagues who volunteered their time to help. Finally, I would like to thank IFIP WG 6.1 for sponsoring this event, Springer's *Lecture Notes in Computer Science* team for their support and sponsorship, EasyChair for providing the reviewing infrastructure, the Nordic IoT Hub for their sponsorship, and the Technical University of Denmark for providing meeting rooms and additional support.

June 2019   Alberto Lluch Lafuente

Preface

This volume contains the papers presented at DAIS 2019, the 19th IFIP International Conference on Distributed Applications and Interoperable Systems, sponsored by the IFIP (International Federation for Information Processing) and organized by the IFIP Working Group 6.1. The DAIS conference series addresses all practical and conceptual aspects of distributed applications, including their design, modeling, implementation and operation, the supporting middleware, appropriate software engineering methodologies and tools, as well as experimental studies and applications.

DAIS 2019 was held during June 17–21, 2019, in Kongens Lyngby, Denmark, as part of DisCoTec, the 12th International Federated Conference on Distributed Computing Techniques. There were 28 submissions for DAIS. Each submission was reviewed by four Program Committee (PC) members. The review process included an in-depth discussion phase, during which the merits of all papers were discussed by the PC. The committee decided to accept nine full papers and two short papers.

Accepted papers address challenges in multiple application areas, such as the Internet of Things, cloud and edge computing, and mobile systems. A number of papers focus on middleware for managing concurrency and consistency in distributed systems, including data replication and transactions. There is also an emphasis on distributed systems security, including the evaluation and application of trusted execution environments and applications of blockchain technology.

The conference was made possible by the work and cooperation of many people working in several committees and organizations that are listed in these proceedings. In particular, we thank the Program Committee members for their commitment and thorough reviews and for their active participation in the discussion phase, and all the external reviewers for their help in evaluating submissions. Finally, we also thank the DisCoTec general chair, Alberto Lluch Lafuente, and the DAIS Steering Committee chair, Rui Oliveira, for their constant availability, support, and guidance.

June 2019

José Pereira
Laura Ricci

Organization

Steering Committee

Alysson Bessani	Universidade de Lisboa, Portugal
Sara Bouchenak	INSA Lyon, France
Lydia Y. Chen	IBM Research Zurich Lab, Switzerland
Jim Dowling	Swedish Institute of Computer Science, Kista, Sweden
Frank Eliassen	University of Oslo, Norway
Pascal Felber	Université de Neuchâtel, Switzerland
Karl M. Goeschka	FH Technikum Wien, Austria
Evangelia Kalyvianaki	University of Cambridge, UK
Rüdiger Kapitza	Technical University of Braunschweig, Germany
Kostas Magoutis	FORTH-ICS, Greece
Rui Oliveira (Chair)	Universidade do Minho, Portugal
Peter Pietzuch	Imperial College London, UK
Hans P. Reiser	University of Passau, Germany
Romain Rouvoy	University of Lille 1, France
François Taiani	Université de Rennes 1, France

Program Committee

Sonia Ben Mokhtar	LIRIS CNRS, France
Silvia Bonomi	Sapienza University of Rome, Italy
Sara Bouchenak	INSA Lyon, France
Manuel Bravo	IMDEA Software Institute, Madrid, Spain
Frank Eliassen	University of Oslo, Norway
Mohammed Erradi	ENSIAS Rabat, Morocco
David Eyers	University of Otago, New Zealand
Davide Frey	Inria, France
Barbara Guidi	University of Pisa, Italy
Jordi Guitart	Universitat Politècnica de Catalunya, Spain
Mark Jelasity	University of Szeged, Hungary
Vana Kalogeraki	Athens University of Economics and Business, Greece
Boris Koldehofe	TU Darmstadt, Germany
Mark Little	RedHat, UK
Kostas Magoutis	University of Ioannina and FORTH-ICS, Greece
Miguel Matos	INESC-ID and IST Universidade de Lisboa, Portugal
Ibéria Medeiros	LaSIGE, Universidade de Lisboa, Portugal
Claudio Antares Mezzina	Università di Urbino, Italy
Francesc D. Muñoz-Escoí	Instituto Tecnológico de Informática, UPV, Valencia, Spain
Emanuel Onica	Alexandru Ioan Cuza University of Iasi, Romania

Claudio Palazzi	University of Padova, Italy
Marta Patiño-Martinez	Universidad Politécnica de Madrid, Spain
João Paulo	INESC TEC and University of Minho, Portugal
José Pereira (Co-chair)	INESC TEC and University of Minho, Portugal
Hans P. Reiser	University of Passau, Germany
Laura Ricci (Co-chair)	University of Pisa, Italy
Etienne Rivière	UCLouvain, Belgium
Altair O. Santin	PUCPR, Brazil
Valerio Schiavoni	Université de Neuchâtel, Switzerland
Marco Serafini	University of Massachusetts Amherst, USA

DisCoTec Organizing Committee

Alberto Lluch Lafuente (General Chair)	DTU, Denmark
Kiko Fernández-Reyes (Publicity Chair)	Uppsala University, Sweden
Francesco Tiezzi (Publicity Chair)	University of Camerino, Italy
Andrea Vandin (Workshops Chair)	DTU, Denmark
Maurice ter Beek (Workshops Chair)	CNR, Italy
Valerio Schiavoni (Workshops Chair)	Université de Neuchâtel, Switzerland
Ann-Cathrin Dunker (Logistics)	DTU, Denmark

Additional Reviewers

Vilmar Abreu Jr.	Manisha Luthra
Maryem Ait El Hadj	Stewart Sentanoe
Yahya Benkaouz	Maicon Stihler
Christian Berger	Benjamin Taubmann
Johannes Köstler	Dimitrios Tomaras
Tien Dat Le	Eduardo Viegas
Federico Lombardi	Rachid Zennou

DisCoTec Keynotes

Versatile Quantitative Modelling: Verification, Synthesis and Data Inference for Cyber-Physical Systems

Marta Kwiatkowska

University of Oxford, UK

Abstract. Computing systems are becoming ever more complex, encompassing autonomous control of physical processes, stochasticity and inference from sensor data. This lecture will demonstrate the versatility of quantitative modelling and verification to aid the design of cyber-physical systems with machine learning components. Topics discussed will include recent advances in probabilistic/quantitative verification, template-based model synthesis, resource-performance trade off analysis, attacks on biometric security, and robustness guarantees for machine learning components. The lecture will conclude by giving an overview of future challenges in this field.

ALGORAND – The Distributed Ledger for the Borderless Economy

Silvio Micali

MIT, USA

Abstract. A distributed ledger is a tamperproof sequence of data that can be read and augmented by everyone. Distributed ledgers stand to revolutionize the way democratic societies and traditional economies operate. They secure all kinds of traditional transactions –such as payments, asset transfers, titling– in the exact order in which they occur; and enable totally new transactions –such as cryptocurrencies and smart contracts. They can remove intermediaries and usher in a new paradigm for trust. As currently implemented, however, distributed ledgers cannot achieve their enormous potential. The global participation and trust necessary to realize an inclusive and borderless economy require substantially better technology. Algorand is an alternative, democratic, and efficient distributed ledger. Unlike prior ledgers based on 'proof of work', it dispenses with 'miners'. Indeed, Algorand requires only a negligible amount of computation. Moreover, its transaction history does not 'fork' with overwhelming probability: i.e., Algorand guarantees the finality of all transactions. In addition, Algorand guarantees flexible self-governance. A successful society and economy must be able to evolve. A cryptocurrency cannot be an ocean liner on autopilot. By using its hallmark propose-and-agree process, Algorand can consensually correct its course, as necessary or desirable, without any 'hard forks', to meet the current and future needs of the community.

Making Sense of Fast Big Data (DAIS Keynote)

Anne-Marie Kermarrec

Inria Rennes, France

Abstract. Computing systems that make human sense of big data, usually called personalization systems or recommenders, and popularized by Amazon and Netflix, essentially help Internet users extracting information of interest to them. Leveraging machine learning techniques, research on personalization has mainly focused on improving the quality of the information extracted, according to some measure of quality. Yet, building an operational recommender goes far beyond, especially in a world where data is not only big but also changes very fast. This talk will discuss system challenges to scale to a large number of users and a growing volume of fastly changing data to eventually provide real-time personalization.

Contents

Syncpal: A Simple and Iterative Reconciliation Algorithm for File Synchronizers

Marius Shekow[✉][iD]

Fraunhofer FIT, Sankt Augustin, Germany
marius.shekow@fit.fraunhofer.de

Abstract. Today file synchronizers are tools often used to facilitate collaboration scenarios and data management across multiple devices. They replicate the file system, e.g. from a cloud storage to a device disk, achieving convergence by only transmitting detected changes. A popular variant available in a plethora of products are state-based file synchronizers such as the Dropbox client. They detect operations by computing the difference between a previously persisted state and the respective current state. However, state-based synchronization is difficult because we need to detect and resolve conflicting operations as well as the propagation order of non-conflicting operations. This work presents Syncpal, an algorithm that reconciles two divergent file systems using an *iterative* approach. It first handles conflicts, one at a time, making sure that resolving one conflict does not negatively affect other ones, while avoiding conflicts whenever possible. It then finds order dependencies (and breaks cycles) between the remaining non-conflicting operations to avoid the violation of operation preconditions during propagation. This work is relevant for file synchronizer researchers and developers who want to improve their products with an algorithm whose iterative nature reduces the overall complexity and the probability of bugs. In addition to our proposed algorithm and a formal analysis of the underlying problem, our validation approach for the proposed algorithm includes the presentation of a full-scale implementation of an exemplary file system model.

Keywords: File synchronizer · File system · Optimistic replication · Conflict detection

1 Introduction

Today tools like word processors are a core component in digital workflows. They are used to create large parts of the user's data in the form of files, which are stored and distributed on multiple devices in a hierarchical *file system*. However, copying files and directories between storages causes various problems, both for individual users and collaborative settings. For instance, users may fail to locate

© IFIP International Federation for Information Processing 2019
Published by Springer Nature Switzerland AG 2019
J. Pereira and L. Ricci (Eds.): DAIS 2019, LNCS 11534, pp. 1–18, 2019.
https://doi.org/10.1007/978-3-030-22496-7_1

the correct, up to date version of a document on the right device [5,8,22], and files are prone to lose their context and meta-data information when transferred via Email or instant messaging [25]. One convenient solution for such challenges is *data synchronization*. *File synchronizers* [2] are synchronizers whose data is the file system, including its namespace structure and file contents. They provide *optimistic replication* to otherwise isolated file systems, with weak, *eventual consistency* [21] guarantees. In particular, *cloud storage* file synchronizers like Dropbox, Google Backup and Sync, OneDrive, ownCloud and others[1] have become popular over the last ten years, indicated by the high number of their users [9,18]. They synchronize *two* file system replicas—a directory on the local storage of a device, and a directory on a cloud storage server, in near real-time. As they are not integrated on a kernel-level with the operating system, they use a *state-based* approach that detects operations by computing the difference between the current and a persisted file system state.

When using synchronizers files are available on the local disk, thus users can work *offline* for extended time periods (e.g. while traveling). The side effect is an increased chance for conflicting operations as well as long, non-conflicting operation sequences resulting from users reorganizing the folder hierarchies. These are challenging to detect and propagate for the synchronizer. For example, a conflict situation, where the user creates a new file at path '/dir/file' but '/dir' was already deleted on the server, must be detected and resolved in favor of one of the operations. But even non-conflicting operations can be challenging to propagate. Consider the situation where the user swaps two objects at paths '/x' and '/y' on the local disk, using three *rename* operations. The synchronizer's state-based update detection mechanism detects them as *two* operations (*move('/x', '/y')+move('/y', '/x')*. If the corresponding objects were not modified on the server since the last synchronization (which makes the operations *non*-conflicting), the synchronizer cannot apply these two detected *move* operations to the server because they would violate the move operation's precondition that requires the target location to be free.

Contrary to the marketing materials of industrial synchronizers which promise that their product "just works", we observed that they misbehave and make intransparent decisions for the user - especially when attempting to synchronize after a long offline phase. This includes:

- Inexplicable changes made to the file system, convoluting its structure, e.g. with file and folder (conflict) copies where no conflict actually happened,
- Ineffective use of network bandwidth, in particular when *move* operations were not detected correctly in replica X, causing the synchronizer to retransmit large files as new, rather than moving them on replica Y,
- Bugs or crashes of the file synchronizer, resulting in permanently divergent replicas, or even data loss.

All these problems cause frustration because users then have to repair directory structures and file contents manually. The majority of issues can be traced

---

[1] E.g. Amazon Drive, Box, NextCloud, Seafile, SpiderOakOne, LeitzCloud, Tonido, TeamDrive, Strato HiDrive, or Hubic.

back to an incomplete analysis of the underlying file system model (and its operations) by the synchronizer authors. In this work we contribute *Syncpal*, a generic algorithm for file synchronizers that eliminates above side effects, because it provides a simple and iterative solution to solving conflicts and propagating non-conflicting operations. It is based on a formally defined file system model, which makes its individual steps provably correct. Additionally, it is able to avoid conflicts whenever possible, resolves conflicts without side effects for other conflicts, and does not replace detected *move* operations with *delete* and *create* operations. This improves propagation performance, preserves meta-data (which would otherwise be lost due to the *delete* operation) and maintains usability, because users will be able to identify the move operations of their own replica in the respective operations log of the other replica [20].

We start with providing background on file synchronizers, file systems and state-based update detection in Sect. 2. After presenting the generic approach in Sect. 3 we apply it to a concrete file system model in Sect. 4. We briefly present the evaluation of an implementation of our approach in Sect. 5 and conclude in Sect. 6.

2   Background

We begin with a short introduction to file synchronizers in Sect. 2.1. As file systems are the core component being synchronized, we briefly explain differences in how file systems can be modeled and formally present our own, exemplary model in Sect. 2.2, which we use in the remainder of this work. In Sect. 2.3 we briefly explain how operations are detected in a state-based approach.

2.1   File Synchronizers

In [2] the authors describe and coin the term *file synchronizer* as a user-invoked program that performs a pair-wise synchronization of *two* file system replicas. They describe a *state-based* approach [21] with three stages, *update detection*, *reconciliation* and *propagation*. In contrast, *operation-based* approaches like [13,15] rely on a complete log of operations. Because some file systems (e.g. POSIX APIs) do not provide such logs, it is reasonable to assume that cloud storage synchronizers (and other products) use a state-based approach with a similar three-stage process. State-based approaches persist the file system state (structure + meta-data) in a database and compute operations by comparing the persisted and current state, see Sect. 2.3 for more details. Surprisingly, while there is a plethora of file synchronizer products, the topic has not received much attention in comparison within academia (neither state- nor operation-based synchronizers).

2.2   File System Model

Every file synchronizer uses its own internal file system model definition for the state. An analysis of related works reveals several differences:

- *Identity- vs. path-based model*: as discussed in [23, section 3] the file system and its operations can be modeled using the *identity*-based approach where each object is identified by a unique ID, or by a *path*-based approach where objects are only identified by their path. ID-based approaches include [3, 10–13, 23], for path-based approaches see [2, 4, 15, 24].
- *Hardlink* support for files: an identity-based model may support that a specific *file* is linked exactly once, or several times. In the latter case a file's name may be part of the file itself, or be part of the parent-child link.
- *Directory* support: Most file system implementations support directories. However, alternatives exist, e.g. models that only consist of a set of *file* paths and their identities [19, Definition 2.3.1 + section 2.4.4]. Another example is Git [24] which does not support *empty* directories.
- *Operation* support: while the models of all file synchronizers we examined support *create directory*, *create file* and *edit* operations (that update the content of a file), support for other operations varies. For example, the model may or may not offer a *move* operation, or the *delete* operation may be modeled as such, or as a *move* operation to the garbage directory [13].

Because there may be a mismatch between the internal model definition and the definitions of the two underlying replicas being synchronized, file synchronizers belong to the category of *heterogeneous* synchronization [1, 6, 17].

We now present a formal file system model that is used in the remainder of this work. It is ID-based, because the file systems industrial synchronizers are ID-based, too, and because IDs allow to efficiently detect *moved* objects.

We define the file system $\mathcal{F}$ to be a set of tuples where each tuple represents an object with a unique ID $i \in I$, parent directory ID $p \in I$, type $t \in T$ (with $T = \{file, dir\}$), name $n \in \Sigma^+$ (with $\Sigma^+ = \Sigma^* \backslash \{\epsilon\}$), *lastmodified* meta-datum $l \in L$ and content $b \in B$. I is the set of unique IDs, L is the set of all valid lastmodified meta-datum values (e.g. $\mathbb{N}$ or arbitrary strings), and B is the set of arbitrary byte sequences, including ϵ. That is, $\mathcal{F} \subset I \times I \times T \times \Sigma^+ \times L \times B$, with tuples $(i_k, p_k, t_k, n_k, l_k, b_k)$ with $t_k = dir \implies b_k = \epsilon$. Several invariants hold for $\mathcal{F}$:

$$\forall i, j \in I : i \in list(j) \implies type(j) = dir \tag{1}$$

$$\forall i \in I : i \notin list(i) \tag{2}$$

$$\forall i, j, k \in I : j \neq k \wedge i \in list(j) \implies i \notin list(k) \tag{3}$$

$$\forall i \in I : i_{root} \notin list(i) \tag{4}$$

$$\forall i \in I \setminus \{i_{root}\} : type(i) \neq error \iff ancestor(i_{root}, i) \tag{5}$$

$$\forall i, j, k \in I : j \neq k \wedge j \in list(i) \wedge k \in list(i) \implies name(j) \neq name(k) \tag{6}$$

where $list(i)$ returns the set of IDs of all tuples whose $p_k = i$ (i.e., the set of immediate child IDs of i); $type(i)$ returns t_k of the tuple where $i_k = i$, or *error* if no such tuple exists; *name*(i) returns n_k of the tuple where $i_k = i$. We additionally define the predicate

$$ancestor(i,j) = \begin{cases} true & j \in list(i) \\ true & \exists k \in list(i) : ancestor(k,j) \\ false & \text{otherwise} \end{cases}$$

to express whether the object with ID i is an ancestor of the object with ID j. $\mathcal{F}$ is an arborescence rooted in the well-known object $i_{root} \in I$ with $type(i_{root}) = dir$, where each object exists exactly once.

The operations with their pre- and postconditions are defined in Table 1. Function $id(i,n)$ returns the ID of the object with parent i and name n, or *error* if no such object exists. $lastmodified(i)$ returns l_k of the tuple where $i_k = i$, or *error* if no such tuple exists. $content(i)$ returns b_k of the tuple where $i_k = i$, or *error*.

We refer to [14, Section 8.5] for an equivalent formal definition, which the authors proved to be correct using the CISE SMT solver [7].

2.3   State-Based Update Detection

State-based update detection means that operations are computed by comparing the persisted and current state of the tree-shaped data structure. The operations depend on the data model and there might be slight differences between the detected operations and those defined in the file system model. For $\mathcal{F}$ we detect:

- *createdir(i, p, n)*: a directory was created, when we find i with $type(i) = dir$ in the current state, but not in the persisted one
- *createfile' (i, p, n, c)*: a file with content c was created, when we find i with $type(i) = file$ in the current state, but not in the persisted one
- *move(i,u,v,n)*: an object was moved, when we find i in both states, but with varying name or parent
- *edit' (i)*: a file content was edited, when we find i in both states, but with different lastmodified meta-datum l. For update-detection, the exact content, i.e., *how* the file changed, is not relevant yet ($edit' \neq edit$)
- *delete' (i,p)*: an object was deleted when we find i in the persisted state, but not in the current one. *delete'* is a *recursive* operation when it affects a *directory*. It aggregates all other detected $deletefile(j,q)$ and $deletedir(j,q)$ operations that affect objects j situated below i, i.e., where $ancestor(i,j)$ holds. When the synchronizer applies $delete'(i,p)$ to the other replica in the propagation stage, it has to apply the corresponding *deletefile* and *deletedir* operations according to a *post-order* traversal of the file system arborescence.

The computed list of operations does not indicate the exact order of operations, and some operations are affected by consolidation. See [4,20] who identified this problem for file systems without *move* operation support. For $\mathcal{F}$ we find seven consolidation rules presented in Table 2 by examining all operation pairs. Note that $create = createfile \lor createdir$, $delete = deletefile \lor deletedir$.

Table 1. File system operations

Operation	Description, pre- and post-conditions
$createdir(i, p, n)$	Creates new dir with ID i and name n in parent dir with ID p Precondition: $\neg ancestor(i_{root}, i) \land (ancestor(i_{root}, p) \lor p = i_{root}) \land type(p) = dir \land id(p, n) = error$ Postcondition: $i \in list(p) \land type(i) = dir \land lastmodified(i) \neq error$
$createfile(i, p, n)$	Creates new file with ID i and name n in parent dir with ID p Precondition: see $createdir(i, p, n)$ Postcondition: $i \in list(p) \land type(i) = file \land lastmodified(i) \neq error$
$move(i, u, v, n)$	Moves a file or dir with ID i from parent dir with ID u to parent dir with ID v, and/or change the object's name to n Precondition: $type(u) = dir \land i \in list(u) \land type(v) = dir \land id(v, n) = error \land \neg ancestor(i, v)$ Postcondition: $i \in list(v) \land i \notin list(u)$ Note: $\neg ancestor(i, v)$ ensures that the user cannot move a dir to a destination dir below it.
$deletefile(i, p)$	Removes the file with ID i from parent dir with ID p Precondition: $ancestor(i_{root}, i) \land type(i) = file$ Postcondition: $i \notin list(p) \land \neg ancestor(i_{root}, i) \land lastmodified(i) = error$
$deletedir(i, p)$	Removes the empty dir with ID i from parent dir with ID p Precondition: $ancestor(i_{root}, i) \land type(i) = dir \land list(i) = \{\}$ Postcondition: see $deletefile(i, p)$
$edit(i, op)$	Changes the byte content of file with ID i by performing the operation op (e.g. adding, removing or changing bytes at specific positions within the file) Precondition: $ancestor(i_{root}, i) \land type(i) = file$. Let $l_{pre} = lastmodified(i)$ Postcondition: $ancestor(i_{root}, i) \land lastmodified(i) \neq l_{pre}$

3   Approach

This section describes our approach in generic steps, independent of a concrete data model, such as $\mathcal{F}$. It consists of two phases. The preparation phase described in Sect. 3.1 is done offline before implementing the software, whereas the execution phase applies the findings of phase 1, online at run-time of the synchronizer, see Sect. 3.2.

3.1   Phase 1: Preparation

In the preparation phase we get an understanding of the problems that can occur during synchronization by building and closely examining the file system model. We found that an analysis of the operation preconditions reveals two classes of issues: first, two concurrent operations (each applied to a different replica) can

Table 2. Operation consolidation rules

Operation consolidation rule	Explanation
$move(i, u, v_1, n_1) + move(i, v_1, v_2, n_2) \cong$ $move(i, u, v_2, n_2)$	An object moved several times is detected as moved exactly once
$createfile(i, p, n) + edit(i, op) \cong$ $createfile'(i, p, n, c)$	Creating an empty file and changing its content is detected as a non-empty file
$create(i, p, n_1) + move(i, p, v, n_2) \cong$ $create(i, v, n_2)$	Creating and moving an object is detected as if it were created in the move operation's destination
$edit(i, op_1) + edit(i, op_2) \cong edit'(i)$	Editing a file multiple times is detected as a single $edit'$ operation
$create(i, p, n) + delete(i, p) \cong []$	A created object that is subsequently deleted is not detected at all
$edit(i, op) + deletefile(i, p) \cong$ $deletefile(i, p)$	When an edited file is subsequently deleted, only the deletion is detected
$move(i, u, v, n) + delete(i, v) \cong$ $delete'(i, u)$	When a moved object is subsequently deleted, only the deletion is detected

cause *conflicts* that a synchronizer needs to handle. Second, state-based update detection will not detect the actual operations (and their order) applied by the user, but only an equivalent, unordered set. A precondition analysis must extract order dependencies (and even identify cycles), otherwise the synchronization of operations may fail. The following sections describe the individual steps.

Step 1: File System Model Formalization: The first step is to formally define the file system model the synchronizer uses internally, that consists of a formal definition of its elements, invariants and operations (with their pre- and postconditions). We recommend an automated approach where a model (initially built by hand) is iteratively refined via model checking tools, until all invariants and operations are known and free of contradictions. See [14] for an example, who did this for a model equivalent to our $\mathcal{F}$ model.

Step 2: Analysis of Conflicting Operations: An operation o_X detected in replica X is conflicting with operation o_Y detected in replica Y (and thus cannot be applied to Y by the synchronizer) if the preconditions of o_X no longer hold for new state of Y due to the modifications already applied to Y by o_Y.

To find conflicts, let OT be the list of *all* operation types of the model found in step 1. We start from an initially equal state for replicas X and Y. For any two types t_A, t_B from OT we instantiate operations o_X (of type t_A) and o_Y (of type t_B), apply o_X to X (which yields X') and o_Y to Y (yields Y'). We choose the operation parameters (e.g. i, p, u, v, n for $\mathcal{F}$) such that either applying o_Y to X', or o_X to Y' fails, due to violated preconditions.

Finding conflicts can be done manually or in an automated approach. The manual, pragmatic approach examines each individual precondition of each operation type t_A and finds a t_B, o_Y and o_X that produces a conflict. We generally recommend to identify *pseudo* conflicts, where two operations do conflict syntactically, but should not, because both operations have the same effect. In this case the synchronizer does not need to change the replicas, because the effect of both operations is the same anyway. An example for a pseudo-conflict is if o_X, o_Y are both *deletefile(i,p)* operations that affect the same object i.

Step 3: Resolving Conflicts: The general rule of conflict resolution is that the effect of operations o_X and o_Y are preserved as much as possible. There are two general approaches to conflict resolution:

1. Choose one of the operations to *win*, and manipulate the loser operation to resolve the conflict, or
2. Let both operations lose, by manipulating both of them, which avoids having to choose a winner.

We prefer option 1. Even though it is challenging to decide which of the two operations should take precedence in case of *automatic* resolution[2], the advantage is that at least one operation is fully preserved, and only the user who executed the loser operation needs to be informed. Our general approach for resolving conflicts is to perform the simplest possible resolution step, focusing on manipulating the *loser* operation instead of the winner operation. Sometimes the loser operation only has to be changed slightly, in other cases it has to be *undone* completely. Consider an example where o_X deletes a *directory* which was renamed by o_Y, and the strategy is to prefer *delete* over *move* operations. Instead of executing o_X in replica Y, which could cause side effects because the directory may have child-objects that are involved in other conflicts, it is more appropriate to undo o_Y. The winner operation o_X remains and is eventually executed, once all other conflicts have been resolved.

If conflict resolution is *automatic*, we need to make sure that if the preconfigured resolution was inappropriate for the user, the costs of subsequent, manual repair of the file system is manageable. Optimally, automatic resolutions can be changed by the user by a simple click, either before (via configuration) or after the fact.

In this step the synchronizer developer needs to examine each conflict found in step 2 and determine suitable resolution options. The operation(s) the synchronizer generates to resolve a conflict must be designed such that their execution cannot fail (due to violated preconditions), even if other conflicts exist.

---

[2] This is not a problem if the conflict resolution is delegated to the user.

Step 4: Analysis of Operation Order Dependencies: Assume that a file synchronizer has resolved conflicting operations between X and Y, such that the update detection now results in one set of unordered operations per replica $\bar{O}_X$, $\bar{O}_Y$. To be able to propagate the operations in $\bar{O}_X, \bar{O}_Y$, a suitable order needs to be found, which requires an analysis of the operation preconditions because not all operations are commutative. Let OT be the list of considered operation types. For any two types t_A, t_B from OT we instantiate the respective operations o_A, o_B, as they would have been *detected* (see Sect. 2.3) on one specific replica, e.g. X. We choose the parameters (e.g. i, p, u, v, n for $\mathcal{F}$) such that applying the sequence (o_A, o_B) to the other, unchanged replica is feasible, but applying (o_B, o_A) would fail, because a precondition of one of the two operations is violated . We end up with a list of *order dependencies*, where each order dependency contains t_A, t_B (in a specific order) and the violated operation precondition(s). Finally, we examine whether cycles can be built from the *order dependencies*.

3.2   Phase 2: Execution

Figure 1 provides a flow chart of our algorithm. Hexagons illustrate computation steps, table-shaped rectangles represent data structures. The *Current file system state* is provided (and regularly updated) by the update detection component of the synchronizer (not shown). Our algorithm is iterative. Let $\bar{O}_X, \bar{O}_Y$ be the detected operations. Step *Find conflicts* analyzes every operation pair of $\bar{O}_X, \bar{O}_Y$ and generates (1) a list of conflicts C where each $c \in C$ is a tuple of two conflicting operations, and (2) a list of *pseudo*-conflicts P, where each $p \in P$ summarizes two pseudo-conflicting operations. If $C \neq \emptyset$, C is sorted according to some preference (e.g. "resolve conflict type t_1 before type t_2"), if desired. Then a resolution operation is generated and executed that only resolves the first $c \in C$. If $C = \emptyset$ then operations are sorted according to Algorithm 1.

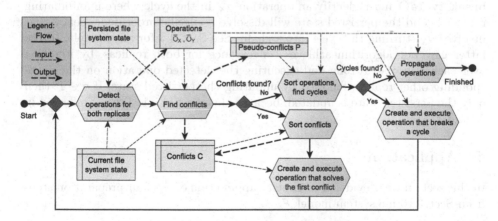

Fig. 1. Synchronization algorithm

Algorithm 1. Sorting operations

```
def sort_operations(Ox, Oy, P) -> L:
  global has_order_changed = False
  operations = [P + (Ox - P) + (Oy - P)]
  complete_cycles = []
  reorderings = []
  while True:
    has_order_changed = False
    find_and_fix_order_violations(operations)
    if not has_order_changed:
      break
    complete_cycles = find_complete_cycles(reorderings)
    if len(complete_cycles) > 0:
      break
  if len(complete_cycles) > 0:
    resolution_operation = break_cycle(complete_cycles[0])
    return [resolution_operation]
  else:
    return operations
```

We build `operations` as an initially unsorted list of pseudo-conflicting operations P and *non*-conflicting operations from $\bar{O}_X, \bar{O}_Y$ (that are not in P). Function `find_and_fix_order_violations()` performs an in-place sorting of `operations`. It checks all operation pairs for order violations as determined in step 4. If a violation is detected, the order of the two operations is swapped, the corrected order is added to `reorderings` and `has_order_changed` is set to *True*. Eventually either a cycle is found in `reorderings` which needs to be broken, or no more order violations were found in `operations`. In the first case `break_cycle()` must identify an operation o_X in the cycle where manipulating replica Y and the persisted state will dissolve a specific order dependency that involves o_X, turning the cycle into a chain. See Sect. 4.4 for an example. In the latter case our algorithm achieves convergence for both replicas, by iterating over each o in `operations` and executing the detected operation on the corresponding other replica, followed by updating the persisted state. If $o \in P$ then only the persisted state is updated, because the effect of o is already reflected in X and Y.

4   Application

In this section we provide an exemplary application of the four preparation steps from Sect. 3 to file system model $\mathcal{F}$.

4.1   Step 1: File System Model Formalization

Refer to the definition of $\mathcal{F}$ presented earlier in this work in Sect. 2.2.

4.2 Step 2: Conflict Detection

By examining the preconditions of the operations from Table 1, we find the conflicts and pseudo-conflicts presented in the following two lists. We use the $\otimes$ symbol for two conflicting operations. We use subscript letters X and Y as placeholders that designate to which replica the operation (or parameter) applies.

- **Create-Create**: On both replicas a new object was created with the same name under the same parent directory.
  Definition: $create_X(i_X, u_X, n_X) \otimes create_Y(i_Y, u_Y, n_Y) = [u_X = u_Y] \wedge [n_X = n_Y] \wedge [type_X(i_X) = dir \vee type_Y(i_Y) = dir \vee content_X(i_X) \neq content_Y(i_Y)]$ with $create := createdir \vee createfile'$.
  Violated precondition: $id(p, n) = error$
- **Edit-Edit**: The content of a file was changed on both replicas.
  Definition: $edit'_X(i_X, op_X) \otimes edit'_Y(i_Y, op_Y) = [i_X = i_Y] \wedge [content_X(i_X) \neq content_Y(i_Y)]$
  Violated precondition: technically no precondition is violated, but overwriting the file content on replica X with the one from replica Y would cause X's changes to be lost
- **Move-Create**: On one replica the user moved an object into a specific parent directory, assigning name n, on the other replica the user created a new object with the same name n in the same parent directory.
  Definition: $create_X(i_X, u_X, n_X) \otimes move_Y(i_Y, u_Y, v_Y, n_Y) = [u_X = v_Y] \wedge [n_X = n_Y]$ with $create := createdir \vee createfile'$
  Violated preconditions: create: $id(p, n) = error$; move: $id(v, n) = error$
- **Edit-Delete**: On one replica a file's content was edited, on the other replica the corresponding file was deleted.
  Definition: $edit'_X(i_X, op_X) \otimes delete'_Y(i_Y, p_Y) = (i_X = i_Y)$
  Violated precondition: On replica Y, $ancestor(i_{root}, i)$ of the $edit'$ operation is violated. On replica X there is no violation on the technical level, but on the semantic level: the changes of the $edit'$ operation would be lost.
- **Move-Delete**: On one replica an object was moved, on the other replica the corresponding object was deleted (either directly or as a consequence of deleting a parent directory).
  Definition: $move_X(i_X, u_X, v_X, n_X) \otimes delete'_Y(i_Y, p_Y) = (i_X = i_Y)$
  Violated precondition: On replica Y, $i \in list(u)$ of the $move$ operation is violated. On replica X there is no violation on the technical level, but on the semantic level: the changes of the structural change of the move operation would be lost. The user who deleted the object would have done so without knowing that it was recently moved by another user on the other replica.
- **Move-Move (Source)**: On both replicas the same object was moved to a *different* location. That is, on each replica either the new name or parent directory (or both) differs.
  Definition: $move_X(i_X, u_X, v_X, n_X) \otimes move_Y(i_Y, u_Y, v_Y, n_Y) = (i_X = i_Y) \wedge [(v_X \neq v_Y) \vee (n_X \neq n_Y)]$
  Violated precondition: on replica X: $i_Y \in list(u_Y)$; on replica Y: $i_X \in list(u_X)$. The source is no longer in the expected location

- **Move-Move (Dest)**: The users of both replicas each moved a *different* object into the same parent directory, assigning the same name. The name of this conflict is Move-Move *(Dest)* because the conflict occurs at the *destination*.
  Definition: $move_X(i_X, u_X, v_X, n_X) \otimes move_Y(i_Y, u_Y, v_Y, n_Y) = (i_X \neq i_Y) \wedge (v_X = v_Y) \wedge (n_X = n_Y)$
  Violated precondition: $id(v, n) = error$
- **Move-ParentDelete**: On one replica the user deleted directory d, on the other replica the user moved another object into d.
  Definition: $move_X(i_X, u_X, v_X, n_X) \otimes delete'_Y(i_Y, p_Y) = (v_X = i_Y)$
  $\wedge ancestor_Y(i_{root}, i_X)$
  Violated precondition: move: $type(v) = dir$
- **Create-ParentDelete**: On one replica the user deleted directory d, on the other replica the user creates a new object in d.
  Definition: $create_X(i_X, p_X, n_X) \otimes delete'_Y(i_Y, p_Y) = (p_X = i_Y)$ with $create :=$ $createdir \vee createfile'$
  Violated precondition: $type(p) = dir$
- **Move-Move (Cycle)**: Given two synchronized directories A and B, A was moved into B's namespace on one replica while B was moved into A's namespace on the other replica. This would create a cyclic parent-child relationship in the merged result.
  Definition: $move_X(i_X, u_X, v_X, n_X) \otimes move_Y(i_Y, u_Y, v_Y, n_Y) = (type(i_X) = type(i_Y) = dir) \wedge \lfloor ancestor(i_Y, v_X) \vee (i_Y = v_X) \rfloor \wedge \lfloor ancestor(i_X, v_Y) \vee (i_X = v_Y) \rfloor$ where *ancestor* refers to the state after all operations were executed.
  Violated precondition: $\neg ancestor(i, v)$

Pseudo-conflicts are presented in the following list, where $\odot$ indicates that two operations are pseudo-conflicting:

- **Edit-Edit**: The content of a file was changed on both replicas, such that the content is now the same.
- **Create-Create**: On both replicas a new *file* was created with the same content and name under the same parent directory. It would also be possible to consider two *createdir* operations to pseudo-conflict and to merge the directory contents recursively. However, if this resolution is done automatically and is inappropriate, manual clean up work is extensive [15].
- **Delete-Delete**: both replicas deleted the same object.
  Definition: $delete'_X(i_X, p_X) \odot delete'_Y(i_Y, p_Y) = (i_X = i_Y)$
- **Move-Move**: A specific object was moved to the same location.
  Definition: $move_X(i_X, u_X, v_X, n_X) \odot move_Y(i_Y, u_Y, v_Y, n_Y) = (i_X = i_Y) \wedge [(v_X = v_Y) \wedge (n_X = n_Y)]$

4.3 Step 3: Resolving conflicts

Who Wins? The winner of a conflict can be chosen in numerous ways. Either the user is explicitly involved in each decision, or conflicts are resolved automatically. For the latter the resolution strategy is pre-configured, typically by the developer. To better customize the synchronizer to the user's workflows, we propose to develop *multiple* conflict resolution strategies to choose from, where the choice may be given to the users or technically-apt administrators.

Name Occupation Conflicts: The **Create-Create**, **Move-Create** and **Move-Move (Dest)** conflicts all have in common that a specific name in a specific directory is being occupied by a *create* or *move* operation in each replica. A simple resolution approach is to modify the loser operation, by renaming the object on the corresponding replica, appending a unique suffix to the name.

Edit-Edit: When a specific file is edited on both replicas, undoing or modifying may not be possible because a replica may not store previous versions of a file. Resolving this conflict can either be achieved by renaming the loser file (and synchronizing it to the other replica, or keep it only on the loser replica), or backing up the loser file and overwriting it with the file of the winner replica, together with updating the *lastmodified* timestamp in the persisted state.

Delete Conflicts: Both **Edit-Delete** and **Move-Delete** are conflicts where one operation changed the object, while the other one deleted it. Thus the resolution approach should be similar for both. When the resolution favors the *delete* operation, a **Move-Delete** conflict can be resolved by undoing the move, but since the *edit* operation of an **Edit-Delete** conflict cannot be undone, the only solution is to delete the file from the loser replica and persisted state, to avoid the redetection of the conflict.

When the resolution favors the *move* or *edit* operation, we suggest the following approach:

- **Edit-Delete**: if the loser replica keeps deleted files in a garbage directory then restoring such files effectively undoes the *delete* operation. Otherwise the synchronizer can remove the file's entry from the persisted state only. In the next iteration, the file will be detected as *createfile'* operation and it will be synchronized to the loser replica.
- **Move-Delete**: the resolution works like for **Edit-Delete** conflicts. One caveat to consider is that when the *move* operation affects a *directory*, removing its entries from the database may cause orphaned entries for those child-objects that were moved out. For instance, given a directory at path '/d' and file '/d/f', with operations $move_X('/d','/e'), move_Y('/d/f','/f'), delete'_Y('/d')$. To restore the directory, deleting *both* the directory and its children from the persisted state is inappropriate, because then one *move* operation would be lost, causing file f to be duplicated. However, removing only those objects that were deleted on replica Y, here: '/d', would also be inappropriate, because f would then be orphaned in the persisted state. We propose to move such orphaned objects temporarily to the root level in the persisted state and solve follow-up **Move-Move (Source)** conflicts in favor of replica Y.

Move-Move (Source): We propose to resolve this conflict type by undoing the loser *move* operation. Note that undoing a *move* operation may not always be possible: the source parent directory *s* might already be deleted, or the original name of the moved object might already be occupied in *s*, or the user could have moved *s* such that it is now a child of the affected object. In case of such issues we propose to move the affected object to the root of the synchronized directory instead, with a random suffix added to its name.

Indirect Conflicts: Two operations indirectly conflict with each other if they don't target two *different* objects, which are always in a hierarchical parent-child relationship. The **Move-Move (Cycle)**, **Move-ParentDelete** and **Create-ParentDelete** conflict belong to this category. **Move-Move (Cycle)** conflicts can be resolved exactly like **Move-Move (Source)** conflicts. **Move-ParentDelete** can be resolved by either undoing the deletion by restoring the deleted directory *in its entirety* (with all sub-objects), if possible, or to prefer the *delete* operation by undoing the *move* operation. The goal is to resolve this conflict in a way that avoids that *both* users are unhappy with the merged result. For instance, the two following resolution approaches would be bad ideas: (1) favor the *move* operation, by restoring only the deleted directory (and all its ancestor directories) targeted by the *move* operation, in order to make the *move* operation possible. This would *partially* undo the *delete* operation and cause an inconsistent namespace that would not be appreciated by either user. (2) Favor the *delete* operation by deleting the directory. This would cause the moved file to be deleted, which was not the intention of either user. In contrast, our solution only discards the intention for the user of the *move* operation.

Resolving **Create-ParentDelete** conflicts works similarly. We also suggest to take precedence to the *delete* operation. Undoing the *create* operation would mean data loss, thus we suggest to back up the created object first, or to move it to the root of the synchronized directory, or to a garbage directory.

Pseudo Conflicts: A pseudo conflict is resolved by updating the entries of the affected objects in the persisted state, such that the two operations are no longer detected in the next iteration. For example, a *Delete-Delete* pseudo-conflict would be resolved by removing the entries of the affected objects from the persisted state.

4.4 Step 4: Analysis of Operation Order Dependencies

For $\mathcal{F}$ we choose $OT = \{createfile', createdir, move, edit', delete'\}$. Figure 2 shows an overview of the eight order dependencies we found for the operation types in OT. The arrows are denoted with a dependency number explained below:

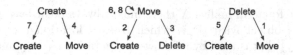

Fig. 2. Operation dependencies

1. *delete'* before *move*, e.g. user deletes an object at path '/x' and moves another object '/a' to '/x'
2. *move* before *create*, e.g. user moves an object '/a' to '/b' and creates another object at '/a'
3. *move* before *delete'*, e.g. user moves object '/X/y' outside of directory '/X' (e.g. to '/z') and then deletes '/X'
4. *create* before *move*, e.g. user creates directory '/X' and moves object '/y' into '/X'
5. *delete'* before *create*, e.g. user deletes object '/x' and then creates a new object at '/x'
6. *move* before *move* (occupation), e.g. user moves file '/a' to '/temp' and then moves file '/b' to '/a'
7. *create* before *create*, e.g. user creates directory '/X' and then creates an object inside it
8. *move* before *move* (parent-child flip), e.g. user moves directory '/A/B' to '/C', then moves directory '/A' to '/C/A' (parent-child relationships are now flipped)

By connecting the dependencies, we're able to construct *cycles*. Figure 3 shows *minimal* cycles (with the smallest possible number of operations) in the first row, and two examples of more elaborate cycles in the second row. We note that it is impossible to build cycles of only *delete* and *create* operations. It is also easy to prove that cycles that exclusively consist of *move* operations connected only by rule *8* are impossible[3]. Cycles always include at least one *move* operation.

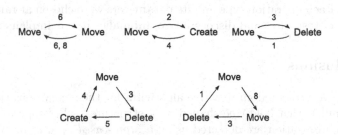

Fig. 3. Operation dependency cycles

---

[3] Intuitively, a proof by contradiction shows that the existence of a *rule 8 cycle* of *n* objects would require that those *n* objects also formed a cyclic parent-child relationship (before and after synchronization), but cycles are not allowed in $\mathcal{F}$.

For any cycle found in replica X there must always be at least one operation o_X (that affects object with ID i) which frees a location (i.e., a name in a specific directory) that is used by a follow-up operation o'_X. o_X must either be a *move* (dependencies $6+2$) or a *delete* (dependencies $1+5$) operation. Instead of executing o_X we generate a different *move* operation r_Y that breaks the cycle. r_Y renames i by appending a unique suffix to its name. We execute r_Y on Y and the persisted state. This way, r_Y is not detected after restarting the algorithm, but o_X still is detected because r_Y did not modify X: if o_X is a *move* operation, changing the name of i in the persisted state to a *unique* name will still find i as moved on X; if o_X is a *delete* operation then it will still be deleted on X. However, the cycle is now broken, because the order dependency (6, 2, 1, or 5) no longer applies. Note that if $o_X \in P$, i.e., o_X is a pseudo-conflicting operation, r_Y may only be executed on the persisted state, leaving both physical replicas X, Y untouched.

5 Evaluation

We implemented the approach presented in Sect. 4 as a user-space Python program that synchronizes folders on the user's local disk to the BSCW groupware [16]. We deployed it to 30 users who have been using it in production for over one year. In addition to hundreds of hand-made tests we applied two automated testing approaches to verify practical correctness of our algorithm. We used a variation of model checking.

In the first test approach we generated all possible operation sequences that can be applied to the 12 start scenarios that consist of three directories and one file. Due to state-space explosion we limited the number of operations to one *createfile*, two *createdir*, three *move* and three *delete* operations. This resulted in 5.5 million test cases computed in a HPC cluster over several weeks. Because local file systems (even RAM disks) are slow, we sped up test generation and execution by implementing a simple in-memory file system used instead.

To overcome the operation count limit resulting from state explosion in the first test approach, the second approach generated a much larger count (up to 30 operations). Each operation type and its parameters were chosen at random. We ran millions of test cases and discovered no anomalies in our implementation.

6 Conclusions

In this work we presented an iterative algorithm for the synchronization of two replicas X and Y that hold tree-shaped data structures, where operations since the last synchronization are detected using a *state-based* approach. We applied it to *file synchronizers* with a concrete file system model.

While the drawback of our iterative algorithm is the increased run-time in those scenarios where multiple iterations are required, we observed that those higher costs only occur after long offline periods. The advantage of the algorithm is that its individual steps are simple to implement, minimal and atomic.

Therefore the synchronization procedure can be interrupted any time, because it avoids long-lasting transactions.

This work demonstrates two challenges during synchronization. First, state-based update detection does not provide the order of the detected operations, which we solve by analyzing the operation preconditions to find a suitable order. The second challenge is that an operation in replica X may conflict with another operation in Y. We provide guidelines for how to identify sensible resolution options, find all possible conflicts, and how to build operations that resolve them. We leave finding a suitable (graphical) representation of the conflicts and their resolution (if automatic) as future work. We consider such conflict awareness an important aspect, as it improves the overall usability of the system.

References

1. Antkiewicz, M., Czarnecki, K.: Design space of heterogeneous synchronization. In: Lämmel, R., Visser, J., Saraiva, J. (eds.) GTTSE 2007. LNCS, vol. 5235, pp. 3–46. Springer, Heidelberg (2008). https://doi.org/10.1007/978-3-540-88643-3_1
2. Balasubramaniam, S., Pierce, B.C.: What is a file synchronizer? In: Proceedings of the 4th Annual ACM/IEEE International Conference on Mobile Computing and Networking, MobiCom 1998, pp. 98–108. ACM, New York (1998). https://doi.org/10.1145/288235.288261
3. Bao, X., Xiao, N., Shi, W., Liu, F., Mao, H., Zhang, H. (eds.): SyncViews: toward consistent user views in cloud-based file synchronization services. In: 2011 Sixth Annual Chinagrid Conference (2011). https://doi.org/10.1109/ChinaGrid.2011.35
4. Csirmaz, E.: Algebraic File Synchronization: Adequacy and Completeness (2016). https://arxiv.org/pdf/1601.01736.pdf
5. Dearman, D., Pierce, J.S.: It's on my other computer! Computing with multiple devices. In: Proceedings of the SIGCHI Conference on Human Factors in Computing Systems, pp. 767–776. ACM, Florence (2008). https://doi.org/10.1145/1357054.1357177
6. Foster, J.N., Greenwald, M.B., Kirkegaard, C., Pierce, B.C., Schmitt, A.: Exploiting schemas in data synchronization. J. Comput. Syst. Sci. **73**(4), 669–689 (2007). https://doi.org/10.1016/j.jcss.2006.10.024
7. Gotsman, A., Yang, H., Ferreira, C., Najafzadeh, M., Shapiro, M.: Cause I'm strong enough: reasoning about consistency choices in distributed systems. In: Proceedings of the 43rd Annual ACM SIGPLAN-SIGACT Symposium on Principles of Programming Languages, pp. 371–384. ACM, St. Petersburg (2016). https://doi.org/10.1145/2837614.2837625
8. Jokela, T., Ojala, J., Olsson, T.: A diary study on combining multiple information devices in everyday activities and tasks. In: Proceedings of the 33rd Annual ACM Conference on Human Factors in Computing Systems, pp. 3903–3912. ACM, Seoul (2015). https://doi.org/10.1145/2702123.2702211
9. Kollmar, F.: The Cloud Storage Report - Dropbox Owns Cloud Storage on Mobile (2016). https://blog.cloudrail.com/cloud-storage-report-dropbox-owns-cloud-storage-mobile/
10. Li, Q., Zhu, L., Zeng, S., Shang, W.Q. (eds.): An improved file system synchronous algorithm. In: 2012 Eighth International Conference on Computational Intelligence and Security (2012). https://doi.org/10.1109/CIS.2012.123

11. Li, Q., Zhu, L., Shang, W., Zeng, S.: CloudSync: multi-nodes directory synchronization. In: 2012 International Conference on Industrial Control and Electronics Engineering (ICICEE 2012), Piscataway, NJ, pp. 1470–1473. IEEE (2012). https://doi.org/10.1109/ICICEE.2012.386

12. Lindholm, T., Kangasharju, J., Tarkoma, S.: A hybrid approach to optimistic file system directory tree synchronization. In: Kumar, V., Zaslavsky, A., Cetintemel, U., Labrinidis, A. (eds.) The 4th ACM International Workshop on Data Engineering for Wireless and Mobile Access, pp. 49–56. ACM, New York (2005). https://doi.org/10.1145/1065870.1065879

13. Molli, P., Oster, G., Skaf-Molli, H., Imine, A.: Using the transformational approach to build a safe and generic data synchronizer. In: Proceedings of the 2003 International ACM SIGGROUP Conference on Supporting Group Work, pp. 212–220. ACM, Sanibel Island (2003). https://doi.org/10.1145/958160.958194

14. Najafzadeh, M.: The analysis and co-design of weakly-consistent applications. Ph.D. thesis, Université Pierre et Marie Curie (2016). https://hal.inria.fr/tel-01351187/document

15. Ng, A., Sun, C.: Operational transformation for real-time synchronization of shared workspace in cloud storage. In: Proceedings of the 19th International Conference on Supporting Group Work, pp. 61–70. ACM, Sanibel Island (2016). https://doi.org/10.1145/2957276.2957278

16. OrbiTeam Software GmbH & Co KG: BSCW Social (2018). https://www.bscw.de/social/

17. Pierce, B.C., Vouillon, J.: What's in unison? A formal specification and reference implementation of a file synchronizer (2004)

18. Price, R.: Google Drive now hosts more than 2 trillion files (2017). http://www.businessinsider.de/2-trillion-files-google-drive-exec-prabhakar-raghavan-2017-5

19. Qian, Y.: Data synchronization and browsing for home environments. Ph.D. thesis, Eindhoven University of Technology (2004)

20. Ramsey, N., Csirmaz, E.: An algebraic approach to file synchronization. In: Tjoa, A.M., Gruhn, V. (eds.) the 8th European Software Engineering Conference Held Jointly with 9th ACM SIGSOFT International Symposium, p. 175 (2001). https://doi.org/10.1145/503209.503233

21. Saito, Y., Shapiro, M.: Optimistic replication. ACM Comput. Surv. **37**(1), 42–81 (2005). https://doi.org/10.1145/1057977.1057980

22. Santosa, S., Wigdor, D.: A field study of multi-device workflows in distributed workspaces. In: Proceedings of the 2013 ACM International Joint Conference on Pervasive and Ubiquitous Computing, pp. 63–72. ACM, Zurich (2013). https://doi.org/10.1145/2493432.2493476

23. Tao, V., Shapiro, M., Rancurel, V.: Merging semantics for conflict updates in geo-distributed file systems. In: Proceedings of the 8th ACM International Systems and Storage Conference, SYSTOR 2015, pp. 10:1–10:12. ACM, New York (2015). https://doi.org/10.1145/2757667.2757683

24. Torvalds, L., Hamano, J.: Git: Distributed Version Control (2010). https://git-scm.com

25. Vonrueden, M., Prinz, W.: Distributed document contexts in cooperation systems. In: Kokinov, B., Richardson, D.C., Roth-Berghofer, T.R., Vieu, L. (eds.) CONTEXT 2007. LNCS (LNAI), vol. 4635, pp. 507–516. Springer, Heidelberg (2007). https://doi.org/10.1007/978-3-540-74255-5_38

Check-Wait-Pounce: Increasing Transactional Data Structure Throughput by Delaying Transactions

Lance Lebanoff, Christina Peterson[(⊠)], and Damian Dechev

University of Central Florida, 4000 Central Florida Blvd, Orlando, FL, USA
{lancelebanoff,clp8199}@knights.ucf.edu, dechev@cs.ucf.edu

Abstract. Transactional data structures allow data structures to support transactional execution, in which a sequence of operations appears to execute atomically. We consider a paradigm in which a transaction commits its changes to the data structure only if all of its operations succeed; if one operation fails, then the transaction aborts. In this work, we introduce an optimization technique called *Check-Wait-Pounce* that increases performance by avoiding aborts that occur due to failed operations. Check-Wait-Pounce improves upon existing methodologies by delaying the execution of transactions until they are expected to succeed, using a thread-unsafe representation of the data structure as a heuristic. Our evaluation reveals that Check-Wait-Pounce reduces the number of aborts by an average of 49.0%. Because of this reduction in aborts, the tested transactional linked lists achieve average gains in throughput of 2.5x, while some achieve gains as high as 4x.

1 Introduction

As multi-core machines are becoming the norm, many software developers turn to multi-threaded solutions to increase the execution speed of their applications. Building concurrent programs is difficult, because the programmer needs to have in-depth knowledge of the pitfalls of multi-threaded programming. Concurrent programs are prone to semantic errors, performance bottlenecks, and progress issues such as deadlock and starvation. Therefore, simplifying the task of concurrent programming has become an important challenge.

Concurrent data structures allow users to reap the benefits of concurrency while avoiding the dangers of multi-threaded programming [5,13]. These data structures support a predefined set of operations (e.g. insert, delete, find) such that any execution of concurrent operations is guaranteed to behave as if those operations were executed atomically. While concurrent data structures provide this guarantee for individual operations, the same guarantee does not hold for sequences of operations known as *transactions*. To overcome this issue, programmers often resort to coarse-grained locking, which hinders parallelism.

© IFIP International Federation for Information Processing 2019
Published by Springer Nature Switzerland AG 2019
J. Pereira and L. Ricci (Eds.): DAIS 2019, LNCS 11534, pp. 19–35, 2019.
https://doi.org/10.1007/978-3-030-22496-7_2

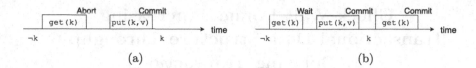

Fig. 1. A scenario in which a transaction experiences a self-abort that is avoidable. In (a), Transaction 1 executes get(k) which fails because k does not exist in the data structure. In (b), Transaction 1 avoids this scenario by waiting until Transaction 2 has inserted k into the data structure.

This issue has motivated the development of transactional data structures [7–10,12]. We recognize a data structure to be transactional if it supports *atomicity* and *isolation*. Atomicity means that a transaction may commit its changes to the data structure only if all its operations succeed. Isolation guarantees that transactions executed concurrently will appear to execute in some sequential order. There are several techniques that can be used to create transactional data structures, and we refer to these techniques as *transactional data structure methodolgies* (TDSMs).

We consider a paradigm of transactional data structures in which each operation in a transaction has a defined precondition [18]. For example, in a reservation system, an operation to reserve an item might require that the item has not already been reserved. If an operation's precondition is not satisfied at the beginning of the operation's execution, then the operation fails. A TDSM must abort a transaction if one of its operations fails, in order to preserve atomicity. We refer to this type of abort as a *self-abort*. Self-aborts waste computation time, as time spent executing transactions that will ultimately abort does not contribute to the overall throughput.

By reordering the execution of transactions, we can reduce the number of self-aborts and improve performance. For example, consider the scenario in Fig. 1. In Part (a), two transactions perform operations on a key-value map M. Transaction 1 consists of one operation get(k) that reads the value associated with a key k, and the operation's precondition requires that the $k \in M$. When the operation executes, it observes that $k \notin M$, so it fails, and the transaction self-aborts. Then, Transaction 2 executes put(k,v) to insert k into M. Part (b) shows that if Transaction 1 had waited until Transaction 2's completion, then its precondition would have been met, and Transaction 1 would avoid a self-abort.

Finding the optimal ordering of transactions would minimize the number of self-aborts. Although this approach might be possible in some cases, the large search space of potential orderings makes this approach computationally expensive [1], possibly more so than the self-aborts themselves.

In this paper, we present an optimization technique called *Check-Wait-Pounce* that reduces the number of self-aborts by delaying transactions. Transactions are analyzed before they execute, and if they are predicted to abort, then they are delayed instead. This results in an ordering of transactions with fewer self-aborts.

The Check-Wait-Pounce algorithm follows three steps. (1) In the *check* step, we heuristically determine the expected chance that a transaction will succeed. We make this prediction based on the transactional data structure's *Likely Abstract State Array* (LASA), which is an auxiliary array introduced in this paper. LASA is a heuristic representation of the transactional data structure's abstract state. A data structure's abstract state refers to the underlying meaning of the data structure. For example, the abstract state of a skip list-based set is a function across the possible range of keys, indicating whether or not the key exists in the data structure. In this case, LASA is an array of bits, where the index of each bit represents a key and the value of each bit represents the presence of that key in the set. When a transaction commits, LASA is updated to match the abstract state of the data structure, but it does so without using costly synchronization mechanisms. Consequently, the operations performed on LASA are not atomic, so it trades accuracy for performance. In Check-Wait-Pounce, the expected chance that a transaction will succeed corresponds to the percentage of operations whose preconditions are satisfied, according to LASA. (2) In the *wait* step, we periodically perform this check until the expected chance of success exceeds a given threshold. While the transaction waits, the thread executes other transactions. (3) When the threshold is reached, we proceed to the *pounce* step, in which we use an underlying TDSM (e.g. Transactional Boosting) to execute the transaction. Check-Wait-Pounce treats the underlying TDSM as a black box.

We employ micro-benchmarks in a variety of test cases to evaluate the effects of our optimization on several transactional data structures, created by four state-of-the-art TDSMs: Lock-free Transactional Transformation (LFTT) [18], Transactional Boosting (TB) [10], Transactional Data Structure Libraries (TDSL) [16], and Software Transactional Memory (STM) [3,6]. The data structures we evaluate are transactional versions of linked lists, skip lists, and multi-dimensional lists created by these TDSMs. With our optimization, the number of self-aborts is reduced by an average of 49.0%. As a result, the transactional linked lists based on LFTT, TB, TDSL, and STM achieve 3.3x, 4.6x, 1.8x, and 41.6% gains in throughput, respectively.

This paper makes the following contributions:

- We present Check-Wait-Pounce, an optimization approach to transactional data structures that reduces the number of aborted transactions. This is achieved by delaying transactions until they are expected to succeed.
- We introduce a new auxiliary data structure called LASA that is used by the Check-Wait-Pounce scheme to heuristically determine a transaction's chance of success.
- Check-Wait-Pounce can be applied to any TDSM. It controls when each transaction should be executed, and then it treats the underlying TDSM as a black box to execute the transaction.

2   Related Work

We use the *strict serializability* correctness condition to verify the correctness of transactional data structures. Strict serializability requires that for each completed transaction, a *serialization point* can be placed between the transaction's first and last operations. A transaction's serialization point is an instantaneous point in time that marks when the transaction effectively occurred. A history of concurrent transactions is strictly serializable if a serialization point can be placed for each transaction to create a sequential history, such that the outcome of the sequential history matches the outcome of the concurrent history.

We present a brief survey of fundamental TDSMs and how they support strict serializability. Then we describe existing techniques that relate to Check-Wait-Pounce because they reorder transactions.

2.1   Transactional Data Structure Methodologies

To guarantee strict serializability, each TDSM employs a unique approach that prevents certain transactions from committing, specifically pairs of transactions that concurrently access the same nodes in the data structure.

Software transactional memory (STM) is a methodology in which each transaction maintains all the memory locations it reads in a *read set* and all the locations that it writes to in a *write set*. If one transaction's write set intersects another transaction's read set or write set, then the transactions *conflict*. One of the conflicting transactions must abort, undoing the changes that it made to the data structure. We refer to this type of abort as a *spurious abort*. Spurious aborts occur as a result of multiple threads that concurrently access the same nodes in the data structure. Transactional Boosting (TB) proposed by Herlihy and Koskinen [10] associates each key in the data structure with a lock. A transaction that performs an operation on a key must first acquire the lock associated with that key. If a transaction fails to acquire a lock, then the transaction spuriously aborts and rolls back completed operations. Lock-free Transactional Transformation (LFTT) proposed by Zhang and Dechev [18] makes each node in the data structure point to a *transaction descriptor object*, which is an object that represents the transaction that last accessed that node. Before a transaction performs an operation on a node, it must help to complete any unfinished transactions that have already accessed that node. Transactional data structure libraries (TDSL) was proposed by Spiegelman et al. [16]. A thread collects a read set and write set, and assigns each node in the read set with a version number. At the end of the transaction, the thread locks all of the nodes in the write set, then checks the version numbers of all the nodes in the read set to validate that they have not been changed. If the thread fails to acquire a lock or the validation fails, then the transaction spuriously aborts.

These TDSMs focus on reducing overhead and spurious aborts, but they do not optimize for use cases in which self-aborts are common. We present Check-Wait-Pounce to optimize these algorithms by reducing the number of self-aborts.

Reducing the number of self-aborts is important because self-aborts waste computation time and do not contribute to the application's overall throughput, similarly to spurious aborts.

2.2 Reordering Transactions

The following techniques reorder the serialization points of conflicting transactions to avoid spurious aborts. Pedone et al. [15] introduced a reordering technique for database transactions that detects conflicts between concurrent transactions and reorders the serialization points of conflicting transactions to remove the conflicts. Chachopo and Rito-Silva [2] proposed an approach for transactional memory that avoids all spurious aborts for read-only and write-only transactions by moving serialization points. Diegues and Romano [4] extend the types of transactions that are reordered to include some read-write transactions.

The technique of reordering serialization points could possibly be applied to the problem of self-aborts. However, all of the TDSMs we study guarantee strict serializability, and to maintain this level of correctness, each transaction's serialization point may only be placed between the invocation of the transaction's first operation and response of the transaction's last operation. Consequently, a serialization point reordering technique may only reorder the serialization points of *concurrent* transactions. This restriction reduces the number of possible orderings of transactions such that the probability of a self-abort being avoided is minuscule. According to our experiments running 64 threads with a micro-benchmark, only 8.6×10^{-4} percent of self-aborts can be avoided by reordering the serialization points of concurrent transactions. On the other hand, our technique of reordering the physical execution of transactions is much more effective, avoiding 49.0% of self-aborts. The details of our experimental setup are given in Sect. 5.

The steal-on-abort technique [1] reorders the physical execution of transactions to prevent spurious aborts. Steal-on-abort has the purpose of reducing the number of spurious aborts, while Check-Wait-Pounce reduces the number of self-aborts. Also, steal-on-abort's method of reordering allows a transaction to execute and abort, *then* it forces the transaction to wait to restart. With Check-Wait-Pounce, we predict whether a transaction will abort *before* it executes in the first place.

3 Check-Wait-Pounce

We provide an overview of Check-Wait-Pounce, followed by detailed descriptions of the algorithm's steps.

3.1 Algorithm Overview

Figure 2 depicts a high-level overview of the life cycle of a transaction in Check-Wait-Pounce. After the transaction is created, we perform the *check step*: we

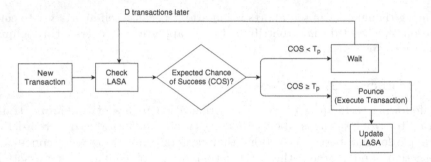

Fig. 2. Transaction life cycle in Check-Wait-Pounce.

determine the transaction's expected chance of success (COS) by checking the Likely Abstract State Array (LASA) of the data structure. LASA is a thread-unsafe representation of the data structure's abstract state. We provide details about LASA and the prediction of a transaction's COS in Sect. 3.2.

A threshold value for the COS called the pounce threshold (T_p) is a user-defined parameter. Based on the COS, we perform one of two actions:

- If the transaction's COS is less than T_p, then the transaction will likely abort if executed immediately. In this case, we proceed to the *wait step*: we delay the transaction's execution, allowing D other transactions to be processed in the meantime (D is an integer provided as an input parameter). After D other transactions complete, the waiting transaction returns to the check step to determine its new COS. We hope that after waiting, the transaction will have a higher chance of success than it had before waiting.
- If the transaction's COS is greater than or equal to T_p, then the transaction will likely commit if executed immediately. In this case, we proceed to the *pounce step*: we execute the transaction. If the transaction commits, then we update LASA to reflect the changes to the data structure's abstract state.

3.2   Algorithm Details

In this paper, we focus on applying Check-Wait-Pounce to transactional data structures that implement the set and map abstract data types. In the case of sets and maps, the available operations are INSERT, DELETE, and FIND.

For clarity, we list the data type definitions and constants of Check-Wait-Pounce in Listing 1. Note, we denote line X of Listing Y as line Y.X.

The TRANSACTION object represents a single transaction. It maintains a list of OPERATION objects, which are used in the check step to determine the transaction's chance of success. Each TRANSACTION object counts *numWaits*, the number of times the transaction has performed the wait step, as well as *waitEndTime*, which is a timestamp indicating when the transaction should stop waiting. Also, the TRANSACTION object has a reference *next* pointing to the next transaction in the wait list. These fields will be explained further in this section.

Listing 1. Type Definitions

```
1  enum OpType                      8  struct Transaction
2  │  Insert;                       9  │  Operation[] ops;
3  │  Delete;                      10  │  int numWaits ← 0;
4  │  Find;                        11  │  int waitEndTime;
5  struct Operation                12  │  Transaction* next = NULL;
6  │  OpType type;                 13  struct TxnWaitList
7  │  int key;                     14  │  int timestamp ← 0;
                                   15  │  Transaction head ← new Transaction();
                                   16  │  Transaction tail ← new Transaction();
```

The TxnWaitList object is a thread-local queue that facilitates the wait step. It is implemented as a linked list, and it maintains an integer *timestamp* to track when transactions have finished waiting.

Each thread is given a stream of transactions to process. We show the procedure that the thread performs on each transaction in Algorithm 2. First, the thread calls the CheckWaitPounce function to process the transaction from the stream (line 2.2). We predict the transaction's COS and proceed to either the wait step or the pounce step. After processing the transaction from the stream, we re-process any transactions that have reached the end of their wait steps (line 2.3). We describe these functions in detail later in this section.

Check Step. The CheckWaitPounce method begins with the check step, in which we predict the transaction's chance of success (COS). This prediction is made based on the number of operations in the transaction that will succeed. Each operation in the transaction has a given precondition. If that precondition is satisfied, then the operation succeeds; otherwise, the operation fails. For a set S and the operation Insert(k) on a given key k, the operation's precondition is $k \notin S$. Conversely, Find(k) and Delete(k) require $k \in S$.

We predict whether or not each operation will succeed based on the LASA auxiliary data structure. LASA represents the abstract state of the transactional data structure, and its implementation may vary for different data structures. For a set, the abstract state is a list of keys that exist in the set. We implement LASA as a bitmap, where each index i represents a key k that could possibly exist in the set, and the LASA[i] is true if $k \in S$, otherwise false. This boolean array representation allows for fast constant-time traversal while keeping memory usage low. In the case of a vastly large key range, LASA can be converted from an array for bits to a hash set or bloom filter to further decrease memory usage.

First, we count the number of operations that are expected to succeed. For each operation, we compare its precondition to the data structure's abstract state, represented by LASA (line 2.14). If they match, then we predict the operation will succeed; otherwise it will fail. Next, we calculate the transaction's chance of success (COS), which is equal to the ratio of successful operations to total operations (line 2.17). The transaction's next step is chosen based on the relation between COS and the pounce threshold (T_p), as detailed in Sect. 3.1.

Algorithm 2. Check-Wait-Pounce

---

1 **Function** ProcessTxn(*Transaction txn*)
2   CHECKWAITPOUNCE(txn);
3   PROCESSWAITINGTXNS();
4 **end**
5 **Function** CheckWaitPounce(*Transaction txn*)
6   //Check step
7   **int** $successfulOps \leftarrow 0$;
8   **foreach** $op \in txn.ops$ **do**
9   **bool** $precondition$;
10   **if** $op.type = Insert$ **then**
11             $precondition \leftarrow False$;
12   **else if** $op.type = Delete \parallel op.type = Find$ **then**
13             $precondition \leftarrow True$;
14   **if** $LASA[op.key] = precondition$ **then**
15             $successfulOps$++;
16   **end**
17   **float** $COS \leftarrow successfulOps\ /\ txn.ops.length$;
18   **if** $COS < T_p$ **and** $txn.numWaits < MAX\_WAITS$ **then**
19   //Wait step
20   **if** $TWL.head = NULL$ **then**
21             $TWL.head \leftarrow txn$;
22             $TWL.tail \leftarrow txn$;
23   **else**
24             $TWL.tail.next \leftarrow txn$;
25         $txn.waitEndTime \leftarrow TWL.timestamp + D$;
26         $txn.numWaits$++;
27   **else**
28   //Pounce step
29   **if** $TDSM.\text{EXECUTETXN}(txn) = True$ **then**
30   **foreach** $op \in txn.ops$ **do**
31   **if** $op.type = Insert \parallel op.type = Find$ **then**
32                    $LASA[op.key] \leftarrow True$;
33   **else if** $op.type = Delete$ **then**
34                    $LASA[op.key] \leftarrow False$;
35   **end**
36 **end**
37 **Function** ProcessWaitingTxns()
38   **Transaction** $txn \leftarrow TWL.head.next$;
39   **while** $txn \neq NULL$ **and** $txn.waitEndTime = TWL.timestamp$ **do**
40   CHECKWAITPOUNCE($TWL.head$);
41         $txn \leftarrow txn.next$;
42   **end**
43      $TWL.head.next \leftarrow txn$;
44      $TWL.timestamp + +$;
45 **end**

Wait Step. If a transaction's COS is less than T_p, then it proceeds to the wait step. Two parameters are given by the user to tune the wait step. D represents the amount of time that each transaction is delayed in the wait step, measured by the number of other transactions that are processed by the calling thread during the transaction's wait step. MAX_WAITS places a bound on the number of times that a transaction enters the wait step to avoid situations in which a transaction waits indefinitely. If a transaction has entered the wait step more than MAX_WAITS times, then it proceeds to the pounce step (line 2.18).

In the common case, we add the transaction to the Transaction Wait List (TWL), at the tail of the queue (line 2.25) or the head if the queue is empty (line 2.21). The transaction waits until D other transactions have been processed. To achieve this, the transaction calculates its *wait end time*—the specific *timestamp* value in which the transaction should finish waiting, which is equal to the current *timestamp* value plus D (line 2.20).

The PROCESSWAITINGTXNS function is called each time a thread processes a transaction from the stream as in Algorithm 2 (line 2.3). This function dequeues transactions from TWL if they have reached their *wait end time* and returns them to the check step (lines 2.35−2.42)

Pounce Step. Once Check-Wait-Pounce chooses the point in time to execute the transaction, we use a transactional data structure methodology (TDSM) to actually perform the execution (line 2.28). This underlying TDSM is treated as a black box to handle the conflict management that ensures strict serializability. The TDSM returns true if the transaction commits, or false if the transaction aborts. If the transaction commits, then its operations take effect, so we must update LASA to match the data structure's new abstract state (lines 2.30–2.33).

Note that LASA is shared among all threads, yet Check-Wait-Pounce uses simple read and write instructions when dealing with LASA. Consequently, LASA is not thread-safe. As a result, multiple threads performing concurrent updates to LASA might encounter a data race and cause LASA to incorrectly reflect the data structure's abstract state. Because of the possibility of such disparities, we only use LASA as a heuristic to choose the point in time to execute a transaction, rather than using it to actually perform the execution.

4   Correctness

We use the correctness condition *strict serializability* for our correctness discussion. The four TDSMs we focus on in this paper—LFTT, STM, TDSL, and TB—all guarantee strict serializability. TDSL guarantees opacity, which is a stricter correctness condition, so our correctness proof holds for TDSL as well. First, we provide background definitions for strict serializability, then we prove that Check-Wait-Pounce does not alter the correctness of the strictly serializable TDSMs.

A *transaction* is a sequence of operations that the user desires to be executed atomically. An *event* is (1) a transaction invocation (the start of a transaction) or response (the end of a transaction), or (2) an operation invocation or response. A *history* is a finite series of instantaneous events [11].

Definition 1. *A history h is strictly serializable if the subsequence of h consisting of all events of committed transactions is equivalent to a legal history in which these transactions execute sequentially in the order they commit [14].*

Definition 2. *Two method calls I, R and I′,R′ commute if for all histories h, if $h \cdot I \cdot R$ and $h \cdot I′ \cdot R′$ are both legal, then $h \cdot I \cdot R \cdot I′ \cdot R′$ and $h \cdot I′ \cdot R′ \cdot I \cdot R$ are both legal and define the same abstract state.*

Definition 3. *For a history h and any given invocation I and response R, let I^{-1} and R^{-1} be the inverse invocation and response. Then I^{-1} and R^{-1} are the inverse operations of I and R such that the state reached after the history $h \cdot I \cdot R \cdot I^{-1} \cdot R^{-1}$ is the same as the state reach after history h.*

Definition 4. *A method call denoted $I \cdot R$ is disposable if, $\forall g \in G$, if $h \cdot I \cdot R$ and $h \cdot g \cdot I \cdot R$ are legal, then $h \cdot I \cdot R \cdot g$ and $h \cdot g \cdot I \cdot R$ are legal and both define the same state.*

4.1 Rules

Any software transactional memory system that obeys the following correctness rules is strictly serializable [10].

Rule 1 *Linearizability: For any history h, two concurrent invocations I and I′ must be equivalent to either the history $h \cdot I \cdot R \cdot I′ \cdot R′$ or the history $h \cdot I′ \cdot R′ \cdot I \cdot R$.*

Rule 2 *Commutativity Isolation: For any non-commutative method calls $I_1, R_1 \in T_1$ and $I_2, R_2 \in T_2$, either T_1 commits or aborts before any additional method calls in T_2 are invoked, or vice-versa.*

Rule 3 *Compensating Actions: For any history h and transaction T, if $\langle T \text{ aborted} \rangle \in h$, then it must be the case that $h - T = \langle T \text{ init} \rangle \cdot I_0 \cdot R_0 \cdots I_i \cdot R_i \cdot \langle T \text{ aborted} \rangle \cdot I_i^{-1} \cdot R_i^{-1} \cdots I_0^{-1} \cdot R_0^{-1} \cdot \langle T \text{ aborted} \rangle$ where i indexes the last successfully completed method call.*

Rule 4 *Disposable Methods: For any history h and transaction T, any method call invoked by T that occurs after $\langle T \text{ commit} \rangle$ or after $\langle T \text{ abort} \rangle$ must be disposable.*

4.2 Strict Serializability and Recovery

We now show that Check-Wait-Pounce satisfies the correctness rules required to guarantee strict serializability. The concrete state of a map is denoted as a node set N.

Lemma 1. *The set operations* INSERT, DELETE, *and* FIND *are linearizable, satisfying Rule 1.*

Proof. It is assumed that the underlying TDSM is strictly serializable. It is therefore guaranteed that any history generated by the TDSM is equivalent to a legal history in which these transactions execute sequentially in the order they commit, so they are linearizable.

Lemma 2. *Check-Wait-Pounce satisfies commutativity isolation as defined in Rule 2.*

Proof. Two set operations commute if they access different keys. The one-to-one mapping from nodes to keys is formally stated as $\forall n_x, n_y \in N, x \neq y \implies n_x \neq n_y \implies n_x.key \neq n_y.key$. This implies that two set operations commute if they access different nodes.

Since a transaction is only executed by the underlying TDSM, then Check-Wait-Pounce satisfies commutativity isolation if the underlying TDSM satisfies commutativity isolation.

Lemma 3. *When a transaction aborts, Check-Wait-Pounce ensures that the resulting history is equivalent to performing the inverse operations of all computed operations of the aborted transaction, satisfying Rule 3.*

Proof. Let T denote a transaction that executes the operations $I_0 \cdot R_0 \cdots I_i \cdot R_i$ on nodes $n_0 \cdots n_i$ and then aborts. Let S_0 denote the abstract state immediately before I_0. By Rule 3, T must execute the inverse operations of the successful method calls $I_i^{-1} \cdot R_i^{-1} \cdots I_0^{-1} \cdot R_0^{-1}$ after those method calls have succeeded. This is equivalent to requiring that the current abstract state S_i be restored to its original state S_0. We prove that the current abstract state S_i is restored to its original state S_0 following an aborted transaction.

In the pounce step, the transaction is executed by the underlying TDSM. Since the TDSM is assumed to be strictly serializable, it follows that the partial effects of an aborted transaction are rolled back to the original abstract state S_0 to guarantee that the resulting history is equivalent to a legal history. Therefore, when the TDSM aborts a transaction, $S_i = S_0$.

Lemma 4. *The LASA update operation is disposable, so Check-Wait-Pounce satisfies Rule 4.*

Proof. After a transaction executed by the underlying TDSM commits, LASA is updated using atomic reads and atomic writes to reflect the expected abstract state based on the operations performed by the transaction. We prove that the LASA update operation is disposable by showing that it does not change the abstract state of the data structure. LASA affects the outcome of the check step. Since the transactional execution by the underlying TDSM does not incorporate LASA, the LASA update operation does not change the abstract state of the data structure, making it disposable.

Theorem 1. *For a data structure that is generated using Check-Wait-Pounce, the history of committed transactions is strictly serializable.*

Proof. Follow Lemmas 1, 2, 3, 4, and the main theorem of Herlihy et al.'s work [10], the theorem holds.

Table 1. Experimental variables tested.

Variable	Values tested
Data structure	Linked list, Skip list, MDList-based dictionary [17]
TDSM	LFTT, TB, TDSL, STM
Transaction size (# operations)	1, 2, 4, 8, 12, 16
Sleep between operations	$0\,\mu s$, $10\,\mu s$, $100\,\mu s$, 1 ms
T_p	0, 0.25, 0.5, 0.75, 1
D	2, 50, 100, 300
MAX_WAITS	2, 50, 100, 300
CPU architecture	Intel Xeon Platinum 8160, SMP, 24 cores @ 2.1 GHz,
	AMD Opteron 6272, NUMA, 64 cores @ 2.1 GHz

5   Evaluation

We compare the performance of several transactional data structures created using four different TDSMs, and evaluate the performance impact of Check-Wait-Pounce when applied to each data structure.

5.1   Experimental Setup

To evaluate the performance impact of Check-Wait-Pounce, we use a micro-benchmark in a similar manner to other evaluations of TDSMs [3,16]. Several threads are spawned, each one continuously executing transactions for 5 s. Each operation in a transaction is randomly assigned an operation type (INSERT, DELETE, or FIND) and a key. All code is compiled with GCC 7.3 with C++17 features and O3 optimizations.

We perform our experiments in a variety of scenarios, outlined in Table 1. We compare the performance of three concurrent data structures made transactional by four TDSMs. We observe the effect of Check-Wait-Pounce on these data structures in different environments, such as the transaction size (the number of operations per transaction), user-defined parameters, and CPU architectures. We also perform tests in which threads execute transactions with different amounts of extra work in between each data structure operation. This means that the number of data structure operations remains the same (e.g. 4 operations) but the time taken to execute each transaction increases. We simulate these kinds of transactions by tasking the threads to sleep for a certain amount of time per operation.

When evaluating STM, we test Fraser STM [6] for the skiplist and NOrec [3] for the other data structures. We denote Check-Wait-Pounce as CWP for the remainder of this section.

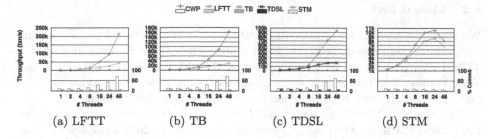

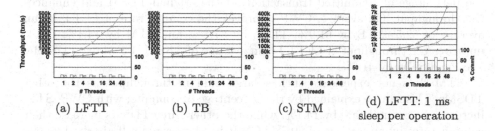

Fig. 3. Linked list performance: throughput and commit rate.

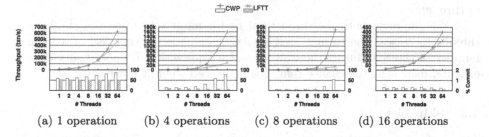

Fig. 4. Skip list performance: throughput and commit rate.

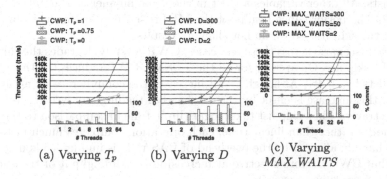

Fig. 5. Comparison using different transaction sizes (number of operations per transaction).

Fig. 6. Linked list performance varying user-defined parameters.

5.2 Linked List

We show the throughput and commit rate for the transactional linked lists in a standard environment in Fig. 3. Each graph displays the performance of one TDSM compared to the performance of that TDSM when optimized by Check-Wait-Pounce. The throughput is the number of committed transactions per second. The commit rate is the percentage of transactions that commit.

For the linked lists, the key range is set to 10^4. The tests are run on the Intel Xeon Platinum 8160 using a uniform distribution, 20% write operations, transaction size of 4, T_p set to 1, D set to 50, and MAX_WAITS set to 100.

In almost every scenario across these test cases, CWP significantly increases the percentage of committed transactions of the original TDSM and enhances the throughput. On average, CWP improves the commit rate of LFTT by an average of 62.5%, TB by 61.9%, TDSL by 57.8%, and STM by 14.1%. CWP improves the throughput of LFTT by an average of 3.3x, TB by 4.6x, TDSL by 1.8x, and STM by 41.6%.

STM does not experience such a large gain in throughput as the other TDSMs. This can be explained by the percentage of commits; with CWP, STM increases its commit rate by 14.1%, while the other three TDSMs increase their commit rates by an average of 60.7%. CWP helps to avoid self-aborts, but one of the main disadvantages of STM is its high number of spurious aborts. Consequently, CWP achieves smaller gains in commit rate, resulting in smaller gains in throughput.

CWP improves both the throughput and commit rate when the number of threads increases, due to increased activity per node. In the case of a higher number of threads, during the wait step of a transaction T, more transactions execute, increasing the chance that T will succeed when it finishes waiting.

5.3 Skip List

The performance of the transactional skip lists in a standard environment is shown in Fig. 4. For the skip lists, we set the key range to 10^6, as the logarithmic nature of traversal for skip lists allows them to handle larger key ranges than linked lists. All other variables are set in the same manner as the linked lists in Sect. 5.2. The performance results of the MDList-based dictionary is similar to those of the skip list, so we do not show its results.

In every scenario across these test cases, CWP severely degrades the throughput of the skip list. On average for all the TDSMs, CWP reduces the throughput of skip lists by 79.4%. Although CWP increases the commit rate by an average of 9.8%, this increase is offset by the overhead of reading and writing to LASA. Because traversal in a skip list takes logarithmic time in comparison to the number of nodes rather than linear time, each operation completes much faster and is more harshly affected by the overhead of LASA. This finding leads us to postulate that CWP is more effective at increasing the throughput of transactions that take more time to execute.

We support this hypothesis by performing tests in which the threads are tasked to sleep for a certain amount of time before each operation. In Fig. 4d we show the performance of the LFTT skip list with 1 ms of sleep per operation. We tested sleep times of 10 and $100\,\mu s$ as well but do not display these results for space. The results show that CWP improves the performance of the data structure more for cases in which transactions take more time to execute. In the case of 1 ms of sleep, CWP improves the throughput of the skip list by 194%.

5.4   Transaction Size

In Fig. 5, we compare the effects of CWP on transactions of different sizes. Before each test run, we fill the data structure until it is 50% full of nodes, and then the number of insert and delete operations are equal during the test. Under these circumstances, the probability of success for each operation is 0.5, so an increased transaction size results in a lower commit rate. Namely, a transaction with size n has a probability of $1/2^n$ to commit.

Our results indicate that CWP performs more effectively for higher transaction sizes until a size of 8, and then its effectiveness declines for higher sizes. For sizes lower than 8, each transaction has a relatively high chance of succeeding, so CWP does not improve the commit rate drastically. For sizes higher than 8, each transaction has such a low chance of succeeding that it needs to wait a high number of wait steps before it succeeds, often greater than the value of MAX_WAITS, which also reduces the effectiveness of CWP.

5.5   Check-Wait-Pounce Parameters

We vary the user-defined parameters for CWP: T_p, D, and MAX_WAITS. The results are shown in Fig. 6. In Fig. 6a, we see that CWP is most effective when T_p is set to 1, which signifies that 100% of the operations in a transaction must be predicted to succeed in order to proceed to the pounce step. If a lower value of T_p is used, transactions with any fail-prone operations are allowed to proceed to the pounce step, and they usually abort, which hurts performance.

In Fig. 6b and c, we see that increasing the values of D and MAX_WAITS improves the throughput and commit rate of CWP. However, increasing these parameters leads to higher latency, as CWP allows transactions to wait for longer periods of time before executing. For applications that tolerate high latency, D and MAX_WAITS can be set to high values.

6   Conclusion

We present an optimization to transactional data structures called Check-Wait-Pounce that reduces the number of self-aborts by delaying transactions. In test cases with linked lists, our optimization improves the throughput of the data structure by an average of 2.5x. Our optimization uses a thread-unsafe heuristic called a Likely Abstract State Array to predict the chance of success of a transaction. Based on our findings, the use of thread-unsafe heuristics for concurrent data structures is promising and can be the focus of future work.

Acknowledgments. This material is based upon work supported by the National Science Foundation under Grant No. 1717515 and Grant No. 1740095. Any opinions, findings, and conclusions or recommendations expressed in this material are those of the author and do not necessarily reflect the views of the National Science Foundation.

References

1. Ansari, M., Luján, M., Kotselidis, C., Jarvis, K., Kirkham, C., Watson, I.: Steal-on-abort: improving transactional memory performance through dynamic transaction reordering. In: Seznec, A., Emer, J., O'Boyle, M., Martonosi, M., Ungerer, T. (eds.) HiPEAC 2009. LNCS, vol. 5409, pp. 4–18. Springer, Heidelberg (2009). https://doi.org/10.1007/978-3-540-92990-1_3
2. Cachopo, J., Rito-Silva, A.: Versioned boxes as the basis for memory transactions. Sci. Comput. Program. **63**(2), 172–185 (2006)
3. Dalessandro, L., Spear, M.F., Scott, M.L.: NOrec: streamlining STM by abolishing ownership records. In: ACM Sigplan Notices, no. 5. ACM (2010)
4. Diegues, N., Romano, P.: Time-warp: lightweight abort minimization in transactional memory. In: Symposium on Principles and Practice of Parallel Programming (2014)
5. Ellen, F., Fatourou, P., Ruppert, E., van Breugel, F.: Non-blocking binary search trees. In: Proceedings of the 29th ACM SIGACT-SIGOPS Symposium on Principles of Distributed Computing, pp. 131–140. ACM (2010)
6. Fraser, K.: Practical lock-freedom. Ph.D. thesis, Cambridge University Computer Laboratory (2003). Also available as Technical report UCAM-CL-TR-579 (2004)
7. Golan-Gueta, G., Ramalingam, G., Sagiv, M., Yahav, E.: Automatic scalable atomicity via semantic locking. In: Proceedings of the 20th ACM SIGPLAN Symposium on Principles and Practice of Parallel Programming, pp. 31–41. ACM (2015)
8. Gramoli, V., Guerraoui, R., Letia, M.: Composing relaxed transactions. In: Parallel & Distributed Processing (IPDPS), pp. 1171–1182. IEEE (2013)
9. Hassan, A., Palmieri, R., Ravindran, B.: On developing optimistic transactional lazy set. In: Aguilera, M.K., Querzoni, L., Shapiro, M. (eds.) OPODIS 2014. LNCS, vol. 8878, pp. 437–452. Springer, Cham (2014). https://doi.org/10.1007/978-3-319-14472-6_29
10. Herlihy, M., Koskinen, E.: Transactional boosting: a methodology for highly-concurrent transactional objects. In: Proceedings of the 13th ACM SIGPLAN Symposium on Principles and practice of parallel programming, pp. 207–216. ACM (2008)
11. Herlihy, M., Shavit, N.: The Art of Multiprocessor Programming. Morgan Kaufmann, Burlington (2011)
12. Koskinen, E., Parkinson, M., Herlihy, M.: Coarse-grained transactions. ACM Sigplan Not. **45**(1), 19–30 (2010)
13. Lindén, J., Jonsson, B.: A skiplist-based concurrent priority queue with minimal memory contention. In: Baldoni, R., Nisse, N., van Steen, M. (eds.) OPODIS 2013. LNCS, vol. 8304, pp. 206–220. Springer, Cham (2013). https://doi.org/10.1007/978-3-319-03850-6_15

14. Papadimitriou, C.H.: The serializability of concurrent database updates. J. ACM (JACM) **26**(4), 631–653 (1979)
15. Pedone, F., Guerraoui, R., Schiper, A.: Transaction reordering in replicated databases. In: Proceedings of the IEEE Symposium on Reliable Distributed Systems, pp. 175–182 (1997)
16. Spiegelman, A., Golan-Gueta, G., Keidar, I.: Transactional data structure libraries. In: Proceedings of the 37th ACM SIGPLAN Conference on Programming Language Design and Implementation, pp. 682–696. ACM (2016)
17. Zhang, D., Dechev, D.: An efficient lock-free logarithmic search data structure based on multi-dimensional list. In: 2016 IEEE 36th International Conference on Distributed Computing Systems (ICDCS), pp. 281–292, June 2016. https://doi.org/10.1109/ICDCS.2016.19
18. Zhang, D., Dechev, D.: Lock-free transactions without rollbacks for linked data structures. In: Proceedings of the 28th ACM Symposium on Parallelism in Algorithms and Architectures, SPAA 2016, pp. 325–336. ACM, New York (2016)

Putting Order in Strong Eventual Consistency

Kevin De Porre[1]([✉]), Florian Myter[1], Christophe De Troyer[1],
Christophe Scholliers[2], Wolfgang De Meuter[1], and Elisa Gonzalez Boix[1]

[1] Vrije Universiteit Brussel, Pleinlaan 2, 1050 Brussel, Belgium
kevin.de.porre@vub.be
[2] Ghent University, Sint Pietersnieuwstraat 33, Ghent, Belgium

Abstract. Conflict-free replicated data types (CRDTs) aid programmers develop highly available and scalable distributed systems. However, the literature describes only a limited portfolio of conflict-free data types and implementing custom ones requires additional knowledge of replication and consistency techniques. As a result, programmers resort to ad hoc solutions which are error-prone and result in brittle systems. In this paper, we introduce strong eventually consistent replicated objects (SECROs), a general-purpose data type for building available data structures that guarantee strong eventual consistency (SEC) without restrictions on the operations. To evaluate our solution we compare a real-time collaborative text editor built atop SECROs with a state-of-the-art implementation that uses JSON CRDTs. This comparison quantifies various performance aspects. The results show that SECROs are truly general-purpose and memory efficient.

Keywords: Distribution · Eventual consistency ·
Replicated data types

1 Introduction

According to the CAP theorem [4,5] distributed systems that are prone to partitions can only guarantee availability or consistency. This leads to a spectrum of distributed systems that ranges from highly available systems (AP) to strongly consistent systems (CP) with hybrid systems - that are partly AP and partly CP - in the middle. A substantial body of research has focused on techniques or protocols to propagate updates [7,16,19,20]. In this paper, we focus on *language abstractions* that ease the development of highly available and partition tolerant systems, the so-called AP systems.

A state-of-the-art approach towards high availability are conflict-free replicated data types (CRDTs) [19]. CRDTs rely on commutative operations to guarantee strong eventual consistency (SEC), a variation on eventual consistency that

© IFIP International Federation for Information Processing 2019
Published by Springer Nature Switzerland AG 2019
J. Pereira and L. Ricci (Eds.): DAIS 2019, LNCS 11534, pp. 36–56, 2019.
https://doi.org/10.1007/978-3-030-22496-7_3

provides an additional *strong convergence* guarantee[1]. This avoids the need for synchronisation, yielding high availability and low latency.

The literature has proposed a portfolio of basic conflict-free data structures such as counters, sets, and linked lists [17,18,22]. However, advanced distributed systems require replicated data types that are tailored to the needs of the application. Consider, for example, a real-world collaborative text editor that represents documents as a balanced tree of characters, allowing for logarithmic time lookups, insertions, and deletions. To the best of our knowledge, the only tree CRDT has been proposed in [12]. In this approach, balancing the tree requires synchronising the replicas. However, this is not possible in AP systems as it implies giving up on availability.

When the current portfolio of CRDTs falls short, programmers can resort to two solutions. One is to manually engineer the data structure as a CRDT. This requires rethinking the data structure completely such that all operations commute. If the operations cannot be made commutative, programmers need to manually implement conflict resolution. This has shown to be error-prone and results in brittle systems [1,9,19]. Alternatively, programmers can use JSON CRDTs [9] or Lasp [14] to design custom CRDTs. JSON CRDTs let programmers arbitrarily nest linked lists and maps into new CRDTs, whereas Lasp supports functional transformations over existing CRDTs. However, these constructs are not general enough. Consider again the case of a collaborative text editor. Using lists and maps one cannot implement a balanced tree CRDT, nor can one derive a balanced tree from existing CRDTs.

In this paper, we explore a new direction which consists in devising a general-purpose language abstraction for high availability. We design a novel replicated data type called *strong eventually consistent replicated object* (SECRO). SECROs guarantee SEC by reordering *conflicting* operations in a way that solves the conflict. To find a conflict-free ordering of the operations, SECROs rely on application-specific information provided by the programmer through *concurrent pre and postconditions* defined over the operations of the SECRO. Our approach is based on the idea that conflict detection and resolution naturally depends on the semantics of the application [21].

We evaluate our approach by implementing a real-time collaborative text editor using SECROs and comparing it to a JSON CRDT implementation of the text editor, as proposed in [9]. We present various experiments that quantify the memory usage, execution time, and throughput of both implementations.

2   Strong Eventually Consistent Replicated Objects

In this section, we describe strong eventually consistent replicated objects from a programmer's perspective. All code snippets are in CScript[2], a JavaScript

---

[1] Strong convergence states that correct replicas that received the same updates must be in an equivalent state.

[2] CScript is available at https://gitlab.com/iot-thesis/framework/tree/master.

extension embodying our implementation of SECROs. We introduce the necessary syntax and features of CScript along with our explanation on SECROs.

2.1 SECRO Data Type

A SECRO is an object that implements an abstract data type and can be replicated to a group of devices. Like regular objects, SECROs contain state in the form of fields, and behaviour in the form of methods. It is not possible to directly access a SECRO's internal state. Instead, the methods defined by the SECRO need to be used. These methods form the SECRO's public interface. Methods can be further categorised in *accessors* (i.e. methods querying internal state) and *mutators* (i.e. methods updating the internal state).

As an example, consider the case of a collaborative text editor which organises documents as a balanced tree of characters [15,22]. Listing 1.1 shows the structure of the Document SECRO. In order to create a new SECRO, programmers extend the SECRO abstract data type. Instead of implementing our own balanced tree data structure, we re-use an existing AVL tree data structure provided by the Closure library[3].

```
1   class Document extends SECRO {
2     constructor(tree = new AvlTree((c1, c2) => c1.id - c2.id)) {
3       this._tree = tree;
4     }
5     @accessor
6     containsId(id) {
7       const dummyChar = {char: '', id: id};
8       return this._tree.contains(dummyChar);
9     }
10    @accessor
11    generateId(prev) { /* see appendix */ }
12    @accessor
13    indexOf(char) {
14      return this._tree.indexOf(char);
15    }
16    // serialisation methods
17    tojson() {
18      return this._tree; // AVL tree is serialisable
19    }
20    static fromjson(tree) {
21      return new Document(tree);
22    }
23    // operations to manipulate the tree
24    insertAfter(id, char) { /* see listing 1.2 */ }
25    delete(id) { /* see listing 1.3 */ }
26    // SECRO's state validators
27    pre insertAfter(doc, args) {/*listing 1.2*/}
28    post insertAfter(originalDoc, doc, args, newChar) {/*listing 1.2*/}
29    post delete(originalDoc, doc, args, res) {/*listing 1.3*/}
30  }
31  Factory.registerAvailableType(Document);
```

Listing 1.1. Structure of the text editor.

---

[3] https://developers.google.com/closure/library/.

The Document SECRO defines three accessors (containsId, generateId and indexOf) and two mutators (insertAfter and delete). containsId returns a boolean that indicates the presence or absence of a certain identifier in the document tree. generateId uses a boundary allocation strategy [15] to compute stable identifiers based on the reference identifiers. Finally, indexOf returns the index of a character in the document tree. Note that side-effect free methods are annotated with @accessor, otherwise, CScript treats them as mutators.

The Document SECRO also defines methods to serialise and deserialise the document as it will be replicated over the network. Note that deserialisation creates a new replica of the Document SECRO. In order for the receiver to know the Document class, programmers must register their SECRO at the CScript *factory* (line 31).

Finally, the Document SECRO forwards insertAfter and delete operations on the text to the underlying AVL tree (as we describe later in Sect. 2.2). Besides the methods defined in the SECRO's public interface, programmers can also enforce application-specific invariants by associating concurrent preconditions and postconditions to the mutators (Line 27 to 29). We say that pre and postconditions are *state validators*. State validators are used by the SECRO to order concurrent operations such that they do not violate any invariant. Next section further describes them.

2.2 State Validators

State validators let programmers define the data type's behaviour in the face of concurrency. State validators are declarative rules that are associated to mutators. Those rules express invariants over the state of the object which need to uphold in the presence of concurrent operations[4]. Behind the scenes, the replication protocol may interleave concurrent operations. From the programmer's perspective the only guarantee is that these invariants are upheld. State validators come in two forms:

Preconditions. Specify invariants that must hold prior to the execution of their associated operation. As such, preconditions approve or reject the state before applying the actual update. In case of a rejection, the operation is aborted and a different ordering of the operations will be tried.

Postconditions. Specify invariants that must hold after the execution of their associated operation. In contrast to preconditions, an operation's associated postcondition does not execute immediately. Instead, the postcondition executes after all concurrent operations complete. As such, postconditions approve or reject the state that results from a group of concurrent, potentially conflicting operations. In case of a rejection a different ordering is tried.

In CScript, state validators are methods which are prefixed with the pre or post keyword, defining a pre or postcondition, respectively. To illustrate

---

[4] From now on, we use the terms operation and mutator interchangeably, as well as the terms update and mutation.

state validators we again consider the example of a collaborative text editor and present the implementation of the `insertAfter` and `delete` methods and their associated preconditions and postconditions. Listing 1.2 contains the `insertAfter` operation. Listing The `id` argument on Line 1 is the identifier of the reference character. On Line 2 the method generates a new stable identifier for the character it is inserting. Using this identifier the method creates a new character on Line 3. Finally, Line 4 and 5 insert the character in the tree and return the newly added character. Line 7 to 10 define a precondition on insert. The precondition is a method which has the same name as its associated operation and takes as parameters the object's current state followed by an array containing the arguments that are passed to its associated operation. In this case, `id` and `char` as passed to `insertAfter`. The precondition checks that the reference character exists (Line 9).

```
1   insertAfter(id, char) {
2       const newId   = this.generateId(id),
3             newChar = new Character(char, newId);
4       this._tree.add(newChar);
5       return newChar;
6   }
7   pre insertAfter(doc, args) {
8       const [id, char] = args;
9       return id === null || doc.containsId(id);
10  }
11  post insertAfter(originalDoc, newDoc, args, newChar) {
12      const [id, char]  = args,
13            originalChar = {char: "dummy", id: id};
14      return (id === null && doc._tree.contains(newChar)) ||
15             doc.indexOf(originalChar) < doc.indexOf(newChar);
16  }
```

Listing 1.2. Inserting a character in a tree-based text document.

Lines 11 to 16 define a postcondition for the `insertAfter` operation. Similar to preconditions, postconditions are defined as a method which has the same name as its associated operation (`insertAfter` in this case). However, they take 4 arguments: (1) the SECRO's initial state, (2) the state that results from applying the operation (`insertAfter`), (3) an array with the operation's arguments, and (4) the operation's return value (`newChar` in this case). This postcondition checks that the newly added character occurs at the correct position in the resulting tree, i.e. after the reference character that is identified by `id`. According to this postcondition any interleaving of concurrent character insertions is valid, e.g. two users may concurrently write "foo" and "bar" resulting in one of: "foobar", "fboaor", etc. If the programmer only wants to allow the interleavings "foobar" and "barfoo" the SECRO must operate on the granularity of words instead of single character manipulations.

Listing 1.3 contains the implementation of the `delete` method and its associated postcondition. Lines 1 to 3 show that characters are deleted by removing them from the underlying AVL tree. Recall that the character's stable identifier uniquely identifies the character in the tree. Afterwards, the postcondition on Lines 4 to 7 ensures that the character no longer occurs in the tree.

```
1  delete(id) {
2      return this._tree.remove(id);
3  }
4  post delete(originalDoc, doc, args, res) {
5      const [id] = args;
6      return !doc.containsId(id);
7  }
```

Listing 1.3. Deleting a character from a tree-based text document.

Notice that preconditions are less expressive than postconditions but, they avoid unnecessary computations by rejecting invalid states prior to the execution of the operation. Preconditions are also useful to prevent operations from running on a corrupted state, thus improving the system's robustness.

3   SECRO's Replication Protocol

A SECRO is a general-purpose language abstraction that guarantees SEC, i.e. eventual consistency and strong convergence. To provide this guarantee SECROs implement a dedicated optimistic replication protocol. For the purpose of this paper, we describe the protocol in pseudocode[5].

SECRO's protocol propagates update operations to all replicas. In contrast to CRDTs, the operations of a SECRO do not necessarily commute. Therefore, the replication protocol totally orders the operations at all replicas. This order may not violate any of the operations' pre or postconditions.

For the sake of simplicity we assume a causal order broadcasting mechanism without loss of generality, i.e. a communication medium in which messages arrive in an order that is consistent with the happened-before relation [10]. Note that even though we rely on causal order broadcasting, concurrent operations arrive in arbitrary orders at the replicas.

Intuitively, replicas maintain their *initial state* and a sequence of operations called the *operation history*. Each time a replica receives an operation, it is added to the replica's history, which may require reordering parts of the history. Reordering the history boils down to finding an ordering of the operations that fulfils two requirements. First, the order must respect the causality of operations. Second, applying all the operations in the given order may not violate any of the concurrent pre or postconditions. An ordering which adheres to these requirements is called a *valid execution*. As soon as a valid execution is found each replica resets its state to the initial one and executes the operations in-order. Reordering the history is a deterministic process, hence, replicas that received the same operations find the same valid execution.

The existence of a valid execution cannot be guaranteed if pre and postconditions contradict each other. It is the programmer's responsibility to provide correct pre and postconditions.

---

[5] The implementation is part of CScript and can be found at https://gitlab.com/iot-thesis/framework/tree/master/src/Application/CRDTs/SECRO.

The replication protocol provides the following guarantees:

1. Eventually, all replicas converge towards the same valid execution (i.e. eventual consistency).
2. Replicas that received the same updates have identical operation histories (i.e. strong convergence).
3. Replicas eventually perform the operations of a valid execution if one exists, or issue an error if none exists.

The operation histories of replicas may grow unboundedly as they perform operations. In order to alleviate this issue we allow for replicas to periodically *commit* their state. Concretely, replicas maintain a *version number*. Whenever a replica commits, it clears its operation history and increments its version number. The replication protocol then notifies all other replicas of this commit, which adopt the committed state and also empty their operation history. All subsequent operations received by a replica which apply to a previous version number are ignored. As we explain in Sect. 3.1, the commit operation does not require synchronising the replicas and thus does not affect the system's availability. However, commits come at the price of certain operations being dropped for the sake of bounded operation history size.

3.1 Algorithm

We now detail our replication protocol which makes the following assumptions:

- Each node in the network may contain any number of replicas of a SECRO.
- Nodes maintain vector clocks to timestamp the operations of a replica.
- Nodes are able to generate globally unique identifiers using lamport clocks.
- Reading the state of a replica happens side-effect free and mutators solely affect the replica's state (i.e. the side effects are confined to the replica itself).
- Eventually, all messages arrive, i.e. reliable communication: no message loss nor duplication (e.g., TCP/IP).
- There are no byzantine failures, i.e. no malicious nodes.

A replica r is a tuple $r = (v_i, s_0, s_i, h, id_c)$ consisting of the replica's version number v_i, its initial state s_0, its current state s_i, its operation history h, and the id of the latest commit operation id_c. A mutator m is represented as a tuple $m = (o, p, a)$ consisting of the update operation o, precondition p, and postcondition a. We denote that a mutation m_1 happened before m_2 using $m_1 \prec m_2$. Similarly, we denote that two mutations happened concurrently using $m_1 \parallel m_2$. Both relations are based on the clocks carried by the mutators [8].

We now discuss in detail the three kinds of operations that are possible on replicas: reading, mutating, and committing state.

Reading Replicas. Reading the value of a replica (v_i, s_0, s_i, h, id_c) simply returns its latest local state s_i.

ALGORITHM 1. Handling *mutate* messages

---

arguments: A *mutate* message m $= (o, p, a, c, id)$, a replica $= (v_i, s_0, s_i, h, id_c)$

```
1   h' = h ∪ {m}
2   for ops ∈ LE(sort_{>>}(h')) do
3       s'_i = s_i
4       pre = 0
5       post = 0
6       for m ∈ ops do
7           concurrentClosure = TC(m, h') ∪ {m}
8           for m' = (o, p, a, c, id) ∈ concurrentClosure do
9               if p(s'_i) then
10                  pre += 1
11                  s'_i = o(s'_i)
12              end
13          end
14          for m' = (o, p, a, c, id) ∈ concurrentClosure do
15              if a(s'_i) then
16                  post += 1
17              end
18          end
19          ops = ops \ concurrentClosure
20      end
21      if pre == |ops| ∧ post == |ops| then
22          return (v_i, s_0, s'_i, h', id_c)
23      end
24  end
        // throw faulty program exception
```

Mutating Replicas. When a mutator $m = (o, p, a)$ is applied to a replica a *mutate* message is broadcast to all replicas. Such a message is an extension of the mutator (o, p, a, c, id) which additionally contains the node's logical clock time c and a unique identifier id.

As mentioned before, operations on SECROs do not need to commute by design. Since operations are timestamped with logical clocks they exhibit a partial order. Algorithm 1 governs the replicas' behaviour to guarantee SEC by ensuring that all replicas execute the same valid ordering of their operation history.

Algorithm 1 starts when a replica receives a *mutate* message. The algorithm consists of two parts. First, it adds the *mutate* message to the operation history, sorts the history according to the $>>$ total order, and generates all *linear extensions* of the replica's sorted history (see Lines 1 and 2). We say that $m_1 = (o_1, p_1, a_1, c_1, id_1) >> m_2 = (o_2, p_2, a_2, c_2, id_2)$ iff $c_1 \succ c_2 \lor (c_1 \parallel c_2 \land id_1 > id_2)$. The generated linear extensions are all the permutations of h' that respect the partial order defined by the operations' causal relations. Since replicas deterministically compute linear extensions and start from the same sorted operation history, all replicas generate the same sequence of permutations.

Second, the algorithm searches for the first *valid* permutation. In other words, for each operation within such a permutation the algorithm checks that the preconditions (Lines 8 to 13) and postconditions (Lines 14 to 18) hold. Remember that postconditions are checked only after all concurrent operations executed since they happened independently (e.g. during a network partition) and may thus conflict. For this reason, Line 7 computes the transitive closure of concurrent operations[6] for every operation in the linear extension.

Since the "is concurrent" relation is not transitive, one might wonder why we consider operations that are not directly concurrent. To illustrate this, consider a replica r_1 that executes operation o_1 followed by o_2 ($o_1 \prec o_2$) while concurrently replica r_2 executes operation o_3 ($o_3 \parallel o_1 \land o_3 \parallel o_2$). Since o_3 may affect both o_1 and o_2 we take into account all three operations. This corresponds to the transitive closure $\{o_1, o_2, o_3\}$. We refer the reader to Appendix A for a proof that no operation can break this transitive closure of concurrent operations.

Finally, the algorithm returns the replica's updated state as soon as a valid execution is found, otherwise, it throws an exception.

Committing Replicas. In a nutshell, commit clears a replica's operation history h, increments the replica's version and updates the initial state s_0 with the replica's current state s_i. This avoids unbounded growth of operation histories, but operations concurrent with the commit will be discarded[7].

When a replica is committed a *commit* message is broadcast to all replicas (including the committed one). This message is a quadruple $(s_i, v_i, clock, id)$ containing the committed state, the replica's version number, the current logical clock time, and a unique id.

ALGORITHM 2. Handling *commit* messages

---

    arguments: A *commit* message $= (s_c, v_c, clock, id)$, a replica $= (v_i, s_0, s_i, h, id_c)$
1 **if** $v_c = v_i$ **then**
2 | **return** $(v_i + 1, s_c, s_c, \emptyset, id)$
3 **end**
4 **if** $v_c = v_i - 1 \land id < id_c$ **then**
5 | **return** $(v_i, s_c, s_c, \emptyset, id)$
6 **end**

To ensure that replicas converge in the face of concurrent commits we design commit operations to commute. As a result, commit does not compromise availability. Algorithm 2 dictates how replicas handle *commit* messages. The algorithm distinguishes between two cases. First, the commit operation commits the current state (see Line 1). The replica's version is incremented, its initial and current state are set to the committed state, the operation history is cleared and the id of the last performed commit is updated. Second, the commit operation commits the previous state (see Line 4). This means that the commit operation applies to the previous version v_{i-1}. As a result, the newly received commit operation is concurrent with the last performed commit operation (i.e. the one that

---

[6] The transitive closure of a mutate message m with respect to an operation history h is denoted $TC(m, h)$ and is the set of all operations that are directly or transitively concurrent with m. A formal definition is provided in Appendix A.

[7] Since commit may drop operations, one can argue that SECROs are similar to last-writer-wins (LWW) strategies. However, SECROs guarantee invariant preservation, which is not the case with CRDTs.

caused the replica to update its version from v_{i-1} to v_i). To ensure convergence, replicas perform the commit operation with the smallest ID. This ensures that the order in which commits are received is immaterial and hence that commit operations commute. Note that the algorithm does not need to tackle the case of committing an elder state since it cannot happen under the assumption of causal order broadcasting.

4 Evaluation

We now compare our novel replicated data type to JSON CRDTs, a state-of-the-art approach providing custom CRDTs built atop lists and maps. We perform a number of experiments which quantify the memory usage, execution time and throughput of the collaborative text editor. We implemented it twice in JavaScript, once using SECROs[8] and once using JSON CRDTs[9]. The JSON CRDT implementation uses a list to represent text documents. The SECRO implementation comes in two variants: one that uses a list and one that uses a balanced tree (described in Sect. 2).

Note that SECROs are designed to ease the development of custom replicated data types guaranteeing SEC. Hence, our goal is not to outperform JSON CRDTs, but rather to evaluate the practical feasibility of SECROs.

4.1 Methodology

All experiments are performed on a cluster consisting of 10 worker nodes which are interconnected through a 10 Gbit twinax connection. Each worker node has an Intel Xeon E3-1240 processor at 3.50 GHz and 32 GB of RAM. Depending on the experiment, the benchmark is either run on a single worker node or on all ten nodes. We specify this for each benchmark.

To get statistically sound results we repeat each benchmark at least 30 times, yielding a minimum of 30 samples per measurement. Each benchmark starts with a number of warmup rounds to minimise the effects of program initialisation. Furthermore, we disable NodeJS' just-in-time compiler optimisations to obtain more stable execution times.

We perform statistical analysis over our measurements as follows. First, depending on the benchmark we discard samples that are affected by garbage collection (e.g. the execution time benchmarks). Then, for each measurement including at least 30 samples we compute the average value and the corresponding 95% confidence interval.

---

[8] CScript code presented in Sect. 2 compiles to JavaScript and runs atop NodeJS.

[9] The implementations are available at https://gitlab.com/iot-thesis/framework/tree/master.

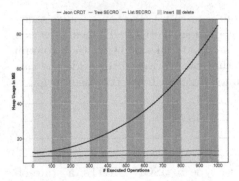 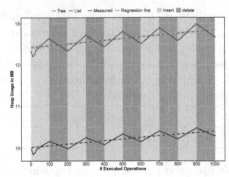

(a) Comparison between the memory usage of the SECRO and JSON CRDT text editors.

(b) Comparison between the list and tree implementations of the SECRO text editor.

Fig. 1. Memory usage of the collaborative text editors. Error bars represent the 95% confidence interval for the average taken from 30 samples. These experiments are performed on a single worker node of the cluster. (Color figure online)

4.2 Memory Usage

To compare the memory usage of the SECRO and JSON CRDT text editors, we perform an experiment in which 1000 operations are executed on each text editor. We continuously alternate between 100 character insertions followed by deletions of those 100 characters. We force garbage collection after each operation[10], and measure the heap usage. The resulting measurements are shown in Fig. 1. Green and red columns indicate character insertions and deletions respectively.

Figure 1a confirms our expectation that the SECRO implementations are more memory efficient than the JSON CRDT one. The memory usage of the JSON CRDT text editor grows unbounded since CRDTs cannot delete characters, but merely mark them as deleted using tombstones. Conversely, SECROs support true deletions by reorganising concurrent operations in a non-conflicting order. Hence, all 100 inserted characters are deleted by the following 100 deletions. This results in lower memory usage.

Figure 1b compares the memory usage of the list and tree-based implementations using SECROs. We conclude that the tree-based implementation consumes more memory than the list implementation. The reason is that nodes of a tree maintain pointers to their children, whereas nodes of a singly linked list only maintain a single pointer to the next node. Interestingly, we observe a staircase pattern. This pattern indicates that memory usage grows when characters are inserted (green columns) and shrinks when characters are deleted (red columns). Overall, memory usage increases linearly with the number of executed operations, even though we delete the inserted characters and commit the replica

---

[10] Forcing garbage collection is needed to get the real-time memory usage. Otherwise, the memory usage keeps growing until garbage collection is triggered.

after each operation. Hence, SECROs cause a small memory overhead for each executed operation. This linear increase is shown by the dashed regression lines.

4.3   Execution Time

We now benchmark the time it takes to append characters to a text document. Although this is not a realistic edition pattern, it showcases the worst case performance. From Fig. 2a we notice that the SECRO versions exhibit a quadratic performance, whereas the JSON CRDT version exhibits a linear performance. The reason for this is that reordering the SECRO's history (see Algorithm 1 in Sect. 3.1) induces a linear overhead on top of the operations themselves. Since insert is also a linear operation, the overall performance of the text editor's insert operation is quadratic. To address this performance overhead the replica needs to be committed. The effect of commit on the execution time of insert operations is depicted in Appendix B.

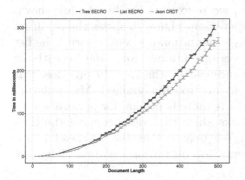 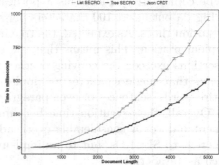

(a) Execution time of an operation that appends one character to a document.

(b) Execution time of an operation that appends 100 characters to a document.

Fig. 2. Execution time of character insertions in the collaborative text editors. Replicas are never committed. Error bars represent the 95% confidence interval for the average taken from a minimum of 30 samples. Samples affected by garbage collection are discarded. (Color figure online)

Figure 2b also shows that the SECRO implementation that uses a linked list is faster than its tree-based counterpart. To determine the cause of this counterintuitive observation, we measure the different parts that make up the total execution time:

Execution time of operations. Total time spent on append operations.
Execution time of preconditions. Total time spent on preconditions.
Execution time of postconditions. Total time spent on postconditions.

Copy time. Due to the mutability of JavaScript objects our prototype implementation in CScript needs to copy the state before validating the potential history. The total time spent on copying objects (i.e. the document state) is the copy time.

Figures 5a and b in Appendix C depict the detailed execution time for the list and tree implementations respectively. The results show that the total execution time is dominated by the copy time. We observe that the tree implementation spends more time on copying the document than the list implementation. The reason being that copying a tree entails a higher overhead than copying a linked list as more pointers need to be copied. Furthermore, the tree implementation spends considerably less time executing operations, preconditions and postconditions, than the list implementation. This results from the fact that the balanced tree provides logarithmic time operations.

Unfortunately, the time overhead incurred by copying the document kills the speedup we gain from organising the document as a tree. This is because each insertion inserts only a single character but requires the entire document to be copied. To validate this hypothesis, we re-execute the benchmark shown in Fig. 2a but insert 100 characters per operation. Figure 2b shows the resulting execution times. As expected, the tree implementation now outperforms the list implementation. This means that the speedup obtained from 100 logarithmic insertions exceeds the copying overhead induced by the tree. In practice, this means that single character manipulations are too fine-grained. Manipulating entire words, sentences or even paragraphs is more beneficial for performance.

Overall, the execution time benchmarks show that deep copying the document induces a considerable overhead. We believe that the overhead is not inherent to SECROs, but to its implementation on top of a mutable language such as JavaScript.

4.4   Throughput

The experiments presented so far focused on the execution time of sequential operations on a single replica. To measure the throughput of the text editors under high computational loads we also perform distributed benchmarks. To this end, we use 10 replicas (one on each node of the cluster) and let them simultaneously perform operations on the text editor. The operations are equally spread over the replicas. We measure the time to convergence, i.e. the time that is needed for all replicas to process all operations and reach a consistent state. Note that replicas reorder operations locally, hence, the throughput depends on the number of operations and is independent of the number of replicas.

Figure 3 depicts how the throughput of the list-based text editor varies in function of the load. We observe that the SECRO text editor scales up to 50 concurrent operations, at which point it reaches its maximal throughput. Afterwards, the throughput quickly degrades. On the other hand, the JSON CRDT implementation achieves a higher throughput than the SECRO version

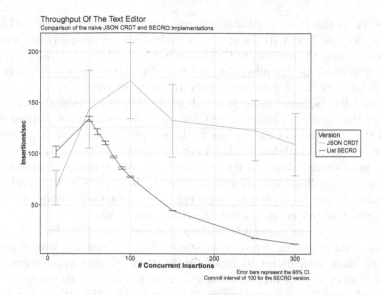

Fig. 3. Throughput of the list-based SECRO and JSON CRDT text editors, in function of the number of concurrent operations. The SECRO version committed the document replica at a commit interval of 100. Error bars represent the 95% confidence interval for the average of 30 samples.

under high loads (100 concurrent operations and more). Hence, the JSON CRDT text editor scales better than the SECRO text editor, but SECROs are general-purpose which allowed us to organise documents as balanced trees of characters.

5   Related Work

We now discuss work that is closely related to the ideas presented in this paper. Central to SECROs is the idea of employing application-specific information to reorder conflicting operations. Bayou [21] was the first system to use application-level semantics for conflict resolution by means of merge procedures provided by users. Our work, however, does not require manual resolution of conflicts. Instead, programmers only need to specify the invariants the application should uphold in the face of concurrent updates, and the underlying update algorithm deterministically orders operations.

Within the CRDT literature, the research on JSON CRDTs [9] is the most closely related to our work. JSON CRDTs aim to ease the construction of CRDTs by hiding the commutativity restriction that traditionally applies to the operations. Programmers can build new CRDTs by nesting lists and maps in arbitrary ways. The major shortcoming is that nesting lists and maps does not suffice to implement arbitrary replicated data types. Hence, JSON CRDTs are not truly general-purpose as opposed to SECROs.

Lasp [14] is the first distributed programming language where CRDTs are first-class citizens. New CRDTs are defined through functional transformations over existing ones. In contrast, SECROs are not limited to a portfolio of existing data types that can be extended. Any existing data structure can be turned into a SECRO by associating state validators to the operations.

Besides CRDTs, cloud types [6] are high-level data types that can be replicated over the network. Similar to SECROs, cloud types do not impose restrictions on the operations of the replicated data type. However, cloud types hardcode how to merge updates coming from different replicas of the same type. As such, programmers have no means to customise the merge process of cloud types to fit the application's semantics. Instead, they are bound to implement a new cloud type and the accompanying merge procedure that fits the application. Hence, conflict resolution needs to be manually dealt with.

Some work has considered a hybrid approach offering SEC for commutative operations, and requiring strong consistency for non-commutative ones [2,3]. There are some similarities to SECROs as they employ application-specific invariants to classify operations as safe or unsafe under concurrent execution. In this work, unsafe operations are synchronised while SECROs reorder unsafe operations as to avoid conflicts without giving up on availability. Partial Order-Restrictions (PoR) consistency [13] uses application-specific restrictions over operations but cannot guarantee convergence nor invariant preservation since these properties depend on the restrictions over the operations specified by the programmer.

6   Conclusion

In this work, we propose strong eventually consistent replicated objects (SECROs), a data type that guarantees SEC without imposing restrictions on the operations. SECROs do not avoid conflicts by design, but instead compute a global total order of the operations that is conflict-free, without synchronising the replicas. To this end, SECROs use *state validators*: application-specific invariants that determine the object's behaviour in the face of concurrency.

To the best of our knowledge, SECROs are the first approach to support truly general-purpose replicated data types while still guaranteeing SEC. By specifying state validators arbitrary data types can be turned into highly available replicated data types. This means that replicated data types can be implemented similarly to their sequential local counterpart, with the addition of preconditions and postconditions to define concurrent semantics. We showcase the flexibility of SECROs through the implementation of a collaborative text editor that stores documents as a tree of characters. The implementation re-uses a third-party AVL tree and turns into a replicated data type using SECROs.

We compared our SECRO-based collaborative text editor to a state-of-the-art implementation that uses JSON CRDTs. The benchmarks reveal that SECROs efficiently manage memory, whereas the memory usage of JSON CRDTs grows unbounded. Time complexity benchmarks reveal that SECROs induce a linear time overhead which is proportional to the size of the operation history. Performance wise, SECROs can be competitive to state-of-the-art solutions if committed regularly.

Acknowledgments. Kevin De Porre is funded by an SB Fellowship of the Research Foundation - Flanders. Project number: 1S98519N.

A   Proof: Operations Cannot Break the Transitive Closure of Concurrent Operations

Recall from Algorithm 1 in Sect. 3.1 that checking preconditions and postconditions requires computing the transitive closure of concurrent operations. We now formally define the transitive closure of concurrent operations and prove that operations cannot break this closure.

Definition 1. *An operation $m_1 = (o_1, p_1, a_1, c_1, id_1)$ happened before an operation $m_2 = (o_2, p_2, a_2, c_2, id_2)$ iff the logical timestamp of m_1 happened before the logical timestamp of m_2: $m_1 \prec m_2 \iff c_1 \prec c_2$.*

Definition 2. *Two operations m_1 and m_2 are concurrent iff neither one happened before the other [11]: $m_1 \parallel m_2 \iff m_1 \nprec m_2 \wedge m_2 \nprec m_1$.*

Definition 3. *We define $\parallel^+$ as the transitive closure of $\parallel$.*

Definition 4. *The set of all operations that are transitively concurrent to an operation m with respect to a history h is defined as: $TC(m, h) = \{m' \mid m' \in h \wedge m' \parallel^+ m\}$.*

Definition 5. *An operation m happened before a set of operations T iff it happened before every operation of the set: $m \prec T \iff \forall m' \in T : m \prec m'$.*

Definition 6. *An operation m happened after a set of operations T iff it happened after all operations of the set: $T \prec m \iff \forall m' \in T : m' \prec m$.*

Definition 7. *A set of operations T_1 happened before a set of operations T_2 iff every operation from T_1 happened before every operation of T_2: $T_1 \prec T_2 \iff \forall m_1 \in T_1 \forall m_2 \in T_2 : m_1 \prec m_2$*

Theorem 1. *For any operation m' and any non-empty transitive closure $TC(m, h)$ it holds that $m' \in TC(m, h) \vee m' \prec TC(m, h) \vee TC(m, h) \prec m'$.*

Proof. Proof by contradiction.

Assume that an operation m' exists for which Theorem 1 does not hold: $\exists m'$: $m' \notin TC(m, h) \wedge m' \not\prec TC(m, h) \wedge TC(m, h) \not\prec m'$. This means that operation m' breaks the concurrent transitive closure into two disjoint sets of operations: $\exists T_1 \exists T_2 : T_1 \prec m' \wedge m' \prec T_2$ where $T_1 = \{m_1, m_2, \ldots, m_i\} \subset TC(m, h)$ and $T_2 = \{m_{i+1}, \ldots, m_n\} \subset TC(m, h)$ and $T_1 \cap T_2 = \emptyset$ and $T_1 \cup T_2 = TC(m, h)$. Then by transitivity of the happened-before relation ($\prec$) we find that $T_1 \prec T_2$. This leads to a contradiction since we know that $T_1 \in TC(m, h) \wedge T_2 \in TC(m, h) \implies \exists m_i \in T_1 \exists m_j \in T_2 : m_i \parallel m_j$, i.e., there must be a link $m_i \parallel m_j$ between T_1 and T_2. Therefore, T_1 cannot have happened before T_2. $\square$

B   The Effect of Commit on the Execution Time

In this appendix, we present two benchmarks. The first quantifies the performance overhead of SECROs that results from reordering the operation history. The second illustrates the effect of commit on the execution time of the collaborative text editor and how commit improves its performance.

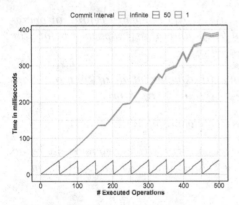
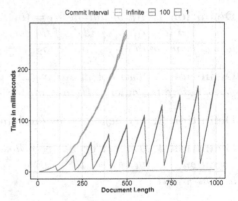

(a) Execution time of a constant time operation in function of the number of executed operations.

(b) Time to append a character to the text document using the list implementation of the SECRO text editor.

Fig. 4. Execution time of SECROs for different commit intervals, performed on a single worker node of the cluster. Error bands represent the 95% confidence interval for the average taken from a minimum of 30 samples. Samples affected by garbage collection were discarded. (Color figure online)

To quantify the performance overhead of SECROs we measure the execution times of 500 *constant* time operations, for different commit intervals. Each operation computes 10 000 tangents and has no associated pre- or postcondition. Hence, the resulting measurements reflect the best-case performance of SECROs.

Figure 4a depicts the execution time of the aforementioned constant time operation. If we do not commit the replica (red curve), the operation's execution time increases linearly with the number of operations. Hence, SECROs induce a linear overhead. This results from the fact that the replica's operation history grows with every operation. Each operation requires the replica to reorganise the history. To this end, the replica generates linear extensions of the history until a valid ordering of the operations is found (see Algorithm 1 in Sect. 3.1). Since we defined no preconditions or postconditions, every order is valid. The replica thus generates exactly one linear extension and validates it. To validate the ordering, the replica executes each operation. Therefore, the operation's execution time is linear to the size of the operation history.

As mentioned previously, commit implies a trade-off between concurrency and performance. Small commit intervals lead to better performance but less concurrency, whereas large commit intervals support more concurrent operations at the cost of performance. Figure 4a illustrates this trade-off. For a commit interval of 50 (blue curve), we observe a sawtooth pattern. The operation's execution time increases until the replica is committed, whereafter it falls back to its initial execution time. This is because *commit* clears the operation history. When choosing a commit interval of 1 (green curve), the replica is committed after every operation. Hence, the history contains a single operation and does not need to be reorganised. This results in a constant execution time.

We now analyse the execution time of insert operations on the collaborative text editor. Figure 4b shows the time it takes to append a character to a text document in function of the document's length, for various commit intervals. If we do not commit the replica (red curve), append exhibits a quadratic execution time. This is because the SECRO induces a linear overhead and append is a linear operation. Hence, append's execution time becomes quadratic. For a commit interval of 100 (blue curve) we again observe a sawtooth pattern. In contrast to Fig. 4a the peaks increase linearly with the size of the document, since append is a linear operation. If we choose a commit interval of 1 (green curve) we get a linear execution time. This results from the fact that we do not need to reorganise the replica's history. Hence, we execute a single append operation.

From these results, we draw two conclusions. First, SECROs induce a linear overhead on the execution time of operations. Second, commit is a pragmatic solution to keep the performance of SECROs within acceptable bounds for the application at hand.

C   Detailed Execution Time

In this appendix we show the detailed execution time of character insertions in the list and tree versions of the collaborative text editor. This is a breakdown of the green and blue curves respectively in Fig. 2a. The replica is never committed. The plotted execution time is the average taken from a minimum of 30 samples. Samples affected by garbage collection are discarded. The complete explanation can be found in Sect. 4.3.

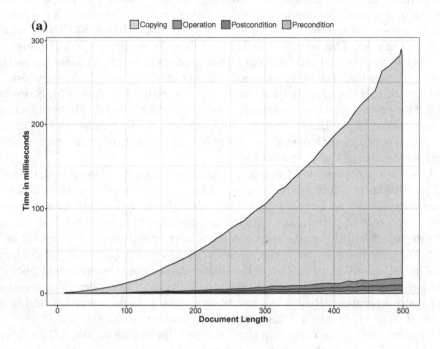

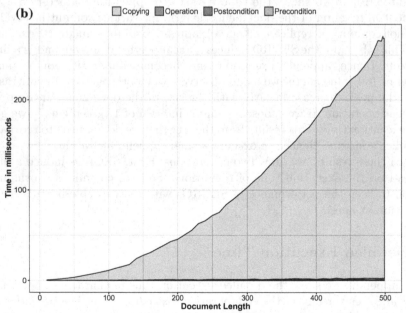

Fig. 5. (a) List implementation (b) Tree implementation

References

1. Almeida, P.S., Shoker, A., Baquero, C.: Efficient state-based CRDTs by delta-mutation. In: Bouajjani, A., Fauconnier, H. (eds.) NETYS 2015. LNCS, vol. 9466, pp. 62–76. Springer, Cham (2015). https://doi.org/10.1007/978-3-319-26850-7_5
2. Balegas, V., et al.: Putting consistency back into eventual consistency. In: 10th European Conference on Computer Systems, EuroSys 2015, pp. 6:1–6:16 (2015)
3. Balegas, V., et al.: Geo-replication: fast if possible, consistent if necessary. IEEE Data Eng. Bull. **39**(1), 12 (2016)
4. Brewer, E.: Towards robust distributed systems. In: 19th Annual ACM Symposium on Principles of Distributed Computing, PODC 2000, p. 7 (2000)
5. Brewer, E.: CAP twelve years later: how the "rules" have changed. Computer **45**(2), 23–29 (2012)
6. Burckhardt, S., Fähndrich, M., Leijen, D., Wood, B.P.: Cloud types for eventual consistency. In: Noble, J. (ed.) ECOOP 2012. LNCS, vol. 7313, pp. 283–307. Springer, Heidelberg (2012). https://doi.org/10.1007/978-3-642-31057-7_14
7. Burckhardt, S., Leijen, D., Protzenko, J., Fähndrich, M.: Global sequence protocol: a robust abstraction for replicated shared state. In: Boyland, J.T. (ed.) 29th European Conference on Object-Oriented Programming (ECOOP 2015), vol. 37, pp. 568–590. Schloss Dagstuhl-Leibniz-Zentrum fuer Informatik, Dagstuhl (2015)
8. de Juan-Marín, R., Decker, H., Armendáriz-Íñigo, J.E., Bernabéu-Aubán, J.M., Muñoz-Escoí, F.D.: Scalability approaches for causal multicast: a survey. Computing **98**(9), 923–947 (2016)
9. Kleppmann, M., Beresford, A.R.: A conflict-free replicated JSON datatype. IEEE Trans. Parallel Distrib. Syst. **28**(10), 2733–2746 (2017)
10. Lamport, L.: Time, clocks, and the ordering of events in a distributed system. Commun. ACM **21**(7), 558–565 (1978)
11. Lamport, L.: The temporal logic of actions. ACM Trans. Program. Lang. Syst. **16**(3), 872–923 (1994)
12. Letia, M., Preguiça, N., Shapiro, M.: CRDTs: consistency without concurrency control. Technical report, INRIA, Rocquencourt, France (2009). rR-6956
13. Li, C., Preguiça, N., Rodrigues, R.: Fine-grained consistency for geo-replicated systems. In: 2018 USENIX Annual Technical Conference (USENIX ATC 2018), pp. 359–372. USENIX Association, Boston (2018)
14. Meiklejohn, C., Van Roy, P.: Lasp: a language for distributed, coordination-free programming. In: 17th International Symposium on Principles and Practice of Declarative Programming, PPDP 2015, pp. 184–195 (2015)
15. Nédelec, B., Molli, P., Mostefaoui, A., Desmontils, E.: LSEQ: an adaptive structure for sequences in distributed collaborative editing. In: Proceedings of the 2013 ACM Symposium on Document Engineering, DocEng 2013, Florence, Italy, pp. 37–46 (2013)
16. Petersen, K., Spreitzer, M.J., Terry, D.B., Theimer, M.M., Demers, A.J.: Flexible update propagation for weakly consistent replication. In: 16th ACM Symposium on Operating Systems Principles, SOSP 1997, pp. 288–301 (1997)
17. Roh, H.G., Jeon, M., Kim, J.S., Lee, J.: Replicated abstract data types: building blocks for collaborative applications. J. Parallel Distrib. Comput. **71**(3), 354–368 (2011)
18. Shapiro, M., Preguiça, N., Baquero, C., Zawirski, M.: A comprehensive study of convergent and commutative replicated data types. Research report RR-7506, Inria - Centre Paris-Rocquencourt, INRIA, January 2011

19. Shapiro, M., Preguiça, N., Baquero, C., Zawirski, M.: Conflict-free replicated data types. In: Défago, X., Petit, F., Villain, V. (eds.) SSS 2011. LNCS, vol. 6976, pp. 386–400. Springer, Heidelberg (2011). https://doi.org/10.1007/978-3-642-24550-3_29
20. Sun, C., Ellis, C.: Operational transformation in real-time group editors: issues, algorithms, and achievements. In: Proceedings of the 1998 ACM Conference on Computer Supported Cooperative Work, CSCW 1998, pp. 59–68 (1998)
21. Terry, D.B., Theimer, M.M., Petersen, K., Demers, A.J., Spreitzer, M.J., Hauser, C.H.: Managing update conflicts in bayou, a weakly connected replicated storage system. In: Jones, M.B. (ed.) 15th ACM Symposium on Operating Systems Principles, SOSP 1995, pp. 172–182 (1995)
22. Weiss, S., Urso, P., Molli, P.: Logoot-Undo: distributed collaborative editing system on P2P networks. IEEE Trans. Parallel Distrib. Syst. 21(8), 1162–1174 (2010)

Composable Actor Behaviour

Sam Van den Vonder$^{(\boxtimes)}$, Joeri De Koster, and Wolfgang De Meuter

Vrije Universiteit Brussel, Pleinlaan 2, 1050 Brussels, Belgium
{svdvonde,jdekoste,wdmeuter}@vub.be

Abstract. Code reusability is the cornerstone of object-oriented programming. Reuse mechanisms such as inheritance and trait composition lay at the basis of a whole range of software engineering practices with the goal to improve software quality and reliability. In this paper we investigate code reuse mechanisms for actors, and find that it is currently difficult to specify the behaviour of an actor out of reusable parts. We discuss different kinds of code reuse mechanisms in different kinds of actor model, and we motivate why these mechanisms are currently unsatisfactory. As a possible solution we define a new reuse mechanism based on delegation-based trait composition. In a nutshell, the mechanism allows programmers to compose the behaviour of actors, and every time a compound behaviour is spawned into an actor, it will cause multiple actors to be spawned (one for each independent behaviour). Some messages will be automatically delegated to the actor that implements the desired functionality. We provide an implementation of this model in a prototype Active Object language called Stella, and we formalise a subset of Stella using a small-step operational semantics to unambiguously define the different steps involved in our reuse mechanism.

Keywords: Actors · Delegation · Active Objects · Code reusability

1   Introduction

In object-oriented programming, the principle of "programming against an interface" helps to foster code reuse and reduce complexity, thus increasing the reliability of individual components [20]. Essentially it is beneficial for the overall complexity of the program to design components as black boxes, because it is then the sole responsibility of each individual component to ensure the functionality it offers through its interface is correct. This principle manifests itself in many reuse mechanisms, such as inheritance [15] and trait composition [12] for class-based languages, and delegation for prototype-based languages [19]. In actor-based programs, using components as black boxes is equally important but for reasons other than just modularity and code reuse.

The *behaviour* of an actor is usually a combination of its internal state and its interface, which is the set of messages that an actor can process [18]. The only way to communicate with an actor is to send it a message that matches an entry in its interface, which is important for two reasons. First, it makes it

© IFIP International Federation for Information Processing 2019
Published by Springer Nature Switzerland AG 2019
J. Pereira and L. Ricci (Eds.): DAIS 2019, LNCS 11534, pp. 57–73, 2019.
https://doi.org/10.1007/978-3-030-22496-7_4

easier for actors to protect their internal state from race conditions via *interface control* [17] (essentially by asynchronously processing messages one by one). Second, a message-passing communication model is beneficial for (among others) concurrency, fault tolerance, and distribution over a network.

Despite the principle of "programming against an interface" being ingrained in the actor model almost by definition, it is rarely leveraged to facilitate modularisation and code reuse among actors. More specifically, currently there is limited language support for composing the behaviour of an actor, i.e. its interface, out of reusable parts.

Since code reuse is an important aspect of software engineering, we argue that actor-based programs can benefit from a simple and well-defined code reuse mechanism to control and reduce their complexity. To this end we introduce Stella, a prototype language that implements an actor composition mechanism based on asynchronous message delegation. The main contributions of this paper are the design and definition of Stella, and a formalisation of a subset of Stella that captures the precise semantics of the reuse mechanism.

In Sect. 2 we discuss the requirements of a suitable code reuse mechanism for actors, and we discuss reuse mechanisms in a number of state-of-the-art actor languages. In Sect. 3 we define Stella, and in Sect. 4 we define an operational semantics for a subset of Stella.

2   Code Reuse in Actor-Based Languages

Before we look into existing reuse mechanisms, we define the term actor *behaviour* and we specify the requirements of a reuse mechanism suitable for actors. We adopt the terminology of [18] that defines the behaviour of an actor as the description of its interface and state. The *interface* defines the list (and possibly types) of messages that an actor can process, as well as the program logic to process them. The state of an actor is defined as all the program state that is synchronously accessible by the actor.

From a software engineering point of view it is beneficial to split up a monolithic behaviour into multiple "reusable components" that can be composed using a composition mechanism. We devise 2 goals or requirements for such a mechanism that is suitable for the actor model, which we base on well-established design principles for object-oriented programming [24, Chapter 14].

Extensibility. The interface of behaviours can be extended to accept new messages, and a behaviour can specialise the acquired components to adapt them to its own needs. Relating this to object-oriented programming, this is similar to how a class can add, override, and specialise methods of a superclass, or to how traits can add methods to a class which may also be further specialised.

Reusability. Pre-existing behaviours can be reused by extending, adapting or specialising them via new behaviour definitions, without modifying the original behaviour. In object-oriented programming this is similar to how a class may be specialised via subclassing, while it remains independently instantiatable regardless of new class definitions that rely on it.

Over the years a number of reuse mechanisms have been proposed in different kinds of actor languages that implement different kinds of actor model. In the following sections we discuss inheritance, trait composition, function composition, and reuse via prototypes in the Communicating Event-Loops model.

2.1 Inheritance

The relation between inheritance and concurrent object-oriented programming has been thoroughly researched. Part of this research is focussed specifically on inheritance in actor-based languages such as Act3 [4] and ACT++ [16], which are based on the work of Agha [3]. In these languages, a `become` statement (fundamental to the model) is used to replace the behaviour of the current actor with a new behaviour. This statement causes severe reusability issues due to the *Actor-Inheritance Conflict* [17]. Consider a behaviour as being similar to a class, then the conflict describes a fundamental issue where adding a new method to a subclass may invalidate many superclass methods.

Classes in combination with inheritance fulfil the requirements of extensibility and reusability. However, inheritance is known to have reusability issues when used as the sole reuse mechanism [12]. Furthermore, nowadays it is generally accepted as a good design principle in object-oriented programming to favour object composition over class inheritance [7,14]. For these reasons we do not consider inheritance by itself to be a suitable reuse mechanism for actors.

2.2 Trait Composition

The Active Objects model is based on the work on ABCL/1 [27], and has modern implementations in languages such as Pony [9] and Encore [8]. Here, actors are typically instances of an *active object class* which describes mutable fields and a set of methods that can be asynchronously invoked via message passing. Pony and Encore support neither a `become` statement (which caused the Actor-Inheritance Conflict from the previous section) nor reuse via inheritance. In the case of Pony it is mentioned that composition is preferred to inheritance [1].

Instead of inheritance, Pony and Encore support stateless traits [12]. Traits can be composed with behaviours and other traits to add new methods to the composer. However, they do not fulfil our 2 requirements. Extensibility is only partially fulfilled because, while traits can be used to extend a behaviour with new functionality, they have a number of drawbacks. Most notably, stateless traits are likely to be an incomplete implementation of some functionality unless it is completely stateless [6]. The follow-up work on stateful traits also has some drawbacks such as possibly breaking black-box encapsulation, and difficulties regarding a linear object layout in memory [6]. Reusability is unfulfilled because the trait composition mechanism cannot be used to compose behaviours.

2.3 Function Composition

Popular languages and libraries such as Erlang [5], Elixir [26] and Akka [23] closely link behaviours and functional programming. In Erlang and Elixir, a blocking `receive` statement is used as part of a function body to dequeue 1 message from the mailbox of the current actor, and local actor state is encapsulated via lexical scoping. In Akka (a library for Scala), the behaviour of an actor is represented as a Scala *partial function* that is continually applied to messages by the receiving actor. Consequentially, behaviour composition is based on function composition. For example, in Akka, the Scala `andThen` and `orElse` function combinators compose two behaviours by respectively chaining two functions (pass the output of 1 into the next) or switching over 2 functions (if the given argument is not in the domain of the first, try the second).

We do not consider function composition to be a suitable reuse mechanism because it does not support extensibility. Logically switching over behaviours can be used to emulate some features of extensibility, e.g. the behaviour that is the result of the composition (`behaviourA orElse behaviourB`) will accept the union of messages accepted by both behaviours. However, the end result is highly susceptible to the composition order; messages matched by both behaviours will always be processed exclusively by `behaviourA`. Furthermore, there is no mechanism to deal with conflict resolution, for example when `behaviourA` accidentally captures messages that should be processed by `behaviourB`.

2.4 Communicating Event-Loops

The Communicating Event-Loops model (CEL) originated in the E [22] language and was later adopted by AmbientTalk [11]. Here, an actor is not described by a behaviour. Instead, an actor is a *vat* of plain objects that are said to be owned by the actor. Objects owned by one actor can have *near references* to objects within the same vat and *far references* to objects in another vat. Method calls via a near reference are synchronous; method calls via a far reference are asynchronous, are sent to the actor that owns the object, which will eventually invoke the method. In this model, the behaviour of an actor depends on which of its objects are accessible via far references, since those determine which messages are accepted.

Both E and AmbientTalk define a prototype-based object model, which relies on functions and lexical scoping for object instantiation and information hiding. A problem occurs when two similar actors attempt to share a behaviour, which in this model amounts to sharing an object. If two actors could reference the same behaviour, they would have access to shared mutable state either via the shared lexical scope, or via the shared object. Therefore, a CEL model in combination with a prototype-based object model does not offer a suitable reuse mechanism because, idiomatically, behaviours cannot be freely reused by different actors.

A possible avenue to explore could be to design a class-based CEL language which can eliminate shared mutable state. While we consider this to be a viable approach to our problem, in this paper we opt for a different approach that we consider to be simpler and more applicable to other actor languages.

2.5   Problem Statement

In the previous sections we discussed different kinds of reuse mechanisms in different kinds of actor model. In Sect. 2.1 we discussed the relationship between inheritance and actors, and concluded that inheritance by itself is not a suitable reuse mechanism for actors. For Active Objects (Sect. 2.2) we discussed trait composition and how it does not fulfil our requirements, because traits have a number of drawbacks and cannot be used to compose behaviours themselves. We discussed actor languages where behaviours are encapsulated by functions (Sect. 2.3), where we motivated that function composition is not a suitable composition mechanism. Finally, for the Communicating Event-Loops model (Sect. 2.4) we discussed that a prototype-based object model would lead to shared mutable state between actors if behaviours could be reused.

The problem that we tackle in this paper is to define a code reuse mechanism for behaviours that fulfils the requirements of extensibility and reusability. The mechanism defines (1) how the interface of behaviours can be extended with functionality defined by different components (extensibility), and (2) how behaviours themselves can be reused to define new behaviours (reusability).

3   Delegation-Based Actor Composition in Stella

In this section we introduce Stella, a prototype language based on the Active Objects model, where behaviours can be composed with a mechanism based on delegation-based trait composition [10]. We opted for a language-based approach (rather than a library) to convey the mechanism in a clear and concise manner. It also ensures consistent run-time semantics, particularly with respect to the definition of behaviours and message sending between actors. We first give a motivating example that benefits from reusable behaviours, and in the sections thereafter we gradually introduce the different aspects of Stella. For brevity we only implement parts of the motivating example to introduce the base language and to explain behaviour composition (the precise semantics of which are formalised in Sect. 4)[1].

3.1   Motivating Example

A modern approach to building "real-time" or "live" applications are stream-based frameworks such as ReactiveX, which describes the API of a class of streaming frameworks in over 18 languages [2]. These frameworks provide abstractions for data streams together with an extensive collection of built-in operators to transform and combine them. Consider a temperature monitoring application that visualises live measurements of many heterogenous sensors. Depending on units of measurement and user preferences, measurements may have to be transformed from one unit to another. This can be done by mapping a conversion function over a stream of measurements using some built-in `map` operator, resulting in a new stream of data.

---

[1] The code for the complete example is available and can be run at http://soft.vub.ac.be/~svdvonde/examples/DAIS19/.

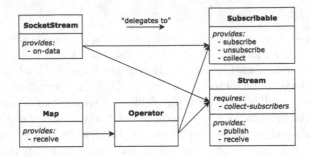

Fig. 1. Composition of behaviours in an actor-based streaming framework.

Streaming frameworks are often designed sequentially, i.e. new input data is first propagated to all connected streams before the next input can be accepted, and parallelising this process is non-trivial. With composable behaviours we can design a simple framework where streams and operators are actors, such that multiple computations can run in parallel.

Figure 1 depicts the different behaviours involved in our streaming framework. Every behaviour lists the methods that it provides, and for clarity we also list when a behaviour expects a certain method to be present in its composer that it does not implement itself. The framework provides a `SocketStream` behaviour to abstract over a typical socket connection as a data stream, and also 1 built-in `Map` operator to map a function over a stream. Common functionality for operators is factored out into an `Operator` behaviour (which also behaves like a stream), and common functionality of streams is factored out into `Stream` and `Subscribable`. `Stream` implements functionality for publishing and receiving values, `Subscribable` simply keeps a list of other streams (actors) that should receive new publications.

3.2   The Base Stella Language

In this section we introduce the base Stella language without behaviour composition. Similar to other Active Object languages, Stella has an active layer of active object classes and actors, and a passive layer of regular classes and objects We omit the details of the passive object layer since its definition is irrelevant to the problem of behaviour composition.

A program written in Stella is a set of top-level behaviour definitions and regular class definitions. Every program must define a `Main` behaviour that is instantiated as the first actor of the program. Listing 1 implements two behaviours `Stream` (Lines 1–5) and `Subscribable` (Lines 7–14). `Stream` implements generic stream functionality for publishing and receiving data. It has two methods called `publish` and `receive` with 1 formal parameter `data` (Lines 2–4 and 5). Publishing data to a stream simply amounts to sending a `receive` message to all subscribers. The logic of sending that message is contained within local definition

```
1  (actor Stream
2    (def-method (publish data)
3      (def f (lambda (subscriber) (send subscriber 'receive data)))
4      (send self 'collect-subscribers f))
5    (def-method (receive data) 'do-nothing))
6
7  (actor Subscribable
8    (fields subscribers)
9
10   (def-constructor (init) (set! subscribers '()))
11
12   (def-method (subscribe subscriber)
13     (set! subscribers (add subscribers subscriber)))
14   (def-method (collect f) (for-each subscribers f)))
```

Listing 1. Implementation of the `Stream` and `Subscribable` behaviours.

`f` (Line 3) that is bound to a `lambda` function[2]. When the lambda is invoked, it sends the `receive` message to `subscriber` with the `data` to be published as single argument. Iterating over subscribers of the stream is done by sending a `collect-subscribers` message to the current actor via pseudo-variable `self` with `f` as argument. The default `receive` method on Line 5 simply returns the symbol `'do-nothing`.

The `Subscribable` behaviour stores a list of subscribers to a stream. Its definition is analogous to `Stream` but shows the use of fields (local actor state) and constructors. In this case there is 1 field `subscribers` (Line 8), a constructor named `init` (Line 10), and 2 methods `subscribe` and `collect` (Lines 12–13 and 14). A constructor is a special method that is called exactly once when an actor is spawned. Behaviours without a constructor will be initialized by a `default` constructor. In this case the `init` constructor initializes the local field `subscribers` to an empty list via the special form `set!` (assignment).

Bodies of constructors and methods contain either special forms (like `set!`) or synchronous method invocations on regular objects. Here, we use the following syntax where `methodName` is invoked on object `target` with the given argument expressions.

> (*methodName target arg₁ ... argₙ*)

In that vein, the invocation of `send` in `Stream` (Listing 1 Line 3 and 4) is simply the invocation of the `send` method on an object that represents a reference to an actor. Similarly, the `add` and `for-each` methods (Line 13 and 14) are invocations on a list object.

Actors can be spawned via a `spawn` special form that returns a reference object that can be used to send asynchronous messages to the newly spawned actor. For example, the following expression spawns an actor with the `Subscribable` behaviour that is initialized by calling the `init` constructor.

> (spawn Subscribable 'init)

---

[2] Stella does not have functions. Using a process similar to Lambda Lifting, a `lambda` statement is transformed to an object with an `apply` method.

```
1  (actor Operator
2    (delegate-to Stream)
3    (delegate-to Subscribable (rename 'collect 'collect-subscribers))
4
5    (def-constructor (init stream)
6      (spawn-delegate Subscribable 'init)
7      (spawn-delegate Stream)
8      (send stream 'subscribe self)))
```

Listing 2. Implementation of the `Operator` behaviour.

```
1  (actor Operator
2    (delegate-fields Subscribable Stream)   // run-time syntax
3
4    (def-constructor (init stream)
5      (spawn-delegate Subscribable 'init)   // populate special field
6      (spawn-delegate Stream)               // populate special field
7      (send stream 'subscribe self))
8
9    (def-method (subscribe subscriber)
10     (delegate Subscribable 'subscribe subscriber))
11   (def-method (collect-subscribers f)     // renamed method
12     (delegate Subscribable 'collect f))
13
14   (def-method (publish data) (delegate Stream 'publish data))
15   (def-method (receive data) (delegate Stream 'receive data)))
```

Listing 3. Compile-time expanded version of the `Operator` behaviour.

3.3 Delegation-Based Behaviour Composition in Stella

In this section we introduce a new composition mechanism for behaviours inspired by delegation-based trait composition in AmbientTalk [10]. In a nutshell, a behaviour can statically acquire the methods of other behaviours, and spawning an actor from a compound behaviour creates multiple actors that each run part of the compound behaviour. We will refer to these actors as the *delegate actors*. Messages that match an acquired method are automatically delegated to the corresponding delegate actor. To explain the different aspects of behaviour composition, we implement the `Operator` behaviour from Fig. 1.

The `Operator` behaviour implements common functionality for all streaming operators in our motivating example, which in this case only amounts to ensuring that every instance of an operator behaves like a stream of data. Its implementation is shown in Listing 2. A `delegate-to` statement (Line 2–3) is used to declare that (at compile-time) all methods from the behaviours `Stream` and `Subscribable` are acquired. A conflict may occur when acquiring two or more methods with the same name. These must be explicitly resolved by aliasing or excluding certain methods using a `rename` or `exclude` statement respectively. In this case, the `collect` method from `Subscribable` is renamed to `collect-subscribers` for clarity rather than solving a conflict.

Before we can explain the run-time semantics of acquired methods (which is different from traditional trait composition), we first show the effects of a `delegate-to` statement at compile-time. Listing 3 shows the compile-time expanded version of the `Operator` behaviour of Listing 2, which incorporates the acquired methods. The added lines of code are Line 2 – a pseudocode statement to explain the run-time semantics – that declares 2 new (special) fields,

Lines 9–12 which are the acquired methods from the Subscribable behaviour (note that the collect method is renamed), and finally Lines 14–15 which are the acquired methods from the Stream behaviour.

The 2 new fields on Line 2 are generated by the compiler and carry the name of the delegate behaviours. They are populated by the spawn-delegate statements in the constructor (Lines 5–6), which is a special version of a regular spawn. Instead of returning the address of the new actor, it is stored in the corresponding (generated) field that carries the name of the spawned behaviour. Thus, when Operator is spawned, it also spawns 2 delegate actors, and by storing their addresses in generated fields we can guarantee that the contents of these fields cannot be directly modified or retrieved. Consequentially, because the address of delegate actors can never be shared with other actors, we keep the process of spawning delegates completely transparent to users of a behaviour.

In contrast with regular trait composition for object-oriented programming, the implementation of acquired methods is not copied over. Instead, a delegate statement is generated that serves 2 purposes. First, delegate retrieves the delegate actor (from the generated fields) referenced by its first argument. Second, it sends a special message to the delegate actor that, when the message is executed, changes the self pointer of the delegate actor to that of the sender. This is a crucial mechanism of trait composition that allows the delegate to communicate with its delegator, which is similar to the unchanged this pointer for regular trait composition in object-oriented programming [10,12]. The effect is that, any time the delegate actor sends a message to self, the message is actually received by its delegator. An example of where this mechanism is necessary is the Stream behaviour of Listing 1 Line 4, where a collect-subscribers message is sent to self to iterate over a list of subscribers stored in another behaviour.

4 Operational Semantics of Stella

In this section we formalise a subset of Stella via an operational semantics. The formalisation entails the necessary details about actors, behaviours and delegation. For brevity we omit the sequential class-based object-oriented subset of the language, since this concern is orthogonal to actors and behaviours. The goal of this formalisation is to describe the precise semantics of the composition mechanism such that it can be reproduced in other languages. Our semantics is based on the formalisation of JCoBox [25] and AmbientTalk [11].

4.1 Syntax

The abstract syntax of Stella is shown in Fig. 2. Capital letters denote sets, and overlines denote sequences (ordered sets). We may implicitly treat single elements as sequences or sets of size 1 (e.g. $\mathcal{A}(\ldots)$ is equivalent to $\{\mathcal{A}(\ldots)\}$). Most of the syntax is shown in Sect. 3. Note that in this section we talk about (active object) classes instead of behaviours.

$$p \in \textbf{Program} ::= B$$
$$B \subseteq \textbf{ClassDecl} ::= (\text{actor } n \; D \; (\text{fields } \overline{f}) \; H)$$
$$D \subseteq \textbf{DelegationDecl} ::= \overline{(\text{delegate-to } n \; (\text{exclude } \overline{m}) \; \overline{(\text{rename } m \; m')})}$$
$$H \subseteq \textbf{MethodDecl} ::= (\text{def-method } (m \; \overline{x}) \; e)$$
$$e \in E \subseteq \textbf{Expression} ::= \begin{array}{l} x \mid self \mid (\text{get } f) \mid (\text{set! } f \; e) \mid (\text{spawn } n) \mid \\ (\text{delegate } d \; m \; \overline{e}) \mid (\text{send } e \; m \; \overline{e}) \end{array}$$

$$x \in \textbf{Variable}, f, d \in \textbf{FieldName}, n \cup Main \in \textbf{ClassName}, m \in \textbf{MethodName}$$

Fig. 2. Abstract syntax.

$k \in K \in \textbf{Configuration} ::= \mathcal{K}(A, C)$	Configurations
$C \subseteq \textbf{ActorClass} ::= \mathcal{C}(n, \overline{f}, \overline{d}, M)$	Actor Classes
$a \in A \subseteq \textbf{Actor} ::= \mathcal{A}(i, M, Q, F, F_d, e)$	Actors
$Q \subseteq \textbf{Queue} ::= \overline{msg}$	Queues
$F, F_d \subseteq \textbf{Field} ::= \mathcal{F}(f, v)$	Fields
$msg \in \textbf{Message} ::= \mathcal{M}sg(i, m, \overline{v})$	Messages
$M \subseteq \textbf{Method} ::= \mathcal{M}(m, \overline{x}, e)$	Methods
$v \in \textbf{Value} ::= i \mid null$	Values
$e \in E \subseteq \textbf{Expression} ::= \ldots \mid v$	Runtime Expressions

$$i \in \textbf{ActorId}$$

Fig. 3. Semantic entities.

- A program p is a set actor class declarations, one of which we assume will be called `Main`.
- For simplicity, classes have no constructor.
- Because there are no constructors, there is no explicit `spawn-delegate` statement required in the syntax because delegate actors can now be created ex nihilo (i.e. without initializing them with run-time values).
- Methods have just one expression as their body, and there are no variable definitions (e.g. via a `let` statement).
- Fields are accessed explicitly via `get` and `set!` statements.

4.2   Semantic Entities

The static and dynamic semantics are formulated as a small-step operational semantics whose semantic entities are listed in Fig. 3. Calligraphic letters such as $\mathcal{K}$ and $\mathcal{C}$ are used as "constructors" to distinguish different semantic entities syntactically.

The state of a program is represented by a configuration k which contains a set of concurrently executing actors and a set of classes.

A class has a unique name n, fields $\overline{f}$, delegate fields $\overline{d}$ (these are the generated fields to store references to delegate actors, see Sect. 3.3), and a set of methods M. In Sect. 4.4 we show how a class is produced from the abstract syntax.

An actor has a unique identifier i that we use as its address, a set of methods M that can be invoked by the actor, a queue Q that holds a sequence of messages to be processed, a set F that maps fields to values, a set F_d that maps delegate fields to delegate actors, and an expression e that the actor is currently executing.

A message msg is a triplet of a `self` address i to be used during execution of the message (either the message receiver or the delegator), the name m of a method to invoke, and a sequence of values $\overline{v}$ which are the method arguments.

A method M is a triplet containing the name of the method m, a sequence of formal parameters $\overline{x}$, and a body e.

Our reduction rules in Sect. 4.5 operate on "runtime expressions" which are simply all expressions e extended with run-time values v, which can be actor references i and $null$.

4.3   Notation

We use the $\uplus$ (disjoint union) operator to lookup and extract values from sets. For example, $S = S' \uplus s$ splits the set S into element s and the set $S' = S \setminus \{s\}$. When the order of elements is important (e.g. for representing the message queue of an actor) we use the notation $S = S' \cdot s$ to deconstruct a sequence S into sequence $S' = S \setminus \{s\}$ and s which is the last element of S. We denote both the empty set and the empty sequence as $\emptyset$.

4.4   Static Semantics

Our reuse mechanism requires an additional compilation step to transform a class declaration from the abstract syntax into a class that can be used at run-time. In Fig. 4 we define a number of auxiliary functions in a declarative style to generate such a run-time class. We sum up their purpose:

gen. Generates a set of methods (to be acquired by a class) based on a set of pre-existing methods and a set of `delegate-to` statements. M represents a set of pre-existing (non-acquired) methods of a class, C is a set of compiled run-time classes, and D a set of delegation declarations. For each delegation declaration, lookup the corresponding run-time class and generate a set of methods to be acquired for this particular delegate.

genMethods. Given a set of pre-existing methods M, a classname n, a set of excluded methods m_{excl}, a set of aliased methods m_{alias} and a set of methods M' to acquire, return a new set of methods possibly extended with newly acquired ones. Methods in M' with name m are excluded if $m \in \overline{m_{excl}}$, or if a method m already exists in the pre-existing set of methods M. The latter ensures that methods from the base class take precedence over acquired methods (they are not "overridden" by the delegate).

genMethod. Generate the method to be acquired by a class. $\mathcal{M}$ is the original method from the delegate class, n is the name of said class, and m_{alias} is a set of tuples to possibly rename the generated method. The body of the generated method is a `delegate` expression where n will refer to the delegate actor.

$\text{gen}(M, C, \emptyset) = \emptyset$

$\text{gen}(M, C, D \uplus (\text{delegate-to } n \ (\text{exclude } \overline{m_{excl}}) \ \overline{m_{alias}})) =$
  $\text{genMethods}(M, n, \overline{m_{excl}}, \overline{m_{alias}}, M') \cup \text{gen}(M, C, D)$

  with $\mathcal{C}(n, \overline{f}, \overline{d}, M') \in C$

$\text{genMethods}(M, n, \overline{m_{excl}}, \overline{m_{alias}}, \emptyset) = \emptyset$

$\text{genMethods}(M, n, \overline{m_{excl}}, \overline{m_{alias}}, M' \uplus \mathcal{M}(m, \overline{x}, e)) =$

$\begin{cases} \text{genMethods}(M, n, \overline{m_{excl}}, \overline{m_{alias}}, M'), & \text{if } m \in \overline{m_{excl}} \ \vee \ \mathcal{M}(m, \overline{x'}, e') \in M \\ \text{genMethod}(\mathcal{M}(m, \overline{x}, e), n, \overline{m_{alias}}) \ \cup \ \hookleftarrow \\ \quad \text{genMethods}(M, n, \overline{m_{excl}}, \overline{m_{alias}}, M') & \text{otherwise} \end{cases}$

$\text{genMethod}(\mathcal{M}(m, \overline{x}, e), n, \overline{m_{alias}}) = \mathcal{M}(\text{name}(m, \overline{m_{alias}}), \overline{x}, (\text{delegate } n \ m \ \overline{x}))$

$\text{name}(m, \overline{m_{alias}}) = \begin{cases} m', & \text{if } (\text{rename } m \ m') \in \overline{m_{alias}} \\ m & \text{otherwise} \end{cases}$

$\text{methodsOf}((\text{delegate-to } n \ (\text{exclude } \overline{m_{excl}}) \ \overline{m_{alias}}), C) =$
  $\{name(m, m_{alias}) \mid (\mathcal{M}(m, \overline{x}, e) \in M) \wedge (m \notin m_{excl})\}$

  with $\mathcal{C}(n, \overline{f}, \overline{d}, M) \in C$

Fig. 4. Auxiliary functions for class compilation.

$$\forall x_1 \in D : \forall x_2 \in D \setminus \{x_1\} : methodsOf(x_1, C) \cap methodsOf(x_2, C) = \emptyset$$
$$M = \{\mathcal{M}(m, \overline{x}, e) \mid (\text{def-method } (m \ \overline{x}) \ e) \in H\}$$
$$\overline{d} = \{n \mid (\text{delegate-to } n \ (\text{exclude } \overline{m}) \ (\text{rename } m \ m')) \in D\}$$
$$\overline{\langle B \uplus (\text{actor } n \ D \ (\text{fields } \overline{f}) \ H), C\rangle \to_c \langle B, C \cup \{\mathcal{C}(n, \overline{f}, \overline{d}, M \cup \text{gen}(M, C, D))\}\rangle}$$

Fig. 5. Class compilation reduction rule.

name. Given a method name m and a set of possibly aliased methods m_{alius}, return the (possibly aliased) method name.

methodsOf. Given a delegation declaration and a set of run-time classes C, return the set of all method names that would be acquired by C using the delegation declaration.

Figure 5 defines a reduction $\to_c$ to compile a set of class declarations B. The reduction is defined as $\langle B, C\rangle \to_c \langle B', C'\rangle$ where the tuple $\langle B, C\rangle$ initially contains all class declarations B in the program, and C is empty. Compilation fails when the conditions of the rule are not met and no element in B can be reduced. This signifies an error in the program. Another possible error is explicitly formulated by a precondition given on the first line of the premise that prevents method conflicts between delegates, which means that the intersection of the acquired methods for any 2 delegates is empty. A set of delegate fields $\overline{d}$ is created using the classnames of delegates.

$$\text{Field-Get} \frac{\mathcal{F}(f,v) \in F}{\mathcal{A}(i,M,Q,F,F_d,e_\square[(\text{get } f)]) \to_a \mathcal{A}(i,M,Q,F,F_d,e_\square[v])}$$

$$\text{Field-Set} \frac{F = F' \uplus \mathcal{F}(f,v_0) \quad F'' = F' \cup \{\mathcal{F}(f,v)\}}{\mathcal{A}(i,M,Q,F,F_d,e_\square[(\text{set! } f \; v)]) \to_a \mathcal{A}(i,M,Q,F'',F_d,e_\square[v])}$$

$$\text{Process-Msg} \frac{Q = Q' \cdot \mathcal{M}sg(i',m,\overline{v}) \quad \mathcal{M}(m,\overline{x},e) \in M}{\mathcal{A}(i,M,Q,F,F_d,v) \to_a \mathcal{A}(i,M,Q',F,F_d,e[i'/self][\overline{v}/\overline{x}])}$$

Fig. 6. Actor-local reduction rules.

4.5 Dynamic Semantics

Evaluation Contexts. We use evaluation contexts [13] to abstract over the context of an expression, and to indicate which subexpressions should be fully reduced before a compound expression can be reduced. The expression $e_\square$ denotes an expression with a "hole" to identify the next subexpression to be reduced. The notation $e_\square[e]$ indicates that expression e is part of an abstracted compound expression $e_\square$, and that e should be reduced first before $e_\square$ can be reduced.

$$e_\square ::= \begin{array}{l} \square \mid (\text{set! } f \; e_\square) \mid (\text{send } e_\square \; m \; \overline{e}) \mid \\ (\text{send } v \; m \; \overline{v} \; e_\square \; \overline{e}) \mid (\text{delegate } d \; m \; \overline{v} \; e_\square \; \overline{e}) \end{array}$$

Evaluation Rules. Our evaluation rules are defined in terms of a reduction on sets of configurations $K \to K'$. For clarity we split the rules defining this reduction in two parts. Actor-local rules are defined in terms of a reduction $a \to_a a'$ and can be applied in isolation (within one actor). Actor-global rules are defined in terms of a reduction $K \to_k K'$ and indicate interactions between actors.

Actor-Local Evaluation Rules. Actors continually dequeue the first message from their message queue, retrieve the correct expression to process this message, and reduce this expression to a value. The next message can only be processed after the expression is reduced to a value. An actor is considered idle when its message queue is empty and its current expression has been completely reduced. This is the only situation in which no rules apply to a particular actor. Otherwise, if an actor is not idle and no rules can reduce its current expression, there is an error in the program. We summarise the actor-local reduction rules in Fig. 6.

Field-Get, Field-Set. Values of fields are stored in a set F of 2-tuples that map fields to values. A get expression is a simple lookup of the field, and set! replaces the current association with a new one.

Process-Msg. Processing a message is only possible when the message queue Q is not empty and the current expression is reduced to a value. The last entry of the queue is removed and the corresponding method is retrieved. To evaluate the body of the method we substitute the formal parameters $\overline{x}$ and

$$\text{Send} \frac{A = A' \uplus \mathcal{A}(i', M', Q', F', F'_d, e') \qquad Q'' = \mathcal{M}sg(i', m, \overline{v}) \cdot Q'}{\mathcal{K}(A \uplus \mathcal{A}(i, M, Q, F, F_d, e_\square[(\text{send } i' \ m \ \overline{v})]), C) \to_k \\ \mathcal{K}(A' \cup \{\mathcal{A}(i, M, Q, F, F_d, e_\square[null]), \mathcal{A}(i', M', Q'', F', F'_d, e')\}, C)}$$

$$\text{Delegate} \frac{\begin{array}{c} \mathcal{F}(d, i') \in F_d \\ A = A' \uplus \mathcal{A}(i', M', Q', F', F'_d, e') \qquad Q'' = \mathcal{M}sg(i, m, \overline{v}) \cdot Q' \end{array}}{\mathcal{K}(A \uplus \mathcal{A}(i, M, Q, F, F_d, e_\square[(\text{delegate } d \ m \ \overline{v})]), C) \to_k \\ \mathcal{K}(A' \cup \{\mathcal{A}(i, M, Q, F, F_d, e_\square[null]), \mathcal{A}(i', M', Q'', F', F'_d, e')\}, C)}$$

$$\text{Spawn} \frac{\text{makeActor}(n, C) = \mathcal{A}(i', M', Q', F', F'_d, e') \cdot \overline{delegates}}{\mathcal{K}(A \uplus \mathcal{A}(i, M, Q, F, F_d, e_\square[(\text{spawn } n)]), C) \to_k \\ \mathcal{K}(A \cup \{\mathcal{A}(i, M, Q, F, F_d, e_\square[i']), \mathcal{A}(i', M', Q', F', F'_d, e')\} \cup \overline{delegates}, C)}$$

$$\text{Congruence} \frac{a \to_a a'}{K \uplus \mathcal{K}(A \uplus a, C) \to_k K \uplus \mathcal{K}(A \uplus a', C)}$$

Fig. 7. Actor-global reduction rules.

$$\text{zipFields}(\emptyset, \emptyset) = \emptyset$$
$$\text{zipFields}(d \uplus \overline{d}, \mathcal{A}(i, M, Q, F, F_d, e) \uplus \overline{delegates}) = \{\mathcal{F}(d, i)\} \cup \text{zipFields}(\overline{d}, \overline{delegates})$$

$$\text{makeActor}(n, C) = \{\mathcal{A}(i, M, \emptyset, F, F_d, null)\} \cdot \overline{delegates}$$
$$\text{with} \quad i \text{ fresh}, \quad \mathcal{C}(n, \overline{f}, \overline{d}, M) \in C, \quad F = \{\mathcal{F}(f, null) \mid f \in \overline{f}\}$$
$$\overline{delegates} = \{\text{makeActor}(n', C) \mid n' \in \overline{d}\}$$
$$F_d = \text{zipFields}(\overline{d}, \overline{delegates})$$

Fig. 8. Auxiliary functions to create actors.

self with the values contained within the message. Note that self is either the current actor (when the message was sent via a normal message send) or the delegator (when the message was delegated).

Actor-Global Evaluation Rules. We summarise the actor-global evaluation rules of Fig. 7.

Send. Describes an asynchronous message send to an actor. A new message is added at the front of the queue Q' of the receiving actor i'. The address of the self reference passed as an argument in the message is also i'. This means that the receiving actor will execute the message using its own address as self parameter. Semantically, all arguments $\overline{v}$ are passed to the other actor via a (deep) copy, but in our case there is no assignment other than local fields, and therefore we do not explicitly create copies in this formalisation. The send expression reduces to null.

Delegate. Describes delegating messages. This rule is almost identical to Send, except that the address of the receiver i' is stored in a delegate field d in F_d,

$$\frac{\text{makeActor}(Main, C) = \mathcal{A}(i, M, Q, F, F_d, null)}{\langle \emptyset, C \rangle \to \mathcal{K}(\mathcal{A}(i, M, \{\mathcal{M}sg(i, start, \emptyset)\}, F, F_d, null), C)}$$

Fig. 9. Program initialization.

and that the address of the sender i is passed in the message instead of i'. Thus, when the receiver eventually processes this message, any messages it sends to `self` during execution will be sent to the delegator i.

Spawn. This rule describes the spawning of an actor given a classname n. Spawning an actor may add multiple actors to the program, namely the actor with the spawned behaviour and all of its delegates (and all of their delegates, ...). To create these actors in a single evaluation step we define an auxiliary function `makeActor` in Fig. 8 that, given a classname n and all classes C, returns a sequence of newly created actors. The first element of this sequence is the actor spawned from behaviour n, whose address i' is the value of the reduced spawn expression. All newly created actors are added to the configuration.

Congruence. This rule relates the local and global reduction rules such that reductions of local rules also progress the global system.

Finally, the rule in Fig. 9 bridges compilation and evaluation, and shows how to reduce a fully compiled program represented by a tuple $\langle \emptyset, C \rangle$ into the first configuration of the program. The first actor is an instance of the `Main` class and contains a `start` message in its mailbox.

5 Conclusion

Code reusability is an important aspect of software engineering that can improve software quality and reliability of actor-based systems. We approach this topic in Sect. 2 by discussing different kinds of code reusability mechanisms in different kinds of actor models. The discussed mechanisms do not fulfil 2 requirements that we find essential for programming actor-based systems: extensibility and reusability.

We introduce a prototype language in Sect. 3 called Stella with a behaviour composition mechanism based on delegation-based trait composition. Here, a compound behaviour essentially describes a collection of actors that are composed at runtime such that some messages are implicitly delegated from one actor to another. It fulfils the requirement of extensibility because behaviours can be easily extended with new methods defined elsewhere, and it fulfils self-containment because every part of a composed behaviour can, by itself, also be used to create new actors.

Acknowledgements. We would like to thank Thierry Renaux for his insightful comments on drafts of this paper. Sam Van den Vonder is supported by the Research Foundation - Flanders (FWO) under grant No. 1S95318N.

References

1. Pony tutorial: What about inheritance? https://web.archive.org/web/201807171 15657/tutorial.ponylang.org/types/classes.html. Accessed 17 July 2018
2. ReactiveX: An API for asynchronous programming with observable streams. http://web.archive.org/web/20180717115824/reactivex.io/ (2018). Accessed 17 July 2018
3. Agha, G.: Concurrent object-oriented programming. Commun. ACM **33**(9), 125–141 (1990)
4. Agha, G.: A Model of Concurrent Computation in Distributed Systems. The MIT Press, Cambridge (1986)
5. Armstrong, J., Virding, R., Williams, M.: Concurrent Programming in ERLANG. Prentice Hall, Upper Saddle River (1993)
6. Bergel, A., Ducasse, S., Nierstrasz, O., Wuyts, R.: Stateful traits and their formalization. Comput. Lang. Syst. Struct. **34**(2–3), 83–108 (2008)
7. Bloch, J.J.: Effective Java. The Java Series... from the Source, 2nd edn. Addison-Wesley, Boston (2008)
8. Brandauer, S., et al.: Parallel objects for multicores: a glimpse at the parallel language ENCORE. In: Bernardo, M., Johnsen, E.B. (eds.) SFM 2015. LNCS, vol. 9104, pp. 1–56. Springer, Cham (2015). https://doi.org/10.1007/978-3-319-18941-3_1
9. Clebsch, S., Drossopoulou, S., Blessing, S., McNeil, A.: Deny capabilities for safe, fast actors. In: Boix, E.G., Haller, P., Ricci, A., Varela, C. (eds.) Proceedings of the 5th International Workshop on Programming Based on Actors, Agents, and Decentralized Control, AGERE! 2015, Pittsburgh, PA, USA, 26 October 2015, pp. 1–12. ACM (2015)
10. Van Cutsem, T., Bergel, A., Ducasse, S., De Meuter, W.: Adding state and visibility control to traits using lexical nesting. In: Drossopoulou, S. (ed.) ECOOP 2009. LNCS, vol. 5653, pp. 220–243. Springer, Heidelberg (2009). https://doi.org/10.1007/978-3-642-03013-0_11
11. Van Cutsem, T., et al.: Ambienttalk: programming responsive mobile peer-to-peer applications with actors. Comput. Lang. Syst. Struct. **40**(3–4), 112–136 (2014)
12. Ducasse, S., Nierstrasz, O., Schärli, N., Wuyts, R., Black, A.P.: Traits: a mechanism for fine-grained reuse. ACM Trans. Program. Lang. Syst. **28**(2), 331–388 (2006)
13. Felleisen, M., Hieb, R.: The revised report on the syntactic theories of sequential control and state. Theor. Comput. Sci. **103**(2), 235–271 (1992)
14. Gamma, E., Helm, R., Johnson, R., Vlissides, J.: Design Patterns: Elements of Reusable Object-Oriented Software. Addison-Wesley, Boston (1994)
15. Johnson, R.E., Foote, B.: Designing reusable classes. J. Object-Orient. Program. **1**(2), 22–35 (1988)
16. Kafura, D.G.: Concurrent object-oriented real-times systems research. SIGPLAN Not. **24**(4), 203–205 (1989)
17. Kafura, D.G., Lee, K.H.: Inheritance in actor based concurrent object-oriented languages. Comput. J. **32**(4), 297–304 (1989)
18. De Koster, J., Van Cutsem, T., De Meuter, W.: 43 years of actors: a taxonomy of actor models and their key properties. In: Clebsch, S., Desell, T., Haller, P., Ricci, A. (eds.) Proceedings of the 6th International Workshop on Programming Based on Actors, Agents, and Decentralized Control, AGERE 2016, Amsterdam, The Netherlands, 30 October 2016, pp. 31–40. ACM (2016)

19. Lieberman, H.: Using prototypical objects to implement shared behavior in object oriented systems. In: Meyrowitz [21], pp. 214–223 (1986)
20. Meyer, B.: Applying "design by contract". IEEE Comput. **25**(10), 40–51 (1992)
21. Meyrowitz, N.K. (ed.): Conference on Object-Oriented Programming Systems, Languages, and Applications (OOPSLA 1986), Portland, Oregon, USA, Proceedings. ACM (1986)
22. Miller, M.S., Tribble, E.D., Shapiro, J.: Concurrency among strangers. In: De Nicola, R., Sangiorgi, D. (eds.) TGC 2005. LNCS, vol. 3705, pp. 195–229. Springer, Heidelberg (2005). https://doi.org/10.1007/11580850_12
23. Roestenburg, R., Bakker, R., Williams, R.: Akka in Action. Manning Publications Co., New York (2015)
24. Rumbaugh, J., Blaha, M., Premerlani, W., Eddy, F., Lorensen, W.E., et al.: Object-Oriented Modeling and Design, vol. 199. Prentice-Hall, Englewood Cliffs (1991)
25. Schäfer, J., Poetzsch-Heffter, A.: JCoBox: generalizing active objects to concurrent components. In: D'Hondt, T. (ed.) ECOOP 2010. LNCS, vol. 6183, pp. 275–299. Springer, Heidelberg (2010). https://doi.org/10.1007/978-3-642-14107-2_13
26. Thomas, D.: Programming Elixir. Pragmatic Bookshelf, Boston (2018)
27. Yonezawa, A., Briot, J., Shibayama, E.: Object-oriented concurrent programming in ABCL/1. In: Meyrowitz [21], pp. 258–268 (1986)

Gossip Learning as a Decentralized Alternative to Federated Learning

István Hegedűs[1], Gábor Danner[1], and Márk Jelasity[1,2]([⊠])

[1] University of Szeged, Szeged, Hungary
jelasity@inf.u-szeged.hu
[2] MTA SZTE Research Group on Artificial Intelligence, Szeged, Hungary

Abstract. Federated learning is a distributed machine learning approach for computing models over data collected by edge devices. Most
importantly, the data itself is not collected centrally, but a master-worker
architecture is applied where a master node performs aggregation and the
edge devices are the workers, not unlike the parameter server approach.
Gossip learning also assumes that the data remains at the edge devices,
but it requires no aggregation server or any central component. In this
empirical study, we present a thorough comparison of the two approaches.
We examine the aggregated cost of machine learning in both cases, considering also a compression technique applicable in both approaches. We
apply a real churn trace as well collected over mobile phones, and we
also experiment with different distributions of the training data over
the devices. Surprisingly, gossip learning actually outperforms federated
learning in all the scenarios where the training data are distributed uniformly over the nodes, and it performs comparably to federated learning
overall.

1 Introduction

Performing data mining over data collected by edge devices, most importantly,
mobile phones, is of very high interest [17]. Collecting such data at a central
location has become more and more problematic in the past years due to novel
data protection rules [9] and in general due to the increasing public awareness to
issues related to data handling. For this reason, there is an increasing interest in
methods that leave the raw data on the device and process it using distributed
aggregation.

Google introduced *federated learning* to answer this challenge [12,13]. This
approach is very similar to the well-known parameter server architecture for
distributed learning [7] where worker nodes store the raw data. The parameter

This work was supported by the Hungarian Government and the European Regional
Development Fund under the grant number GINOP-2.3.2-15-2016-00037 ("Internet of
Living Things") and by the Hungarian Ministry of Human Capacities (grant 20391-
3/2018/FEKUSTRAT).

J. Pereira and L. Ricci (Eds.): DAIS 2019, LNCS 11534, pp. 74–90, 2019.
https://doi.org/10.1007/978-3-030-22496-7_5

server maintains the current model and regularly distributes it to the workers who in turn calculate a gradient update and send it back to the server. The server then applies all the updates to the central model. This is repeated until the model converges. In federated learning, this framework is optimized so as to minimize communication between the server and the workers. For this reason, the local update calculation is more thorough, and compression techniques can be applied when uploading the updates to the server.

In addition to federated learning, *gossip learning* has also been proposed to address the same challenge [10,15]. This approach is fully decentralized, no parameter server is necessary. Nodes exchange and aggregate models directly. The advantages of gossip learning are obvious: since no infrastructure is required, and there is no single point of failure, gossip learning enjoys a significantly *cheaper scalability and better robustness*. The key question, however, is how the two approaches compare in terms of performance. This is the question we address in this work. To be more precise, we compare the two approaches in terms of convergence time and model quality, assuming that both approaches utilize the same amount of communication resources in the same scenarios.

To make the comparison as fair as possible, we make sure that the two approaches differ mainly in their communication patterns. However, the computation of the local update is identical in both approaches. Also, we apply subsampling to reduce communication in both approaches, as introduced in [12] for federated learning. Here, we adapt the same technique for gossip learning.

We learn linear models using stochastic gradient descent (SGD) based on the logistic regression loss function. For realistic simulations, we apply smart-phone churn traces collected by the application Stunner [2]. We note that both approaches offer mechanisms for explicit privacy protection, apart from the basic feature of not collecting data. In federated learning, Bonawitz et al. [3] describe a secure aggregation protocol, whereas for gossip learning one can apply the methods described in [4]. Here, we are concerned only with the efficiency of the different communication patterns and do not compare security mechanisms.

The result of our comparison is that gossip learning is in general comparable to the centrally coordinated federated learning approach, and in many scenarios gossip learning actually outperforms federated learning. This result is rather counter-intuitive and suggests that decentralized algorithms should be treated as first class citizens in the area of distributed machine learning overall, considering the additional advantages of decentralization.

The outline of the paper is as follows. Section 2 describes the basics of federated learning and gossip learning. Section 3 describes the specific algorithmic details that were applied in our comparative study, in particular, the management of the learning rate parameter and the subsampling compression techniques. Section 4 presents our results.

2   Background

Classification is a fundamental problem in machine learning. Here, a data set $D = \{(x_1, y_1), \ldots, (x_n, y_n)\}$ of n examples is given, where an example is represented by a feature vector $x \in R^d$ and the corresponding class label $y \in C$, where d is the dimension of the problem and C is the set of class labels. The problem of classification is often expressed as finding the parameters w of a function $f_w : R^d \to C$ that can correctly classify as many examples as possible in D, as well as outside D (this latter property is called generalization). Expressed formally, the objective function $J(w)$ captures the error of the model parameters w, and we wish to minimize $J(w)$ in w:

$$w^* = \arg\min_w J(w) = \arg\min_w \frac{1}{n} \sum_{i=1}^{n} \ell(f_w(x_i), y_i) + \frac{\lambda}{2} \|w\|^2, \tag{1}$$

where $\ell()$ is the loss function (the error of the prediction), $\|w\|^2$ is the regularization term, and λ is the regularization coefficient. By keeping the model parameters small, regularization helps in avoiding overfitting to the training set.

Perhaps the simplest algorithm to approximate w^* is the gradient descent method. Here, we start with a random weight vector w_0. In each iteration, we compute w_{t+1} based on w_t by finding the gradient of the objective function at w_t and making a step towards the direction opposite to the gradient. One such iteration is called a gradient update. Formally,

$$w_{t+1} = w_t - \eta_t \left(\frac{\partial J}{\partial w}(w_t) \right) = w_t - \eta_t (\lambda w_t + \frac{1}{n} \sum_{i=1}^{n} \frac{\partial \ell(f_w(x_i), y_i)}{\partial w}(w_t)), \tag{2}$$

where η_t is the learning rate at iteration t. Stochastic gradient descent (SGD) is similar, only we use a single example (x_i, y_i) instead of the entire database to perform an update:

$$w_{t+1} = w_t - \eta_t (\lambda w_t + \frac{\partial \ell(f_w(x_i), y_i)}{\partial w}(w_t)). \tag{3}$$

It is also usual to apply a so called *minibatch update*, in which more than one example is used, but not the entire database.

In this study we use *logistic regression* as our machine learning model, where the specific form of the objective function is given by

$$J(w) = -\frac{1}{n} \sum_{i=1}^{n} \ln P(y_i | x_i, w) + \frac{\lambda}{2} \|w\|^2, \tag{4}$$

where $y_i \in \{0, 1\}$, $P(0|x_i, w) = (1 + \exp(w^T x))^{-1}$ and $P(1|x_i, w) = 1 - P(0|x_i, w)$.

2.1   Federated Learning

The pseudocode of the federated learning algorithm [12,13] is shown in Algorithm 1 (master) and Algorithm 2 (worker). The master periodically sends the current model w to all the workers asynchronously in parallel and collects the answers from the workers. Any answers from workers arriving with a delay larger

---

Algorithm 1. Federated Learning Master

1: $(t, w) \leftarrow \text{init}()$
2: **loop**
3:     **for** every node i **in parallel do**   ▷ non-blocking (in separate thread(s))
4:         send (t, w) to i
5:         receive (n_i, h_i) from i ▷ n_i: example count at i; h_i: model gradient
6:     **end for**
7:     $\text{wait}(\Delta_f)$ ▷ the round length
8:     $n \leftarrow \frac{1}{|\mathcal{I}|} \sum_{i \in \mathcal{I}} n_i$ ▷ $\mathcal{I}$: nodes that returned a model in this round
9:     $t \leftarrow t + n$
10:    $h \leftarrow \text{aggregate}(\{h_i : i \in \mathcal{I}\})$
11:    $w \leftarrow w + h$
12: **end loop**

Algorithm 2. Federated Learning Worker

1: **procedure** ONRECEIVEMODEL(t, w)
2:     $(t', w') \leftarrow \text{update}((t, w), D_k)$ ▷ D_k: the local database of examples
3:     $(n, h) \leftarrow (t' - t, w' - w)$ ▷ n: the number of local examples
4:     send $(n, \text{compress}(h))$ to master
5: **end procedure**

---

than Δ_f are simply discarded. After Δ_f time units have elapsed, the master aggregates the received gradients and updates the model. We also send and maintain the model age t (based on the average number of examples used for training) in a similar fashion, to enable the use of dynamic learning rates in the local learning. These algorithms are very generic, the key characteristics of federated learning lie in the details of the update method (line 2 of Algorithm 2) and the compression mechanism (line 4 of Algorithm 2 and line 10 of Algorithm 1). The update method is typically implemented through a minibatch gradient descent algorithm that operates on the local data, initialized with the received model w. The details of our implementation of the update method and compression is presented in Sect. 3.

2.2 Gossip Learning

Gossip Learning is a method for learning models from fully distributed data without central control. Each node k runs Algorithm 3. First, the node initializes

---

Algorithm 3. Gossip Learning Framework

1: $(t_k, w_k) \leftarrow \text{init}()$
2: **loop**
3:     $\text{wait}(\Delta_g)$ 7: **procedure** ONRECEIVEMODEL(t_r, w_r)
4:     $p \leftarrow \text{select}()$ 8: $(t_k, w_k) \leftarrow \text{merge}((t_k, w_k), (t_r, w_r))$
5:     send $(t_k, \text{compress}(w_k))$ to p 9: $(t_k, w_k) \leftarrow \text{update}((t_k, w_k), D_k)$
6: **end loop**   10: **end procedure**

Algorithm 4. Model update rule

1: **procedure** UPDATE$((t, w), D)$
2:    **for all** batch $B \subseteq D$ **do**   ▷ D is split into batches
3:        $t \leftarrow t + |B|$
4:        $w \leftarrow w - \eta_t \sum_{(x,y) \in B} \left(\frac{\partial \ell(f_w(x), y)}{\partial w}(w) + \lambda w \right)$
5:    **end for**
6:    **return** (t, w)
7: **end procedure**

Algorithm 5. Model initialization

1: **procedure** INIT()
2:    $t \leftarrow 0$
3:    $w \leftarrow \mathbf{0}$ ▷ **0** denotes the vector of all zeros
4:    **return** (t, w)
5: **end procedure**

---

a local model w_k (and its age t_k). This is then periodically sent to another node in the network. (Note that these cycles are not synchronized.) The node selection is supported by a so-called sampling service [11,16]. Upon receiving a model w_r, the node merges it with the local model, and updates it using the local data set D_k. Merging is typically achieved by averaging the model parameters; see Sect. 3 for specific implementations. In the simplest case, the received model merely overwrites the local model. This mechanism results in the models taking random walks in the network and being updated when visiting a node. The possible update methods are the same as in the case of federated learning, and compression can be applied as well.

3   Algorithms

In this section we describe the details of the UPDATE, INIT, COMPRESS, AGGRE-GATE, and MERGE methods. Methods UPDATE, INIT and COMPRESS are shared among federated learning and gossip learning. In all the cases we used the implementations in Algorithms 4 and 5. In the minibatch update we compute the sum instead of the average to give an equal weight to all the examples irrespective of batch size. (Note that even if the minibatch size is fixed, actual sizes will vary because the number of examples at a given node is normally not divisible with the nominal batch size.) We used the dynamic learning rate $\eta_t = \eta/t$, where t is the number of instances the model was trained on.

Method AGGREGATE is used in Algorithm 1. Its function is to decompress and aggregate the received gradients encoded with COMPRESS. When there is no actual compression (COMPRESSNONE in Algorithm 7), simply the average of gradients is taken (AGGREGATEDEFAULT in Algorithm 6). The compression technique we employed is subsampling [13]. When using subsampling, workers do not send all of the model parameters back to the master, but only random

---

Algorithm 6. Various versions of the aggregate function

1: **procedure** AGGREGATEDEFAULT(H)   ▷ Average of gradients
2:     **return** $\frac{1}{|H|} \sum_{h \in H} h$
3: **end procedure**
4:
5: **procedure** AGGREGATESUBSAMPLED(H)   ▷ Restore expected value
6:     **return** $\frac{d}{s|H|} \sum_{h \in H} h$ ▷ s: number of model parameters kept by subsampling
7: **end procedure**
8:
9: **procedure** AGGREGATESUBSAMPLEDIMPROVED(H)
10:     $h' \leftarrow 0$
11:     **for** $i \in \{1, ..., d\}$ **do**
12:         $H_i \leftarrow \{h : h \in H \wedge h[i] \neq 0\}$ ▷ $h[i]$ refers to the ith element of the vector h
13:         $h'[i] \leftarrow \frac{1}{|H_i|} \sum_{h \in H} h[i]$ ▷ skipped if $|H_i| = 0$
14:     **end for**
15:     **return** h'
16: **end procedure**

Algorithm 7. Various versions of the compress function

1: **procedure** COMPRESSNONE(h)
2:     **return** h
3: **end procedure**
4:
5: **procedure** COMPRESSSUBSAMPLING(h)
6:     $h' \leftarrow 0$
7:     $X \leftarrow$ random subset of $\{1, ..., d\}$ of size s
8:     **for** $i \in X$ **do**
9:         $h'[i] \leftarrow h[i]$
10:     **end for**
11:     **return** h'
12: **end procedure**

---

subsets of a given size (see COMPRESSSUBSAMPLING). Note that the indices need not be sent, instead, we can send the random seed used to select them. The missing values are treated as zero. Due to this, the gradient average needs to be scaled as shown in AGGREGATESUBSAMPLED to create an unbiased estimator of the original gradient. We introduce a slight improvement to this scaling method in AGGREGATESUBSAMPLEDIMPROVED. Here, instead of scaling based on the theoretical probability of including a parameter, we calculate the actual average for each parameter separately based on the number of the gradients that contain the given parameter.

In gossip learning, MERGE is used to combine the local model with the incoming one. In the simplest variation, the local model is discarded in favor of the received model (see MERGENONE in Algorithm 8). It is usually a better idea to take the average of the parameter vectors [15]. We use average weighted by model age (see MERGEAVERAGE). Subsampling can be used with gossip learning

---

Algorithm 8. Various versions of the merge function

1: **procedure** MERGENONE$((t, w), (t_r, w_r))$
2:    **return** (t_r, w_r)
3: **end procedure**
4:
5: **procedure** MERGEAVERAGE$((t, w), (t_r, w_r))$
6:    $a \leftarrow \frac{t_r}{t + t_r}$
7:    $t \leftarrow max(t, t_r)$
8:    $w \leftarrow (1 - a)w + aw_r$
9:    **return** (t, w)
10: **end procedure**
11:
12: **procedure** MERGESUBSAMPLED$((t, w), (t_r, w_r))$ ▷ averages non-zero values only
13:    $a \leftarrow \frac{t_r}{t + t_r}$
14:    $t \leftarrow max(t, t_r)$
15:    **for** $i \in \{1, ..., d\}$ **do**
16:       **if** $w_r[i] \neq 0$ **then**   ▷ $w[i]$ refers to the ith element of the vector w
17:          $w[i] \leftarrow (1 - a)w[i] + aw_r[i]$
18:       **end if**
19:    **end for**
20:    **return** (t, w)
21: **end procedure**

---

as well, in which case MERGESUBSAMPLED must be used, which considers only the received parameters.

4   Experiments

4.1   Datasets

We used three datasets from the UCI machine learning repository [8] to test the performance of our algorithms. The first is the Spambase (SPAM E-mail Database) dataset containing a collection of emails. Here, the task is to decide whether an email is spam or not. The emails are represented by high level features, mostly word or character frequencies. The second dataset is Pendigits (Pen-Based Recognition of Handwritten Digits) that contains downsampled images of 4×4 pixels of digits from 0 to 9. The third is the HAR (Human Activity Recognition Using Smartphones) [1] dataset, where human activities (walking, walking upstairs, walking downstairs, sitting, standing and laying) were monitored by smartphone sensors (accelerometer, gyroscope and angular velocity). High level features were extracted from these measurement series.

The main properties, such as size or number of features, are presented in Table 1. In our experiments we standardized the feature values, that is, shifted and scaled them to have a mean of 0 and a variance of 1. Note that the standardization can be approximated by the nodes in the network locally if the

Table 1. Data set properties

	Spambase	Pendigits	HAR
Training set size	4140	7494	7352
Test set size	461	3498	2947
Number of features	57	16	561
Number of classes	2	10	6
Class-label distribution	$\approx$6:4	$\approx$uniform	$\approx$uniform
Parameter η	1E+4	1E+4	1E+2
Parameter λ	1E–6	1E–4	1E–2

approximation of the statistics of the features are fixed and known, which can be ensured in a fixed application.

In our simulation experiments, each example in the training data was assigned to one node when the number of nodes was 100. This means that, for example, with the HAR dataset each node gets 73.5 examples on average. When the network size is 1000, we replicate the examples, that is, each example is assigned to 10 different nodes. As for the distribution of class labels on the nodes, we applied two different setups. The first one is *uniform assignment*, which means that we assigned the examples to nodes at random independently of class label. The number of samples assigned to each node was the same (to be more precise, it differed by at most one due to the number of samples not being divisible by 100).

The second one is *single class assignment* when every node has examples only from a single class. Here, the different class labels are assigned uniformly to the nodes, and then the examples with a given label are assigned to one of the nodes with the same label, uniformly. These two assignment strategies represent the two extremes in any real application. In a realistic setting the class labels will likely be biased but much less so than in the case of the single class assignment scenario.

4.2   System Model

In our simulation experiments, we used a fixed random k-out overlay network, with $k = 20$. That is, every node had $k = 20$ fixed random neighbors. Simulations were performed with a network size of 100 and 1000 nodes. In the churn-free scenario, every node stayed online for the whole experiment. The churn scenario is based on a real trace gathered from smartphones (see Sect. 4.3 below). We assumed that a message is successfully delivered if and only if both the sender and the receiver remains online during the transfer. We also assume that the nodes are able to detect which of their neighbors are online at any given time with a delay that is negligible compared to the transfer time of a model.

We assumed uniform upload and download bandwidths for the nodes, and infinite bandwidth on the side of the server. Note that the latter assumption favors federated learning, as gossip learning does not use a server. The uniform bandwidth assumption is motivated by the fact that it is likely that in a real application there will be a configured (uniform) bandwidth cap that is significantly lower than the average available bandwidth. The transfer time of a full model was assumed to be 172 s (irrespective of the dataset used) in the *long transfer time* scenario, and 17.2 s in the *short transfer time* scenario. This allowed for around 1,000 and 10,000 iterations over the course of 48 h, respectively.

The cycle length parameters Δ_g and Δ_f were set based on the constraint that in the two algorithms the nodes should be able to exploit all the available bandwidth. In our setup this also means that the two algorithms transfer the same number of bits overall in the network in the same time-window. This will allow us to make fair comparisons regarding convergence dynamics. The gossip cycle length Δ_g is thus exactly the transfer time of a full model, that is, nodes are assumed to send messages continuously. The cycle length Δ_f of federated learning is the round-trip time, that is, the sum of the upstream and downstream transfer times. When compression is used, the transfer time is proportionally less as defined by the compression rate. Note, however, that in federated learning the master always sends the full model to the workers, only the upstream transfer is compressed.

It has to be noted that we assume much longer transfer times than what would be appropriate for the actual models in our simulation. To put it differently, in our simulations we pretend that our models are very large. This is because in the churn scenario if the transfer times are very short, the network hardly changes during the learning process, so effectively we learn over a static subset of the nodes. Long transfer times, however, make the problem more challenging because many transfers will fail, just like in the case of very large machine learning models such as deep neural networks. In the case of the no-churn scenario this issue is completely irrelevant, since the dynamics of convergence are identical apart from scaling time.

4.3 Smartphone Traces

The trace we used was collected by a locally developed openly available smartphone app called STUNner, as described previously [2]. In a nutshell, the app monitors and collects information about charging status, battery level, bandwidth, and NAT type.

We have traces of varying lengths taken from 1191 different users. We divided these traces into 2-day segments (with a one-day overlap), resulting in 40,658 segments altogether. With the help of these segments, we were able to simulate a virtual 48-h period by assigning a different segment to each simulated node.

To ensure our algorithm is phone and user friendly, we defined a device to be online (available) when it has been on a charger and connected to the internet for at least a minute, hence we never use battery power at all. In addition, we also treated those users as offline who had a bandwidth of less than 1 Mbit/s.

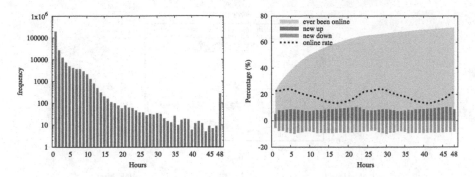

Fig. 1. Online session length distribution (left) and dynamic trace properties (right)

Figure 1 illustrates some of the properties of the trace. The plot on the right illustrates churn via showing, for every hour, what percentage of the nodes left, or joined the network (at least once), respectively. We can also see that at any given moment about 20% of the nodes are online. The average session length is 81.368 min.

4.4 Hyperparameters and Algorithms

The learning rate η and regularization coefficient λ were optimized using grid search assuming the no-failure scenario, no compression, and uniform assignment. The resulting values are shown in Table 1. These hyperparameters depend only on the database, they are robust to the selection of the algorithm. Minibatches of size 10 were used in each scenario. We used logistic regression as our learning algorithm, embedded in a one-vs-all meta-classifier.

4.5 Results

We ran the simulations using PeerSim [14]. We measure learning performance with the help of the 0–1 loss, which gives the proportion of the misclassified examples in the test set. In the case of gossip learning the loss is defined as the average loss over the online nodes.

First, we compare the two aggregation algorithms for subsampled models in Algorithm 6 (Fig. 2) in the no-failure scenario. The results indicate a slight advantage of AGGREGATESUBSAMPLINGIMPROVED, although the performance depends on the database. In the following we will apply AGGREGATESUBSAMPLINGIMPROVED as our implementation of method AGGREGATE.

The comparison of the different algorithms and subsampling probabilities is shown in Fig. 3. The stochastic gradient descent (SGD) method is also shown, which was implemented by gossip learning with no merging (using MERGENONE). Clearly, the parallel methods are all better than SGD. Also, it is very clear that

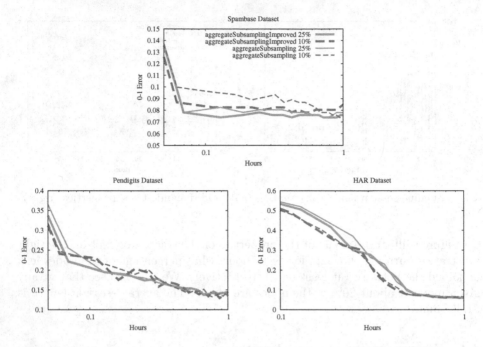

Fig. 2. Federated learning, 100 nodes, long transfer time, no failures, different aggregation algorithms and subsampling probabilities.

subsampling helps both federated learning and gossip learning. However, gossip learning benefits much more from it. The reason is that in the case of federated learning subsampling is implemented only in the worker master direction, the master sends the full model back to the workers [12]. However, in gossip learning, subsampling can be applied to all the messages.

Most importantly, gossip learning clearly *outperforms* federated learning in the case of high compression rates (low sampling probability) over two of the three datasets, and it is competitive on the remaining dataset as well. This was not expected, as gossip learning is fully decentralized, so the aggregation is clearly delayed compared to federated learning. Indeed, with no compression, federated learning performs better. However, with high compression rates, slower aggregation is compensated by a higher communication efficiency. Figure 3 also illustrates scaling. As we can see, the performance with 100 and 1000 nodes is practically identical for both algorithms.

Figure 4 contains our results with the churn trace. In the first hour, the two algorithms behave just like in the no-churn scenario. On the longer range, clearly, federated learning tolerates the churn better. This is because in federated learning nodes always work with the freshest possible models that they receive from the master, even right after coming back online. In gossip learning, outdated

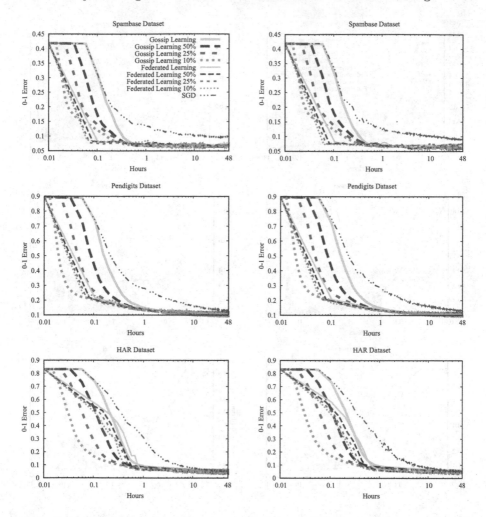

Fig. 3. Federated learning and gossip learning with 100 (left) and 1000 (right) clients, long transfer time, no failures, with different subsampling probabilities. Minibatch Stochastic Gradient Descent (SGD) is implemented by gossip learning with no merging (using MergeNone).

models could temporarily participate in the optimization, albeit with a smaller weight. In this study we did not invest any effort into mitigating this effect, but outdated models could potentially be removed with more aggressive methods as well.

We also include an artificial trace scenario, where online session lengths are exponentially distributed following the same expected length (81 min) as in the smartphone trace. The offline session length is set so we have 10% of the nodes spending any given federated learning round online in expectation, assuming no compression. This is to reproduce similar experiments in [13]. The results

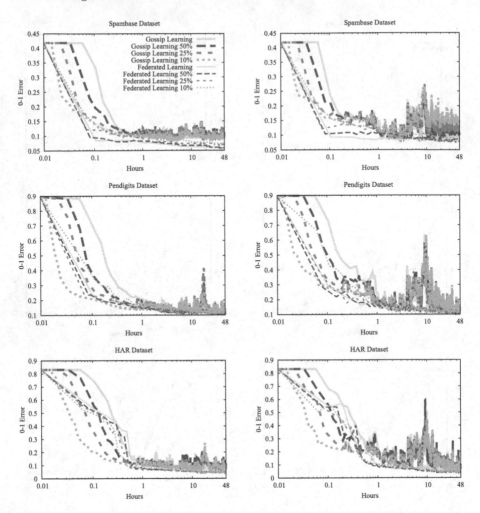

Fig. 4. Federated learning and gossip learning over the smartphone trace (left) and an artificial exponential trace (right), long transfer time, with different subsampling probabilities.

are similar to those over the smartphone trace, only the noise is larger for gossip learning, because the exponential model results in an unrealistically large variance in session lengths.

Figure 5 shows the convergence dynamics when we assume short transfer times (see Sect. 4.2). Clearly, the scenarios without churn result in the same dynamics (apart from a scaling factor) as the scenarios with long transfer time. The algorithms are somewhat more robust to churn in this case, since the nodes are more stable relative to message transfer time.

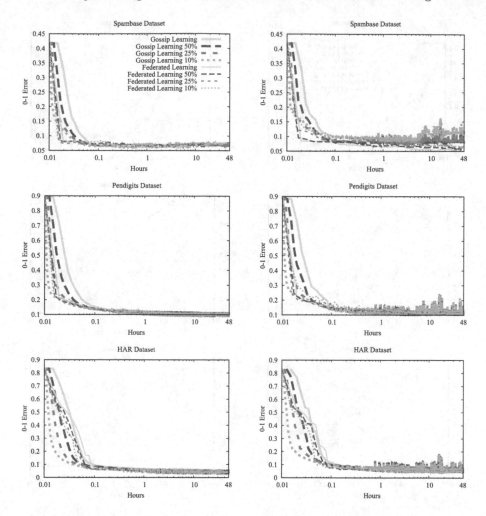

Fig. 5. Federated learning and gossip learning with no churn (left) and over the smartphone trace (right), short transfer time, with different subsampling probabilities.

Figure 6 contains the results of our experiments with the single class assignment scenario, as described in Sect. 4.1. In this extreme scenario, the learning problem becomes much harder. Still, gossip learning remains competitive in the case of high compression rates.

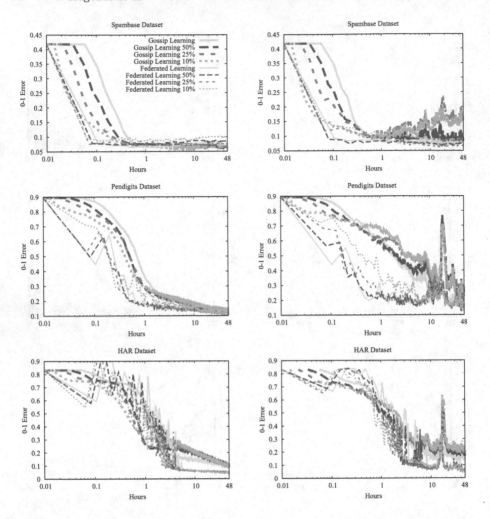

Fig. 6. Federated learning and gossip learning with no churn (left) and over the smartphone trace (right), long transfer time, single class assignment, with different subsampling probabilities.

5   Conclusions

Here, our goal was to compare federated learning and gossip learning in terms of efficiency. We designed an experimental study to answer this question. We compared the convergence speed of the two approaches under the assumption that both methods use the available bandwidth, resulting in an identical overall bandwidth consumption.

We found that in the case of uniform assignment, gossip learning is not only comparable to the centralized federated learning, but it even outperforms it under the highest compression rate settings. In every scenario we examined, gossip learning is comparable to federated learning. We add that this result relies on our experimental assumptions. For example, if one considers the download traffic to be essentially free in terms of bandwidth and time then federated learning is more favorable. This, however, is not a correct approach because it hides the costs at the side of the master node. For this reason, we opted for modeling the download bandwidth to be identical to the upload bandwidth, but still assuming an infinite bandwidth at the master node.

As for future work, the most promising direction is the design and evaluation of more sophisticated compression techniques [5] for both federated and gossip learning. Also, in both cases, there is a lot of opportunity to optimize the communication pattern by introducing asynchrony to federated learning, or adding flow control to gossip learning [6].

References

1. Anguita, D., Ghio, A., Oneto, L., Parra, X., Reyes-Ortiz, J.L.: A public domain dataset for human activity recognition using smartphones. In: 21th European Symposium on Artificial Neural Networks, Computational Intelligence and Machine Learning (ESANN) (2013)
2. Berta, Á., Bilicki, V., Jelasity, M.: Defining and understanding smartphone churn over the internet: a measurement study. In: Proceedings of the 14th IEEE International Conference on Peer-to-Peer Computing (P2P 2014). IEEE (2014)
3. Bonawitz, K., et al.: Practical secure aggregation for federated learning on user-held data. In: NIPS Workshop on Private Multi-Party Machine Learning (2016)
4. Danner, G., Berta, Á., Hegedűs, I., Jelasity, M.: Robust fully distributed mini-batch gradient descent with privacy preservation. Secur. Commun. Netw. **2018**, 15 (2018). Article no. 6728020
5. Danner, G., Jelasity, M.: Robust decentralized mean estimation with limited communication. In: Aldinucci, M., Padovani, L., Torquati, M. (eds.) Euro-Par 2018. LNCS, vol. 11014, pp. 447–461. Springer, Cham (2018). https://doi.org/10.1007/978-3-319-96983-1_32
6. Danner, G., Jelasity, M.: Token account algorithms: the best of the proactive and reactive worlds. In: Proceedings of the 38th International Conference on Distributed Computing Systems (ICDCS 2018), pp. 885–895. IEEE Computer Society (2018)
7. Dean, J., et al.: Large scale distributed deep networks. In: Proceedings of the 25th International Conference on Neural Information Processing Systems, NIPS 2012, vol. 1, pp. 1223–1231. Curran Associates Inc., USA (2012)
8. Dua, D., Graff, C.: UCI machine learning repository (2019). http://archive.ics.uci.edu/ml
9. European Commission: General data protection regulation (GDPR) (2018). https://ec.europa.eu/commission/priorities/justice-and-fundamental-rights/data-protection/2018-reform-eu-data-protection-rules
10. Hegedűs, I., Berta, Á., Kocsis, L., Benczúr, A.A., Jelasity, M.: Robust decentralized low-rank matrix decomposition. ACM Trans. Intell. Syst. Technol. **7**(4), 62:1–62:24 (2016)
11. Jelasity, M., Voulgaris, S., Guerraoui, R., Kermarrec, A.M., van Steen, M.: Gossip-based peer sampling. ACM Trans. Comput. Syst. **25**(3), 8 (2007)

12. Konecný, J., McMahan, H.B., Yu, F.X., Richtárik, P., Suresh, A.T., Bacon, D.: Federated learning: strategies for improving communication efficiency. In: Private Multi-Party Machine Learning (NIPS 2016 Workshop) (2016)
13. McMahan, B., Moore, E., Ramage, D., Hampson, S., y Arcas, B.A.: Communication-efficient learning of deep networks from decentralized data. In: Singh, A., Zhu, J. (eds.) Proceedings of the 20th International Conference on Artificial Intelligence and Statistics. Proceedings of Machine Learning Research, vol. 54, pp. 1273–1282. PMLR, Fort Lauderdale, FL, USA, 20–22 April 2017
14. Montresor, A., Jelasity, M.: PeerSim: a scalable P2P simulator. In: Proceedings of the 9th IEEE International Conference on Peer-to-Peer Computing (P2P 2009), pp. 99–100. IEEE, Seattle, Washington, USA, September 2009. Extended abstract
15. Ormándi, R., Hegedűs, I., Jelasity, M.: Gossip learning with linear models on fully distributed data. Concurr. Comp. Pract. Exp. **25**(4), 556–571 (2013)
16. Roverso, R., Dowling, J., Jelasity, M.: Through the wormhole: low cost, fresh peer sampling for the internet. In: Proceedings of the 13th IEEE International Conference on Peer-to-Peer Computing (P2P 2013). IEEE (2013)
17. Wang, J., Cao, B., Yu, P.S., Sun, L., Bao, W., Zhu, X.: Deep learning towards mobile applications. In: IEEE 38th International Conference on Distributed Computing Systems (ICDCS), pp. 1385–1393, July 2018

Using Trusted Execution Environments for Secure Stream Processing of Medical Data
(Case Study Paper)

Carlos Segarra[1]([✉])(iD), Ricard Delgado-Gonzalo[1](iD), Mathieu Lemay[1],
Pierre-Louis Aublin[2], Peter Pietzuch[2], and Valerio Schiavoni[3](iD)

[1] CSEM, Neuchâtel, Switzerland
{cse,rdg,mly}@csem.ch
[2] Imperial College London, London, UK
{p.aublin,prp}@imperial.ac.uk
[3] University of Neuchâtel, Neuchâtel, Switzerland
valerio.schiavoni@unine.ch

Abstract. Processing sensitive data, such as those produced by body sensors, on third-party untrusted clouds is particularly challenging without compromising the privacy of the users generating it. Typically, these sensors generate large quantities of continuous data in a streaming fashion. Such vast amount of data must be processed efficiently and securely, even under strong adversarial models. The recent introduction in the mass-market of consumer-grade processors with Trusted Execution Environments (TEEs), such as Intel SGX, paves the way to implement solutions that overcome less flexible approaches, such as those atop homomorphic encryption. We present a secure streaming processing system built on top of Intel SGX to showcase the viability of this approach with a system specifically fitted for medical data. We design and fully implement a prototype system that we evaluate with several realistic datasets. Our experimental results show that the proposed system achieves modest overhead compared to vanilla Spark while offering additional protection guarantees under powerful attackers and threat models.

Keywords: Spark · Data streaming · Intel SGX · Medical data · Case-study

1 Introduction

Internet of Things (IoT) devices are more and more pervasive in our lifes [22]. The number of devices owned per user is anticipated to increase by 26× by 2020 [19]. These devices continuously generate all large variety of continuous data. Notable examples include location-based sensors (*e.g.*, GPS), inertial units (*e.g.*, accelerometers, gyroscopes), weather stations, and, the focus of this paper, human-health data (*e.g.*, blood pressure, heart rate, stress).

© IFIP International Federation for Information Processing 2019
Published by Springer Nature Switzerland AG 2019
J. Pereira and L. Ricci (Eds.): DAIS 2019, LNCS 11534, pp. 91–107, 2019.
https://doi.org/10.1007/978-3-030-22496-7_6

These devices usually have very restricted computing power and are typically very limited in terms of storage capacity. Hence, this continuous processing of data must be off-loaded elsewhere, in particular for storage and processing purposes. In doing so, one needs to take into account potential privacy and security threats that stem inherently from the nature of the data being generated and processed.

Cloud environments represent the ideal environment to offload such processing. They allow deployers to hand-off the maintenance of the required infrastructure, with immediate benefit for instance in terms of scale-out with the workload.

Processing privacy-sensitive data on untrusted cloud platforms present a number of challenges. A malicious (compromised) Cloud operator could observe and leak data, if no countermeasures are taken beforehand. While there are software solutions that allow to operate on encrypted data (*e.g.*, partial [33] or full-homomorphic [24] encryption), their current computational overhead makes impractical in real-life scenarios [25].

The recent introduction into the mass market of processors with embedded trusted execution environments (TEEs), *e.g.*, Intel Software Guard Extensions (SGX) [20] (starting from processors with codename Skylake) or ARM Trust-Zone [1], offer a viable alternative to pure-software solutions. TEEs protect code and data against several types of attacks, including a malicious underlying OS, software bugs or threats from co- hosted applications. The application's security boundary becomes the CPU itself. The code is executed at near-native execution speeds inside enclaves of limited memory capacity. All the major Infrastructure-as-a-Service providers (Google [21], Amazon [2], IBM [3], Microsoft [37]) are nowadays offering nodes with SGX processors.

We focus on the specific use case of processing data streams generated by health-monitoring wearable devices on untrusted clouds with available SGX nodes. This setting addresses the fact that algorithms for analyzing cardiovascular signals are getting more complex and computation-intensive. Thus, traditional signal-processing approaches [29] have left the way to deep neural networks [43,45]. This increase in computational expenditure has moved the processing towards centralized centers (*i.e.*, the cloud) when scaling up to a large fleet of wearable devices is needed. In order to illustrate the concept, we present a system that computes in real time several metrics of the heart-rate variability (HRV) steaming from wearable sensors. While existing stream processing solutions exist [27,46], they either lack support for SGX or, if they do support it, are tied to very specific programming frameworks and prevent adoption in industrial settings.

The contributions of this case-study paper are twofold. First, we design and implement a complete system that can process heart-specific signals inside SGX enclaves in untrusted clouds. Our design leverages SGX-SPARK, a stream processing system that exploits SGX to execute stream analytics inside TEEs (described in detail in Sect. 2). Note that our design is flexible enough to be used with different stream processing systems (as further described later).

Second, we compare the proposed system against the vanilla, non-secure Spark. Our evaluation shows that the current overhead of SGX is reasonable even for large datasets and for high-throughput workloads and that the technology is almost ready for production environments.

This paper is organized as follows. In Sect. 2, we introduce Intel SGX, Spark, and SGX-SPARK. The architecture of the proposed system is presented in Sect. 3, while we further provide implementation details in Sect. 4. We evaluate our prototype with realistic workloads in Sect. 5 for which include experimental comparisons also against the vanilla Spark. A summary of related work in the domain of (secure) stream processing is given in Sect. 6. Finally, we present future work (Sect. 7) before concluding in Sect. 8.

2 Background

To better understand the design and implementation details, we introduce some technical background on the underlying technologies that we leverage, as well as some of the specific features interesting for cardiac signals. In Sect. 2.1, we provide background on the technical aspects exploited in the remaining of this paper, specifically describing the operating principles of Intel SGX, Spark and its secure counter-part SGX-SPARK. In Sect. 2.2, we describe the specifics of the data streams that the system has to deal with from the medical domain, such as heart-beat monitoring signals, together with the required processing that our system allows to offload on an untrusted cloud provider.

2.1 Technical Background

Trusted Execution Environments and Intel SGX. A trusted execution environment (TEE) is an isolated area of the processor that offers code and data's confidentiality and integrity guarantees. TEEs are nowadays available in commodity CPUs, such as ARM TRUSTZONE and Intel®SGX.

In comparison with ARM TRUST-ZONE, SGX includes a remote attestation protocol, support multiple trusted applications on the same CPU, and its SDK is easier to program with. As mentioned earlier, all the major IaaS providers offer SGX-enabled instances on their cloud offering, hence we decided to base the design of our system on top of it. Briefly, the SGX extensions are a set of instructions and memory access extensions. These instructions enable applications to create hardware-protected areas in their

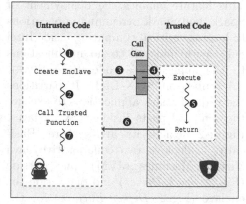

Fig. 1. INTEL SGX execution workflow.

address space, also known as, *enclaves* [31]. At initialization time, the content loaded is measured (via hashing) and sealed. An application using an enclave identifies itself through a remote attestation protocol and, once verified, interacts with the protected region through a call gate mechanism. In particular, Fig. 1 breaks down the typical execution workflow of SGX applications. After the initial attestation protocol, code in the untrusted region creates an enclave and securely loads trusted code and data inside (Fig.-❶). Whenever this untrusted code wants to make use of the enclave, it makes a call to a trusted function (Figs.-❷, -❸) that gets captured by the call gate mechanism and, after performing sanity and integrity checks (Fig.-❹), gets executed (Fig.-❺), the value returned (Fig.-❻) and the untrusted code can resume execution (Fig.-❼). The security perimeter is kept at the CPU package and, as a consequence, all other software including privileged software, OS, hypervisors or even other enclaves are prevented from accessing code and data located inside the enclave. Most notably, the systems' main memory is left untrusted and the traffic between CPU and DRAM over the protected address range is managed by the *Memory Encryption Engine* [26].

Spark and Spark Streaming. Spark is a cluster-computing framework to develop scalable, fault-tolerant, distributed applications. It builds on RDDs, resilient distributed datasets [46], a read-only collection distributed over a cluster that can be rebuilt if one partition is lost. It is implemented in SCALA and provides bindings for PYTHON, JAVA, SQL and R. SPARK STREAMING [47] is an extension of Spark's core API that enables scalable, high-throughput, fault tolerant stream (mini-batch) processing of data streams [16]. The proposed system leverages Spark Streaming to perform file-based streaming, by monitoring a filesystem interface outside the enclave.

SGX-LKL and SGX-Spark. SGX-LKL [11] is a library OS to run unmodified Linux binaries inside enclaves. Namely, it provides system support for managed runtimes, *e.g.*, a full JVM. This feature enables the deployment of Spark, and Spark Streaming applications to leverage critical computing inside Intel SGX with minimal to no modifications to the application's code. SGX-SPARK [15] builds on SGX-LKL. It partitions the code of Spark applications to execute the sensitive parts inside SGX enclaves. Figure 2 depicts its architecture. Basically, it deploys two collaborative Java Virtual Machines (JVM), one outside (Fig. 2, *Spark Driver*) and one inside the enclave (Fig. 2, *Driver Enclave*) for the driver, and two more for each worker deployed. Spark code outside the enclave

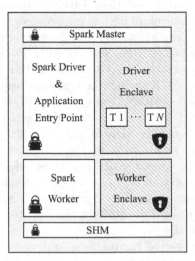

Fig. 2. SGX-SPARK attacker model and collaborative structure scheme.

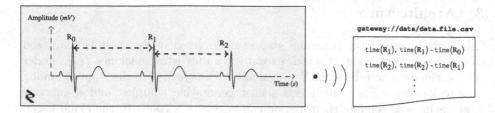

Fig. 3. Schematic representation of an ECG signal. It shows three normal beats and the information transferred from the sensor to the gateway. The most relevant part of the ECG wave are the R peaks and the time elapsed between them. The RR intervals together with the R peaks' timestamp are sent from the sensor to the gateway.

accesses only encrypted data. The communication between the JVMs is kept encrypted and is performed through the host OS shared memory. SGX-SPARK provides a compilation toolchain, and it currently supports the vast majority of the native Spark operators, allowing to transparently deploy and run existing Spark applications into the SGX enclaves.

2.2 Heart Rate Variability Analysis

The data streams used for the evaluation and the algorithms compiled with SGX-SPARK belong to the medical domain and motivate the real need for confidentiality and integrity. As further explained in Sect. 3, our use case contemplates a scenario where multiple sensors track the cardiac activity of different users. The two most standard procedures for monitoring heart activity are electrocardiograms (ECG) and photoplethysmograms (PPG). An ECG measures the heart's electrical activity and is the method used by, for instance, chest bands. A PPG is an optical measure of the evolution of blood volume over time and is the method used by wrist-based sensors [34]. Both procedures lead to an approximation of R peaks' timestamps and the intervals between them (RR intervals). The generation of the approximated diagram and the time measures are done inside the sensor. Figure 3 depicts a schematic representation of an ECG and the values streamed from the sensor to the gateway: R peak's timestamps and RR intervals. With healthy individuals' heart rate (HR) averaging between 60 to 180 beats per minute (bpm), the average throughput per client is between 23 and 69 bytes per second. An interesting use case of RR processing, besides HR approximation, is the study of Heart Rate Variability (HRV). HRV [30] is the variation in the time intervals between heartbeats and it has been proven to be a predictor of myocardial infarction. Finally, despite the proposed system being specifically designed for streams with these data features, its modular design (as we later describe in Sect. 3) makes it easy to adapt to other use-cases.

3   Architecture

The architecture of the proposed system is depicted in Fig. 4. It is composed of a server-side component which executes on untrusted machines (*e.g.*, nodes on the cloud), where Intel SGX is available. The clients are distributed among remote locations. Each client is a sensor generating samples, and a gateway aggregating and sending them periodically every n seconds to the cloud-based component. Similarly, clients fetch the results at fixed time intervals (*i.e.*, every 5 s in our deployments). The interaction between the clients and the server-side components of the system happens over a filesystem interface. Each client data stream is processed in parallel by the SGX-SPARK job. In the reminder, we further detail these components.

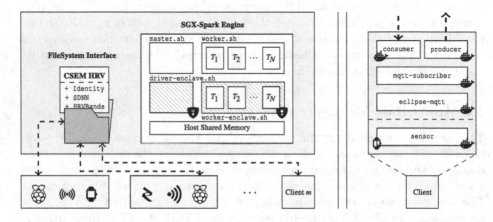

Fig. 4. (Left) Schematic of the system's main architecture. A set of clients bidirectionally stream data to a remote server. The interaction is done via a filesystem interface. On the server side, SGX-SPARK performs secure processing using different HRV analysis algorithms. (Right) Breakdown of a packaged client: it includes a `sensor` and gateway that wrap four different microservices (MQTT broker, `mqtt-subscriber`, `consumer`, `producer`) to interact with the remote end.

3.1   Server-Side

The server-side component is made by three different modules: a filesystem interface, the SGX-SPARK engine, and a set of algorithms to analyze HRV. The filesystem interface acts as a landing point for the batches of data generated by each client. It is monitored by the SGX-SPARK engine. Currently, it is mounted and unmounted, respectively at start-up time and upon the shutdown of the service. The streaming engine and the pool of algorithms are compiled together by the same toolchain, yet they are independent. The SPARK engine (deployed in standalone mode) executes: the master process, the driver process, and an arbitrary number of workers. In the case of SGX-SPARK jobs, two JVMs are deployed per driver and worker process: one inside an enclave and one outside. The communication between JVMs is kept encrypted and is done through the host OS shared memory (see Fig. 2). For each JVM pair, SGX-SPARK will initialize a new enclave. The specific algorithm that the system will execute is currently set at start-up time, although several concurrent ones can be executed, each yielding separated results.

3.2 Clients

The client is a combination of: (1) a data generator that simulates a sensor and (2) a gateway that interacts with the remote end. The data generator streams RR intervals. These samples are gathered by the gateway, which stacks and sends them for processing in a file-based streaming fashion. The typical size of these batches is in the 230–690 Bytes range. Each gateway is composed by: a message broker that handles the samples, a service that handles data pre-processing and batch sending, and a fetcher that directly *greps* from the server's filesystem.

3.3 Threat Model

We assume that the communication between the gateway and the filesystem is kept protected (*e.g.*, encrypted) using secure transfer protocols (more in Sect. 4). Given this assumption, the threat model is the same as typical systems that rely on SGX. Specifically, we assume the system software is untrusted. Our security perimeter only includes the internals of the CPU package. The trusted computing base is Intel's microcode as well as and the code loaded at the enclave, which can be measured and integrity can be checked. We assume that in our case the client package is trusted and tamper-proof. We focus on protecting the areas *outside* user's control. However, if the client package is deployed in, for instance, a RASPBERRY PI, the Trusted Computing Base (TCB) could be further reduced using ARM TRUSTZONE and OP-TEE [9].

3.4 Known Vulnerabilities

As for the known vulnerabilities, SGX (in particular the memory encryption engine) is not designed to be an oblivious RAM. As a consequence and adversary can perform traffic analysis attacks [26]. Moreover, side-channel attacks [38] and speculative execution attacks (*Spectre*-like [13] and *Foreshadow* [42]) have still successful against enclaves and will require in-silicon fixes.

4 Implementation

This section presents the further implementation details. To stress-test our evaluation, we replaced real sensors with synthetic data generators. Additionally, we deploy a large number of Docker containers [5] to mimic a fleet of concurrent clients.

4.1 Server-Side

We rely on the original SGX-SPARK implementation, and we only modify it to support a different in-enclave code deployment path, so that the .jar archive is available inside the enclaves and the shared memory. The application code is implemented in the Scala programming language [14]. Applications must adhere to the RDD API [10] to be usable inside the SGX enclaves. We use SGX-SPARK via Structured Streaming jobs, and must also adhere to the same API. We have implemented two state-of-the-art HRV analysis algorithms, namely SDNN and HRVBands [39]. The SDNN algorithm measures the standard deviation of NN (RR in our case) intervals. HRVBands performs frequency domain calculations: high-frequency (HF) power, low-frequency (LF) power and HF to LF ratio. For the sake of performance comparison, we also include results using an identity algorithm, simply reading the input data stream and outputting it. The implementation of these algorithms rely on basic Spark Streaming operators, and their corresponding Scala implementations. We use the file-based data stream input for SPARK streaming.[1]

4.2 Clients

Clients correspond to body-sensors strapped to the body of a user. These are connected to a gateway, (e.g., a Raspberry Pi) packaged together. Our implementation decouples the clients into into five different microservices (see Fig. 4, right). For evaluation purposes, the sensor is a PYTHON service that generates random RR intervals. These are published into the MQTT queue [6, 8] following a uniform time distribution. The gateway is composed by a MQTT queue and broker service. We rely on eclipse-mosquitto[2], a mqtt-sub service that subscribes to the specific topic and generates data files with several samples, and a producer and consumer services that interact with the remote filesystem. These components are implemented in Python, and consist of 888 Lines of Code (LoC). Our prototype relies on Docker to facilitate the deployment of new clients, and on docker-compose [4] to easily group orchestrate their deployment. The communication between the client and the server happens via SSH/SecureFTP to ensure transport layer security when transferring user's data.

4.3 Deployment

To ease scalability and reproducibility of both server and client, deployment is orchestrated by a single script detached from both execution environments. Specifying the remote location, the SGX-SPARK engine, the streaming algorithm and the filesystem interface are initialized either container-based or on metal. Specifying the number of simulated users and their location, a cluster of clients is dynamically started. On execution time, a Spark streaming service located

---

[1] https://spark.apache.org/docs/2.2.0/api/java/org/apache/spark/streaming.
[2] https://hub.docker.com/_/eclipse-mosquitto/.

in a remote server with a master process and an arbitrary number of Spark workers (or executors) interacts with a standalone Docker Swarm composed by the cluster of clients, a name discovery service and an overlay network. This architecture scales to hundreds of clients.

5 Evaluation

In this section, we present the experimental evaluation. We first present the evaluation settings for both the client and the server components. Then, we describe the metrics of interest on which we focus our experiments. Finally, we present our results. Our experiments answer the following questions: *(i)* is the design of the proposed system sound? *(ii)* is our implementation efficient, *(iii)* what is the overhead of SGX, and *(iv)* is it scalable?

5.1 Settings

Clients. Each client (*e.g.*, a body sensor in real-life) is emulated by a standalone Docker application. We deploy them on a quad-16core (64 hardware cores) AMD EPYC 7281 with 64 GiB of RAM running Ubuntu v18.04 LTS (kernel 4.15.0-42-generic). The client containers are built and deployed using Docker (v18.09.0) and `docker-compose` (v1.23.2). We use `docker-machine` (v0.16.0) with the `virtualbox` disk image. Each machine hosts 20 clients, the maximum number of services supported by its local network, and it registers itself to the Swarm via a name discovery service running on another machine. Inter-container communication rely on the `overlay` network driver. We pull the latest images available on Docker Hub for the Consul name discovery service (v1.4) and the `eclipse-mosquitto` (v1.5) message broker.

Server. The server components run on host machines with Intel ® Xeon ® CPU E3-1270 v6 @ 3.80 GHz with 8 cores and 64 GiB RAM. We use Ubuntu 16.04 LTS (kernel 4.19.0-41900-generic) and the official Intel ® SGX driver v2.0 [7], and SGX-LKL [11]. We use an internal release of the SGX-SPARK framework.

5.2 Experiment Configurations

We compare the results of 3 different systems (or execution modes): the vanilla Spark (our baseline), the SGX-SPARK system with enclaves disabled (*i.e.* collaborative JVMs communicating over SHM which run outside the SGX enclaves) and SGX-SPARK with enclaves enabled. The latter mode is the one the proposed system runs in. The current implementation of SGX-SPARK (still under development) does not provide support for Spark's `Streaming Context` inside enclaves. To overcome this temporary limitation, we evaluate the SDNN and Identity algorithms in batch and stream mode. For the former, all three different execution modes are supported. For the latter, we present estimated results for SGX-SPARK with enclaves enabled, basing the computation time on the batch execution times and the additional overhead against the other modes. The algorithms are fed with a data file or a data stream, respectively. In the streaming scenario, an output file is generated every ten seconds. In a multi-client scenario, each client has a separated data stream (or file) and consequently a different result file. A streaming execution consists of 5 min of the service operating with a specific configuration. We execute our experiments 5 times and report average and standard deviations.

Metrics. To assess performance, scalability, and efficiency, we consider average batch processing times for streaming jobs, and elapsed times for batch executions. Note that we mention *batch* in two different contexts: batch execution (one static input and static output) and streaming batches. Spark Streaming divides live input data in chunks called *batches* determined by a time duration (10 s in our experiments). The time it takes the engine to process the data therein contained is denoted as batch processing time. In order to obtain all batch processing times, we rely on the internal Spark's REST API [12]. Since the GET request fetches the historic of batch processing times for the running job, one single query right before finishing the execution provides all the sufficient informations for our computations. In order to obtain the elapsed times for batch executions, a simple logging mechanism suffices.

Workload. The clients inject streams as cardiac signals, as shown earlier (Sect. 2.2). Each signal injects a modest workload into our system (230–690 bytes per minute). Hence, to assess the efficiency and the processing time as well as to uncover possible bottlenecks, we scale up the output rate of these signals with the goal of inducing more aggressive workloads. We do so in detriment of medical realism, since arbitrary input workloads do not relate to any medical situation or condition. Table 1 shows the variations used to evaluate the various execution modes.

Table 1. Different input loads used for Batch Executions (BE) and Streaming Executions (SE). We present the sample rate they simulate (*i.e.* how many RR intervals are streamed per second) and the overall file or stream size (Input Load).

Experiment	s_rate (samples/s)	Input Load
BE - Small Load	$\{44, 89, 178, 356, 712, 1424\}$	$\{1, 2, 4, 8, 16, 32\}$ kB
SE - Small Load	$\{44, 89, 178, 356, 712, 1424\}$	$\{1, 2, 4, 8, 16, 32\}$ kB/s
BE - Big Load	$\{44, 89, 178, 356, 712, 1424\} * 1024$	$\{1, 2, 4, 8, 16, 32\}$ MB
SE - Big Load	$\{44, 89, 178, 356, 712, 1424\} * 1024$	$\{1, 2, 4, 8, 16, 32\}$ MB/s

5.3   Results

Batch Execution: Input File Size. The configuration for the following experiments is: one client, one master, one driver, one worker, and a variable input file that progressively increases in size. We measure the processing (or elapsed) time of each execution and present the average and standard deviation of experiments with the same configuration. The results obtained are included in Fig. 5.

From the bar plot we highlight that the variance between execution times among same execution modes as we increase the input file size is relatively low. However, it exponentiates as we reach input files of 4–8 MB. We also observe that the slow-down factor between execution modes remains also quite static until reaching the before mentioned load threshold. SGX-SPARK with enclaves, if input files are smaller than 4 MB, increases execution times x4-5 when compared to vanilla Spark and x1.5-2 when compared to SGX-SPARK with enclaves disabled. Note that, since a single client in our real use case streams around 230 to 690 bytes per minute, the current input size limitation already enables several concurrent clients.

Streaming Execution: input load. As done previously, we scale the load of the data streams that feed the system. We deploy one worker, one driver and one client, query the average batch processing time to Spark's REST API, and present the results for the Identity and SDNN algorithms. Results are summarized in Fig. 6.

We obtain results for vanilla Spark, and SGX-SPARK without enclaves, and we estimate them for SGX-SPARK with enclaves. We observe similar behavior as those in Fig. 5. Variability among same execution modes when increasing the input stream size is low until reaching values of around 4 to 8 MB per second. Similarly, the slow-down factor from vanilla Spark to SGX-SPARK without enclaves remains steady at around x2-2.5 until reaching the load threshold. As a consequence, it is reasonable to estimate that the behavior of SGX-SPARK with enclaves will preserve a similar slow-down factor ($\times 4$-$\times 5$) when compared with vanilla Spark in streaming jobs. Similarly, the execution time will increase linearly with the input load after crossing the load threshold of 4 MB. Note as well how different average batch processing times are in comparison with elapsed times, in spite of relatively behaving similar. The average of streaming batch processing times smoothens the initial overhead of starting the Spark engine, and data loading times are hidden under previous batches' execution times.

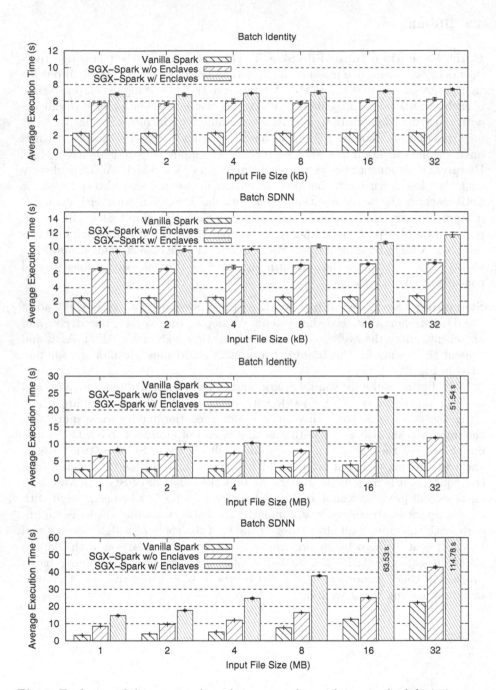

Fig. 5. Evolution of the average elapsed time, together with its standard deviation, as we increase the size of the input file. We compare the three different execution modes for each algorithm. Mode SGX-SPARK w/ enclaves is the mode our system runs in.

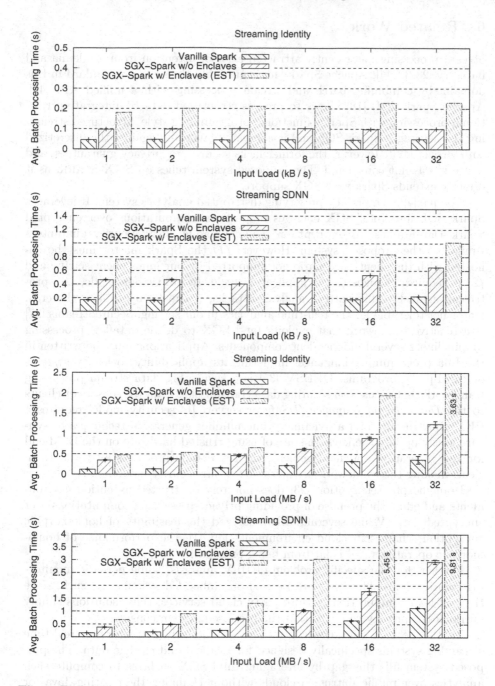

Fig. 6. Evolution of the average batch processing time as we increase the input file size. We compare the results of the three different execution modes. Note that those corresponding to SGX-SPARK w/ enclaves are estimated basing on the results in Fig. 5 and the slow-down with respect to the other execution modes.

6   Related Work

Stream processing has recently attracted a lot of attention from academia and industry [28,32,44]. Apache Spark [46] is arguably the de-facto standard in this domain, by combining batch and stream processing with a unified API [48]. Apache Spark SQL [18] allows to process structured data by integrating relational processing with Spark's functional programming style. Structured streaming [17] leverages Spark SQL and it compares favorably against the discretized counterpart [47]. However, the former lacks security or privacy guarantees, and hence it was not considered. The proposed system relies on SGX-SPARK, as it directly extends Spark with SGX support.

Opaque [49] is a privacy-preserving distributed analytics system. It leverages Spark SQL and Intel SGX enclaves to perform computations over encrypted Spark DataFrames. In encryption mode, Opaque offers security guarantees similar to the proposed system. However, (1) the Spark master must be co-hosted with the client, a scenario not supported by our multi-client setting and (2) it requires changes to the application code. In oblivious mode, i.e., protecting against traffic pattern analysis attacks, it can be up to 46× slower, a factor not tolerable for the real-time analytics in our setting. SecureStreams [27] is a reactive framework that exploits Intel SGX to define dataflow processing by pipelining several independent components. Applications must be written in the Lua programming language, hindering its applicability to legacy systems or third-party programs. DPBSV [35] is a secure big data stream processing framework that focuses on securing data transmission from the sensors or clients to the *Data Stream Manager (DSM)* or server. Its security model requires a PKI infrastructure and a dynamic prime number generation technique to synchronously update the keys. In spite of using trusted hardware on the DSM end for key generation and management, the server-side processes all the data in clear, making the framework not suitable for our security model.

Homomorphic encryption [23] does not rely on trusted execution environments and offers the promise of providing privacy-preserving computations over encrypted data. While several works analyzed the feasibility of homomorphic encryption schemes in cloud environments [40,41], the performance of homomorphic operations [25] is far from being pragmatic.

Further, for the specific problem of HRV analysis, while periodic monitoring solutions exist [36], they are focused on embedded systems. As such, since they off-load computation to third-party cloud services, these solutions simply overlook the privacy concerns that the proposed system considers.

To the best of our knowledge, there are no privacy-preserving real-time streaming systems specifically designed for medical and cardiac data. The proposed system fills this gap by leveraging Intel SGX enclaves to compute such analytics over public untrusted clouds without changing the existing Java- or Scala-based source code.

7 Future Work

The current prototype can be improved along several dimensions. First, we envision to support clients running inside ARM TrustZone: this TEE is widely available in low-power devices (*e.g.*, Raspberry PI), hence makes an ideal candidate to reduce the TCB in the client-side of the architecture. Second, we intend to improve the plug-in mechanism for additional analysis of the data, as currently a given algorithm is set at deploy-time, while it is expected to load/unload those at runtime. Thirdly, we intend to study the cost of deployment of such system over public cloud infrastructures such as AWS Confidential Computing.

8 Conclusion

We presented a stream-processing architecture and implementation that leverage Spark-SGX to overcome privacy concerns of deploying such systems over untrusted public clouds. Its design allows to easily scale to different types of data generators (*e.g.*, the clients). The processing components that execute on the cloud rely on SGX-SPARK, a stream processing framework that can executes Spark jobs within SGX enclaves. Our evaluation shows that for typical signal processing, despite an observed overhead of 4×–5× induced by the current experimental version of SGX-SPARK, the performance is still practical. This suggests that it will be possible in a near-future to deploy such systems on a production-ready environment with performances that can easily satisfy even strict Service Level Agreements, while keeping maintaining the costs to use the cloud infrastructure reasonable. We intend to release the code as open-source.

Acknowledgements. We are grateful to the members of the LSDS Team (https:// lsds.doc.ic.ac.uk/) at Imperial College London to have provided us early access to SGX-SPARK.

References

1. ARM TrustZone Developer. https://developer.arm.com/technologies/trustzone
2. Coming Soon: Amazon EC2 C5 Instances, the next generation of Compute Optimized instances. http://amzn.to/2nmIiH9
3. Data-in-use protection on IBM Cloud using Intel SGX. https://www.ibm.com/blogs/bluemix/2018/05/data-use-protection-ibm-cloud-using-intel-sgx/
4. Docker Documentation: Docker Compose. https://docs.docker.com/compose/
5. Docker: What is a Container? https://www.docker.com/resources/what-container
6. Eclipse Paho MQTT Implementation. https://www.eclipse.org/paho/
7. Intel Software Guard Extension for Linux OS Driver on GitHub. https://github.com/intel/linux-sgx-driver
8. MQTT Communication Protocol. http://mqtt.org/
9. Open Portable Trusted Execution Environment. https://www.op-tee.org
10. RDD Programming Guide. https://spark.apache.org/docs/latest/rdd-programming-guide.html

11. SGX-LKL on Github. https://github.com/lsds/sgx-lkl
12. Spark Documentation: REST API. https://spark.apache.org/docs/latest/monitor
    ing.html#rest-api
13. Spectre Attack SGX on Github. https://github.com/lsds/spectre-attack-sgx
14. The Scala Programming Language. https://www.scala-lang.org/
15. D3.2 SecureCloud: Specification and Implementation of Reusable Secure Microser-
    vices (2017). https://www.securecloudproject.eu/wp-content/uploads/D3.2.pdf
16. Apache Foundation: Spark streaming programming guide. https://spark.apache.
    org/docs/2.2.0/streaming-programming-guide.html
17. Armbrust, M., et al.: Structured streaming: a declarative API for real-time appli-
    cations in Apache Spark. In: ACM SIGMOD 2018 (2018)
18. Armbrust, M., et al.: Spark SQL: relational data processing in Spark. In: ACM
    SIGMOD 2015 (2015)
19. Barbosa, M., et al.: SAFETHINGS: data security by design in the IoT. In: IEEE
    EDCC 2017 (2017)
20. Costan, V., Devadas, S.: Intel SGX explained. IACR 2016 (2016)
21. Darrow, B.: Google is first in line to get Intel's next-gen server chip. http://for.
    tn/2lLdUtD
22. Gartner: Leading the IoT Gartner Insights on how to lead in a connected world
    (2017)
23. Gentry, C.: Fully homomorphic encryption using ideal lattices. In: ACM STOC
    2009 (2009)
24. Gentry, C., Halevi, S., Smart, N.P.: Homomorphic evaluation of the AES circuit. In:
    Safavi-Naini, R., Canetti, R. (eds.) CRYPTO 2012. LNCS, vol. 7417, pp. 850–867.
    Springer, Heidelberg (2012). https://doi.org/10.1007/978-3-642-32009-5_49
25. Göttel, C., et al.: Security, performance and energy trade-offs of hardware-assisted
    memory protection mechanisms. In: IEEE SRDS 2018 (2018)
26. Gueron, S.: A memory encryption engine suitable for general purpose processors.
    IACR 2016
27. Havet, A., et al.: SecureStreams: a reactive middleware framework for secure data
    stream processing. In: ACM DES 2017 (2017)
28. Koliousis, A., et al.: SABER: window-based hybrid stream processing for hetero-
    geneous architectures. In: ACM SIGMOD 2016 (2016)
29. Kumar, A., Shaik, F., Rahim, B.A., Kumar, D.S.: Signal and Image Processing in
    Medical Applications. Springer, Heidelberg (2016). https://doi.org/10.1007/978-
    981-10-0690-6
30. Malik, M.: Heart rate variability: standards of measurement, physiological inter-
    pretation, and clinical use. Circulation 93, 1043–1065 (1996)
31. McKeen, F., et al.: Innovative instructions and software model for isolated execu-
    tion. In: HASP 2013 (2013)
32. Miao, H., Park, H., Jeon, M., Pekhimenko, G., McKinley, K.S., Lin, F.X.: Stream-
    Box: modern stream processing on a multicore machine. In: USENIX ATC 2017
    (2017)
33. Paillier, P.: Public-key cryptosystems based on composite degree residuosity
    classes. In: Stern, J. (ed.) EUROCRYPT 1999. LNCS, vol. 1592, pp. 223–238.
    Springer, Heidelberg (1999). https://doi.org/10.1007/3-540-48910-X_16
34. Parák, J., Tarniceriu, A., Renevey, P., Bertschi, M., Delgado-Gonzalo, R., Korho-
    nen, I.: Evaluation of the beat-to-beat detection accuracy of PulseOn wearable
    optical heart rate monitor. In: IEEE EMBC 2015 (2015)
35. Puthal, D., Nepal, S., Ranjan, R., Chen, J.: DPBSV - an efficient and secure scheme
    for big sensing data stream. In: IEEE TRUSTCOM 2015 (2015)

36. Renevey, P., et al.: Respiratory and cardiac monitoring at night using a wrist wearable optical system. In: IEEE EMBC 2018 (2018)
37. Russinovich, M.: Introducing Azure Confidential Computing. https://azure.microsoft.com/en-us/blog/introducing-azure-confidential-computing/
38. Schwarz, M., Weiser, S., Gruss, D., Maurice, C., Mangard, S.: Malware guard extension: using SGX to conceal cache attacks. In: Polychronakis, M., Meier, M. (eds.) DIMVA 2017. LNCS, vol. 10327, pp. 3–24. Springer, Cham (2017). https://doi.org/10.1007/978-3-319-60876-1_1
39. Shaffer, F., Ginsberg, J.P.: An overview of heart rate variability metrics and norms. Front. Pub. Health **5**, 258 (2017). https://doi.org/10.3389/fpubh.2017.00258
40. Stephen, J.J., Savvides, S., Sundaram, V., Ardekani, M.A., Eugster, P.: STYX: stream processing with trustworthy cloud-based execution. In: ACM SoCC 2016 (2016)
41. Tetali, S.D., Lesani, M., Majumdar, R., Millstein, T.: MrCrypt: static analysis for secure cloud computations. In: ACM OOPSLA 2013 (2013)
42. Van Bulck, J., et al.: Foreshadow: extracting the keys to the Intel SGX kingdom with transient out-of-order execution. In: USENIX Security 2018 (2018)
43. Van Zaen, J., Chételat, O., Lemay, M., Calvo, E.M., Delgado-Gonzalo, R.: Classification of cardiac arrhythmias from single lead ECG with a convolutional recurrent neural network. In: BIOSTEC 2019 (2019)
44. Venkataraman, S., et al.: Drizzle: fast and adaptable stream processing at scale. In: ACM OSP 2017 (2017)
45. Xiong, Z., Nash, M., Cheng, E., Fedorov, V., Stiles, M., Zhao, J.: ECG signal classification for the detection of cardiac arrhythmias using a convolutional recurrent neural network. Physiol. Measur. **39**, 094006 (2018)
46. Zaharia, M., Chowdhury, M., Franklin, M.J., Shenker, S., Stoica, I.: Spark: cluster computing with working sets. In: USENIX HotCloud 2010 (2010)
47. Zaharia, M., Das, T., Li, H., Shenker, S., Stoica, I.: Discretized streams: an efficient and fault-tolerant model for stream processing on large clusters. In: USENIX HotCloud 2012 (2012)
48. Zaharia, M., et al.: Apache spark: a unified engine for big data processing. Commun. ACM 2016 **59**, 56–65 (2016)
49. Zheng, W., Dave, A., Beekman, J.G., Popa, E.A., Gonzalez, J.E., Stoica, I.: Opaque: an oblivious and encrypted distributed analytics platform. In: USENIX NSDI 2017 (2017)

Stunner: A Smart Phone Trace for Developing Decentralized Edge Systems

Zoltán Szabó[1] , Krisztián Téglás[1], Árpád Berta[1] , Márk Jelasity[1,2]([envelope]) ,
and Vilmos Bilicki[1]

[1] University of Szeged, Szeged, Hungary
jelasity@inf.u-szeged.hu
[2] MTA SZTE Research Group on Artificial Intelligence, Szeged, Hungary

Abstract. Conducting research into edge and fog computing often involves experimenting with actual deployments, which is costly and time-consuming, so we need to rely on realistic simulations at least in the early phases of research. To be able to do so we need to collect real data that allows us to perform trace-based simulation and to extract crucial statistics. To achieve this for the domain of distributed smartphone applications, for many years we have been collecting data via smartphones concerning NAT type, the availability of WiFi and cellular networks, the battery level, and many more attributes. Recently, we enhanced our data collecting Android app Stunner by taking actual P2P measurements. Here, we outline our data collection method and the technical details, including some challenges we faced with data cleansing. We present a preliminary set of statistics based on the data for illustration. We also make our new database freely available for research purposes.

1 Introduction

Distributed computing over the edge as part of various smart systems is becoming a popular research topic [4]. Research into algorithms that are suitable to such environments often involves actual deployments, because realistic conditions are non-trivial to model, yet they are crucial for finding an optimally efficient and robust solution. Still, this severely limits the possibilities of exploratory research.

One important domain is smartphone applications that can form a part of many smart systems such as smart city or e-health solutions [14]. In this domain, it is important to fully understand the capabilities and limitations of the devices and their network access as well. This includes battery charging patterns, network availability (churn) and network attributes (for example, NAT type).

This work was supported by the Hungarian Government and the European Regional Development Fund under the grant number GINOP-2.3.2-15-2016-00037 ("Internet of Living Things") and by the Hungarian Ministry of Human Capacities (grant 20391-3/2018/FEKUSTRAT).

J. Pereira and L. Ricci (Eds.): DAIS 2019, LNCS 11534, pp. 108–115, 2019.
https://doi.org/10.1007/978-3-030-22496-7_7

Our team started to develop the smartphone app STUNNER in 2013 to collect data concerning the NAT properties of smartphones using the STUN protocol [2], as well as many other attributes such as battery level and network availability. Since then, we have collected a large trace involving millions of individual measurements. Recently, we also updated the application to collect data concerning direct peer-to-peer capabilities based on a basic WebRTC implementation.

There have been many data collection campaigns targeting smartphones. This included the famous Mobile Data Challenge (MDC) [6], which aimed to collect large amounts of data from smartphones for various research studies, including sensory data, cell towers, calls, etc. and ran between 2009 and 2011, resulting in the largest and most widely known dataset yet. After this, the most prominent project to achieve similar results was the Device Analyzer Experiment. started in 2011 by the University of Cambridge, aiming to not only record similar attributes to the MDC, but also system-level information such as phone types, OS versions, energy and charging [3,13]. This trace has been used, for example, to determine the most energy consuming Android APIs [7] or to reconstruct the states of battery levels on the monitored smartphones [5]. Our dataset is unique in that, apart from being five years long, it contains all the necessary attributes to simulate *decentralized* applications.

Another set of projects are concerned with measuring the network (e.g., detecting NAT boxes) as opposed to collecting a full trace from the devices, which is our main goal. For instance, in 2014 a study was initiated to analyze the deployment rate of carrier-grade NATs that can hide entire areas behind a single public IP address [11]. The measurement was based on NETALYZR, as well as on crawls of BitTorrent DHT tables to detect possible leaked internal addresses due to hairpin NAT traversal. In another study across Europe, an application called NAT REVELIO was developed [9]. Yet another data collection campaign attempted to collect traceroute sessions from smartphones using the custom TRACEBOXANDROID application [12]. The application detects the exact number of middleboxes and NAT translations encountered between the device and a specified test target. In a similar two-week campaign, the NETPICULAR application was deployed [15]. Also, a mobile application called MOBIL TRACEBOX was deployed to carry out traceroute measurements [16]. This campaign ran for an entire year. A summary of these NAT studies can be found in Table 1.

While our NAT measurements are simply based on STUN server feedback [8], thus underestimating the complexity of the network, our P2P measurements indicate that our NAT type data is a good basis for predicting connection success (see Sect. 3).

Our contribution is fourfold: (1) our application STUNNER has been collecting data for a much longer time than any of these applications, which allows us to observe historic trends; (2) in the latest version, we measure direct P2P connections allowing us to collect NAT traversal statistics; (3) we collect a wide range of properties simultaneously, including NAT type, battery level, network availability, and so on, to be able to fully model decentralized protocols; and (4) we make our trace publicly available at http://www.inf.u-szeged.hu/stunner.

Table 1. Comparison between various NAT measurement campaigns

Source	Collected attributes	Length	Public	Tools
[11]	Local, external and public IP addresses	2014–2016	No	Netalyzr
[9]	External IP, mapped port, traceroute results, UPnP query results	2016 May and August	No	NAT Revelio
[16]	Traceroute results	2016 Feb–2017 Feb	No	Mobile Tracebox
[15]	Traceroute results, number of detected middleboxes	2011 Jan., 2 weeks	No	Netpiculet
[12]	Traceroute results, number of detected middleboxes	2014 May–Sep	No	TraceboxAndroid

2 Data Collection Methodology

The functionality of our Android app STUNNER is to provide the user with information about the current network environment of the phone: private and public IP, NAT type, MAC address, and some other network related details [2]. At the same time, the app collects data about the phone and logs it to our servers. The app was launched in April 2014, when it was simply made public without much advertising. Since then, at any point in time we had a user base of a few hundred to a few thousand users, and over 40 million measurements have been collected from all over the world.

In the original version measurements were triggered either by the user (when the app is used) or by specific events that signal the change of some of the properties we measure: battery charging status, network availability. There was periodic measurement as well every 10 min, if no other events occurred.

The latest version was completely redesigned. This was necessary because Android has become very hostile to background processes when the phone is not on a charger, in an effort to save energy. For this reason, we now collect data only when the phone is on a charger. This, however, is not a real issue, because for decentralized applications these are the most useful intervals, when it is much cheaper to communicate and to perform computing tasks in the background. Android event handlers have also became more restricted, so we can use them only under limited circumstances or on early Androids. The events raised by connecting to a charger or a network can still be caught by the Android job scheduler, but the timing of these events is not very reliable.

For this reason, instead of relying on event handlers, we check the state of the phone every minute, and if there is a change in any important locally available networking parameter or in charging availability, we perform a full measurement.

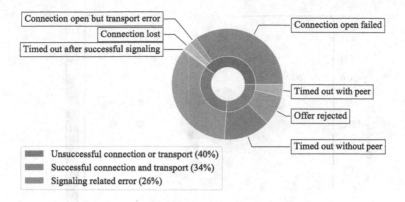

Fig. 1. Proportions of the possible outcomes of P2P connection attempts.

A measurement is still triggered if the user explicitly requests one, and it is also triggered by an incoming P2P measurement request. Also, if there is no measurement for at least 10 min, a full measurement is performed.

P2P connection measurements are also a new feature in the latest version that are performed every time a measurement is carried out. They are based on the WebRTC protocol [1], with Firebase as a signaling server [10], and a STUN server [8]. We build and measure only direct connections, the TURN protocol for relaying is not used. Every node that is online (has network access and is on a charger) attempts to connect to a peer. To do this, the node sends a request to the Firebase server after collecting its own network data. The server attempts to find a random online peer and manages the information exchange using the Session Description Protocol (SDP) to help create a two-way P2P connection over UDP. If the two-way channel is successfully opened then a tiny data massage is exchanged. The channel is always closed at the end of the measurement. One connection is allowed at a time, every additional offer is rejected. The signaling server maintains an online membership list.

3   Some Measurement Results

For illustration, we present some of the interesting patterns in our trace. Figure 1 shows the proportions of the outcomes of 63184 P2P connection attempts. Out of all the attempts, 34% was completed successfully. Let us briefly describe the possible reasons for failure. First, *signaling related error* means that the SDP data exchange via the signaling server failed. This can happen, if the server contacts a possible peer but the peer replies with a reject message (offer rejected), or it does not reply in time (timed out with peer), or we cannot see proof in the trace that any peer was actually contacted (timed out without peer). Note that a peer rejects a connection if it has an ongoing connection attempt of its own.

If the signaling phase succeeds, we have a pair of nodes ready to connect. The most frequent error here is failing to open the channel, most likely due

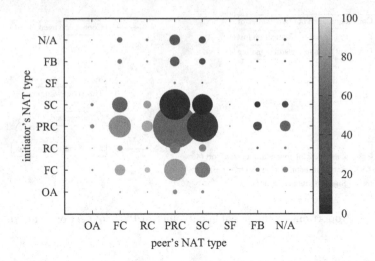

Fig. 2. Statistics over successful connections as a function of NAT type. The area of a disk is proportional to its observed frequency, the color signifies the success rate. Examined NAT types: OA - Open Access, FC - Full Cone, RC - Restricted Cone, PRC - Port Restricted Cone, SC - Symmetric Cone, SF - Symmetric UDP Firewall, FB - Firewall blocks, N/A-missing type (Color figure online)

to incompatible NAT types. After the channel is open, transporting the test message is still not guaranteed to succeed (transport error). Participant nodes may disconnect with an open connection (connection lost). In some rare cases a timeout also occurred after successful signaling, that is, the WebRTC call did not return in time.

Figure 2 shows statistics over successful connections as a function of NAT type. Here, we do not include signaling related errors. Note that NAT type discovery is an independent process executed in parallel with the P2P connection test. Therefore, there are some cases where the NAT type information is missing but the signaling process is completed nevertheless.

We illustrate the dynamics of the NAT distribution over the years in Fig. 3 (left). The distribution is based on continuous sessions of online users. These continuous sessions of homogeneous network conditions were determined based on the measurement records. A session has a start time, a duration, and a NAT type. The distribution is calculated based on the number of aggregated milliseconds of session durations falling on the given day. The distribution of online time per day is near 8% almost every time. Recall, that here the online state is meant to imply that the phone is on a charger.

The plot has gaps because in 2015 the data collector server was down, when the project was temporarily neglected. In addition, the first version of our P2P connection measurement implementation caused lots of downtime in 2018. Also, some of the STUN servers that were initially wired in to the clients disappeared over the years. As a result, the *Firewall blocked* NAT type is not reliable, so we exclude that category from the figure. Note that the distribution is surprisingly stable over the years.

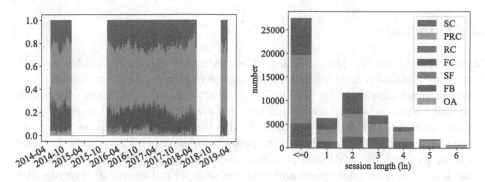

Fig. 3. (1) NAT distribution per day over 5 years (2) Session length distribution

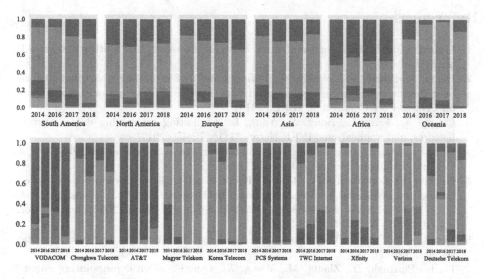

Fig. 4. NAT type distribution by continent in 4 different years (top) and NAT type distribution by the top 10 providers in 4 different years (bottom). Colors represent types as defined in Fig. 3. (Color figure online)

We present session length distribution as well in Fig. 3 (right). Session length is in minutes, the bins for the histogram are defined on a logarithmic scale. Sessions shorter than one minute are not always measured accurately due to our one minute period of observation, so we group such sessions in one bin ($<= 0$).

Figure 4 contains stacked bar charts illustrating the distribution of different NAT types in the 6 continents and in the networks of the top 10 most represented providers in 4 different years. The most common NAT type is the Port Restricted Cone except in Africa where the Symmetric Cone has a relatively larger share.

According to the chart the rarest NAT type is Open Access everywhere. Interestingly, the NAT type distribution is very different among the different providers, unlike in the case of the distributions based on geographic location.

4   Conclusion

Here, we outlined the latest version of our Android app STUNNER for collecting a smartphone trace. Our motivation was to enable exploratory research into decentralized algorithms for edge systems. Our trace contains locally observable attributes such as battery status and network availability, STUN measurements, as well as direct P2P connection data. In this unique combination, we can combine these sources of data to be able to predict, for example, P2P connection success, or to simulate distributed protocols over overlay networks of smartphones. Our trace spans over five years and contains over 40 million measurements. We also make the anonymized version of our trace publicly available.

References

1. Webrtc 1.0: Real-time communication between browsers (2018). https://www.w3.org/TR/webrtc/
2. Berta, A., Bilicki, V., Jelasity, M.: Defining and understanding smartphone churn over the internet: a measurement study. In: 14th IEEE International Conference on Peer-to-Peer Computing. IEEE (2014)
3. Cheng, X., Fang, L., Hong, X., Yang, L.: Exploiting mobile big data: sources, features, and applications. IEEE Netw. **31**(1), 72–79 (2017)
4. Garcia Lopez, P., et al.: Edge-centric computing: vision and challenges. SIGCOMM Comput. Commun. Rev. **45**(5), 37–42 (2015)
5. Gechter, F., Beresford, A.R., Rice, A.: Reconstruction of battery level curves based on user data collected from a smartphone. In: Dichev, C., Agre, G. (eds.) AIMSA 2016. LNCS (LNAI), vol. 9883, pp. 289–298. Springer, Cham (2016). https://doi.org/10.1007/978-3-319-44748-3_28
6. Laurila, J.K., et al.: The mobile data challenge: big data for mobile computing research (2012)
7. Li, L., Beitman, B., Zheng, M., Wang, X., Qin, F.: eDelta: pinpointing energy deviations in smartphone apps via comparative trace analysis. In: 2017 Eighth International Green and Sustainable Computing Conference (IGSC), pp. 1–8. IEEE (2017)
8. MacDonald, D., Bruce, L.: NAT behavior discovery using session traversal utilities for NAT (STUN), No. RFC 5780. (2010). http://www.rfc-editor.org/info/rfc5780
9. Mandalari, A., Lutu, A., Dhamdhere, A., Bagnulo, M., Claffy, K.: Tracking the big NAT across Europe and the U.S. Technical report, Center for Applied Internet Data Analysis (CAIDA), April 2017
10. Moroney, L.: Firebase Cloud Messaging, pp. 163–188. Apress, Berkeley (2017)
11. Richter, P., et al.: A multi-perspective analysis of carrier-grade NAT deployment. In: Proceedings of the 2016 Internet Measurement Conference. ACM (2016)

12. Thirion, V., Edeline, K., Donnet, B.: Tracking middleboxes in the mobile world with traceboxandroid. In: Steiner, M., Barlet-Ros, P., Bonaventure, O. (eds.) TMA 2015. LNCS, vol. 9053, pp. 79–91. Springer, Cham (2015). https://doi.org/10.1007/978-3-319-17172-2_6
13. Wagner, D.T., Rice, A., Beresford, A.R.: Device analyzer: understanding smartphone usage. In: Stojmenovic, I., Cheng, Z., Guo, S. (eds.) MindCare 2014. LNICST, vol. 131, pp. 195–208. Springer, Cham (2014). https://doi.org/10.1007/978-3-319-11569-6_16
14. Wang, J., Cao, B., Yu, P.S., Sun, L., Bao, W., Zhu, X.: Deep learning towards mobile applications. In: IEEE 38th International Conference on Distributed Computing Systems (ICDCS), pp. 1385–1393, July 2018
15. Wang, Z., Qian, Z., Xu, Q., Mao, Z., Zhang, M.: An untold story of middleboxes in cellular networks. In: Proceedings of the ACM SIGCOMM 2011 Conference. ACM (2011)
16. Zullo, R., Pescapé, A., Edeline, K., Donnet, B.: Hic sunt NATs: uncovering address translation with a smart traceroute. In: 2017 Network Traffic Measurement and Analysis Conference (TMA). IEEE (2017)

FOUGERE: User-Centric Location Privacy in Mobile Crowdsourcing Apps

Lakhdar Meftah[1](✉), Romain Rouvoy[2](✉), and Isabelle Chrisment[3](✉)

[1] Inria/Univ. Lille, Lille, France
`lakhdar.meftah@inria.fr`
[2] Univ. Lille/IUF/Inria, Lille, France
`romain.rouvoy@inria.fr`
[3] LORIA-TELECOM Nancy/Univ. Lorraine, Lorraine, France
`isabelle.chrisment@loria.fr`

Abstract. Mobile crowdsourcing is being increasingly used by industrial and research communities to build realistic datasets. By leveraging the capabilities of mobile devices, mobile crowdsourcing apps can be used to track participants' activity and to collect insightful reports from the environment (*e.g.*, air quality, network quality). However, most of existing crowdsourced datasets systematically tag data samples with time and location stamps, which may inevitably lead to user privacy leaks by discarding sensitive information.

This paper addresses this critical limitation of the state of the art by proposing a software library that improves user privacy without compromising the overall quality of the crowdsourced datasets. We propose a decentralized approach, named FOUGERE, to convey data samples from user devices to third-party servers. By introducing an *a priori* data anonymization process, we show that FOUGERE defeats state-of-the-art location-based privacy attacks with little impact on the quality of crowdsourced datasets.

Keywords: Location privacy · Mobile crowdsourcing · LPPM

1 Introduction

Mobile crowdsourcing platforms and applications (or apps) are being widely used to collect datasets in the field for both industrial and research purposes [2, 6,31]. By relying on a crowd of user devices, mobile crowdsourcing delivers an engaging solution to collect insightful reports from the wild. However, the design of such platforms presents some critical challenges related to the management of users, also known as *workers*. In particular, the privacy of the workers is often underestimated by the crowdsourcing platforms and it often fails to be addressed effectively in practice [25].

While data anonymization is commonly achieved *a posteriori* on the server side [7,16,20,22], this approach is subject to adversarial attacks, even when

© IFIP International Federation for Information Processing 2019
Published by Springer Nature Switzerland AG 2019
J. Pereira and L. Ricci (Eds.): DAIS 2019, LNCS 11534, pp. 116–132, 2019.
https://doi.org/10.1007/978-3-030-22496-7_8

protocols for the communication and the data storage are claimed to be secured [11,12]. Furthermore, the workers may be reluctant to share *Sensitive Personal Information* (SPI) with third parties (*e.g.*, students contributing to a crowdsourcing campaign initiated by a professor). Gaining the confidence of workers is extremely difficult and we argue in this paper that the adoption of *a priori* data anonymization mechanisms contributes to delivering a trustable component to better mitigate privacy leaks in the data shared by workers.

For example, the worker's location is not only the most requested but also the most sensitive data collected by mobile crowdsourcing platforms [3]. Our scheme therefore explores the physical proximity of workers to agree on a dissemination strategy for reporting the crowdsourced data. By altering the link between workers and data *consumers* on the server, our approach intends to mix data contributed by several workers within a collaborative data flow that exhibit similar crowd-scale properties and without discarding any SPI. In particular, we propose a system-level service that acts as a proxy within the mobile device for sharing crowdsourced data and from which workers can control their privacy settings. FOUGERE is our implementation of this anonymization scheme and is available as an open source library[1] that can be used by legacy mobile crowdsourcing apps. We illustrate the benefits of FOUGERE by integrating it within the state-of-the-art MOBIPERF mobile crowdsourcing app as well as the APISENSE mobile crowdsourcing platform. We evaluate the effectiveness and the impact of our anonymization scheme on these two mobile crowdsourcing systems by deploying and orchestrating a crowd of 15 emulated mobile devices. More precisely, we replay the SFCABS cab mobility traces [30] and we show that FOUGERE defeats state-of-the-art privacy attacks [18,24,26] with little impact on the quality of the resulting datasets.

The remainder of this paper is organized as follows. Section 2 gives a background on mobile crowdsourcing platforms and discusses the related work in the areas of mobile crowdsourcing and location-based privacy. Section 3 provides an overview of the privacy threats in crowdsourcing apps and platforms. Section 4 introduces our anonymization scheme and the integration of LPPMs to increase the workers' privacy. Section 5 describes the implementation of the FOUGERE open source library on Android. Section 6 introduces our evaluation protocol of FOUGERE on the MOBIPERF mobile crowdsourcing app and discusses the results we obtained on an experimental setup involving 15 emulated workers. Section 7 discusses the threats to validity of our contribution. Finally, Sect. 8 concludes on this paper.

2   Related Work

Thanks to the wide adoption of mobile devices, mobile crowdsourcing has emerged as a convenient approach to gather meaningful and scalable environmental datasets by involving citizens in the process of performing measurements in the wild [2,6,22,31]. While the development of mobile crowdsourcing apps

---

[1] https://github.com/m3ftah/fougere

is clearly leveraged by the *Software Development Kits* (SDK) made available by Android and iOS, mobile crowdsourcing platforms are bringing another level of abstraction to ease the design and the deployment of mobile crowdsourcing campaigns [4, 8, 13, 20].

As depicted in Fig. 1, mobile crowdsourcing campaigns typically consist of several stages: *(i)* the description of the data to be crowdsourced, *(ii)* the deployment and the gathering of the dataset in the wild, *(iii)* the aggregation and storage of datasets in the Cloud, *(iv)* the processing and *(v)* publication of the campaign results. However, along all these stages, SPI can be conveyed by the platform and potentially be subject to attacks from adversaries, therefore motivating the development of a better privacy support.

| Tasking Stage | Collecting Stage | Storing Stage | Mining Stage | Publishing Stage |

Fig. 1. Anatomy of a mobile crowdsourcing campaign

Location Privacy Protection Mechanisms. (LPPMs) are particularly interesting to limit user privacy leaks [5]. A large body of the related work has been devoted towards the latest stages of mobile crowdsourcing campaigns by improving the privacy properties of datasets once uploaded to remote servers [23, 28, 35]. These techniques contribute to preserving the privacy of workers while limiting the impact on the quality of the resulting dataset. However, raw datasets stored on a remote server may be leaked through security breaches.

Collaborative Privacy-Preserving Location-Based Services. In the domain of *Location-Based Services* (LBS), some privacy protection mechanisms can be adapted to mobile crowdsourcing platforms. In particular, we consider the solutions where users collaborate to hide information from the server [10, 29, 32, 33], which share similarities with FOUGERE. In particular, Chow *et al.* [10] use communication over *peer-to-peer* (P2P) protocols, Shokri *et al.* [32] use WiFi *Access Point* connection, and finally, Shokri *et al.* [33] and Peng *et al.* [29] propose to use Wi-Fi Direct communications. Yet, such approaches are not widely adopted by LBS solutions as they fail to demonstrate their effectiveness in a realistic deployment.

Privacy in Mobile Crowdsourcing Platforms. Mobile crowdsourcing platforms are actively working on privacy protection mechanisms [3, 19]. In particular, Cornelius *et al.* [13] have proposed ANONYSENSE: a mobile platform for opportunistic sensing. Because the server hosting the collected dataset can trace the worker's wireless access points, they propose to use an anonymization network to hide worker locations, they rely on a third-party server for routing the data. ANONYSENSE also supports reporting data with a statistical guarantee of k-anonymity. The workers' data are blurred and combined before being reported to the remote server. While their approach hides workers from the server, it exposes them to a third-party server that has to be trusted by the workers. Thus, introducing a single point of failure. Das *et al.* [14] present PRISM: a platform for remote sensing. They use a sandbox to prevent mobile apps from using mobile sensors. Adversaries can still collect geotagged data from workers and apply privacy de-anonymization attacks on the dataset. As discussed in [14], both ANONYSENSE and PRISM suffer from similar privacy leaks as the mobile app collects data local sensors made available by their mobile device, allowing data to be linked to the worker identifier. Hu *et al.* [21] present a collaborative privacy-preserving platform called HP3, which uses social networks to hide workers from the server. In their approach, they rely on third-party servers (the social network) that can store all the exchanged locations along with workers identifiers.

Synthesis. To the best of our knowledge, the state of the art fails to appropriately address the anonymization schemes along the earliest stages of a mobile crowdsourcing campaign in order to limit potential privacy threats. Therefore, in this paper, we intend to address this limitation by proposing an approach that leverages existing privacy protection mechanisms from the mobile device by providing the first decentralized dissemination to adjust location privacy in mobile crowdsourcing systems.

3   Privacy Threats in Mobile Crowdsourcing Systems

This section discusses the potential threats in mobile crowdsourcing systems along 3 axes: the *system model*, the *sensitive personal information*, and the *known location-based attacks*.

Mobile Crowdsourcing System Model. The architecture we consider is a mobile crowdsourcing campaign that involves three components, namely, *mobile devices*, *crowdsourcing apps*, and *storage servers*.

We consider that the mobile *crowdsourcing apps* can be trusted as we believe that the owner of the mobile crowdsourcing app or platform is interested in gathering insightful datasets with the consent of workers, especially if this mobile app is open sourced.

However, we consider that the *storage server* can be compromised and reveal some sensitive personal information on behalf of the owner and the workers. For example, no matter if they are deployed in the cloud or on-premise, the remote storage servers may suffer from security leaks that can be exploited by an adversary. Furthermore, storing the crowdsourced data on the server must comply with *The EU General Data Protection Regulation (GDPR)* and the *Privacy Act of 1974* of the USA. With crowdsourced data, it is difficult to comply with the regulations, for example: giving the users the right to delete their own data whenever they want. FOUGERE does resolve issues related to these regulations as it does not store personal identifiers on the server side.

Sensitive Personal Information in Mobile Crowdsourcing. The goal of a mobile crowdsourcing system is to gather a very large volume of data from measurements produced by third-party workers. These workers are recruited by the owner of the mobile crowdsourcing system to upload crowdsourced data through a dedicated mobile app or device. However, existing mobile crowdsourcing systems may collected some sensitive personal information.

In particular, we identify 4 categories of *sensitive personal information* (SPI) that might be exploited by attackers:

Identifiers group all persistent or transient identifiers that can take the form of a device ID (IMEI) or Google account ID, for example, to explicitly identify a worker from the perspective of a mobile crowdsourcing system. However, such identifiers may directly name the worker or be used to perform context linking attacks by combining several measurements;

Point of Interests (POI) gather all the forms of geolocated data that can deliver some spatial information on the location of a worker. This includes GPS locations, but also places check-in, cell tower ID or location, which are used by some systems to produce maps from crowdsourced measurements. However, these POI may also reveal the home, office, shopping and/or leisure locations of workers that can uniquely identify them [17];

Routines concern any information that can be use to capture a recurrent activity of a worker. This category of SPI covers in particular any form of timestamp, no matter the format and the precision. While this precious information often appears as harmless, it may also be used by context linking attacks to group crowdsourced data and observe correlation along time (*e.g.*, nights, week-ends);

Markers finally focus on information whose entropy in terms of values can be exploited to detect outlier workers and thus be indirectly used as an identifier by an attacker. There can be a wide diversity of such markers depending on the purpose of the mobile crowdsourcing system. For example, in the case of MOBIPERF, the properties of device manufacturer, model, OS version and network carrier can be considered as unique if a worker uses some original/old mobile device.

Location Privacy Attacks. Similarly to [37], we consider that the adversary can exploit two dimensions of knowledge: *temporal information* and *context information*.

In the context of mobile crowdsourcing systems, *temporal information* refers to the capability of the adversary to access a history of crowdsourced data—*i.e.*, several measurements reported by a single worker. In the case of a compromised storage server (or connection to the storage server), such assumption holds as the attacker gets access to sufficiently large volume of crowdsourced data to build some temporal knowledge.

Beyond spatio-temporal information, *context information* refers to any additional information that an attacker can exploit. This covers embedded knowledge that is included in the crowdsourced dataset (*e.g.*, markers) or side knowledge that an attacker can obtain from other information sources (*e.g.*, the number of involved workers).

4   FOURGERE: Empowering Workers with LPPMs

To overcome the above privacy threats and strengthen the location privacy of workers, this paper introduces a new middleware library, named FOUGERE, which acts as an embedded proxy to anonymize and disseminate the workers' crowdsourced data across the network. This section introduces the key design principles we adopted, a description of how crowdsourced data flows across multiple devices, as well as the core *Location Privacy Protection Mechanisms* (LPPMs) that are provided by FOUGERE.

Collaborating with Apps & Workers. In order to be trusted and gather a large crowd of workers, we assume that mobile crowdsourcing apps and platforms are doing their best to enforce privacy and security support. However, developers are not necessarily aware of privacy threats and implementing a comprehensive support for such a support might be time-consuming and error-prone. FOUGERE therefore offers mobile crowdsourcing apps the possibility to offload the management of the worker privacy settings and the data dissemination across the network, thus letting developers focus on the core business of the mobile app. More specifically, FOUGERE offers the workers control over worker's privacy preferences, thus providing a preference panel to *(i)* explore the list of mobile crowdsourcing apps and respective SPI, *(ii)* monitor and control the volume of crowdsourced data reported by each app, and *(iii)* configure the list of LPPMs to be enforced by a given mobile crowdsourcing app.

By following these principles, FOUGERE can collaborate with the mobile app and the worker to ensure the anonymization and the dissemination of crowdsourced data. Figure 2 overviews these principles and illustrates how a mobile app can disseminate crowdsourced data without and with FOUGERE. In particular, mobile crowdsourcing apps that do not fulfill the design principles—or do not integrate FOUGERE—will upload crowdsourced data directly to the remote server, thus exposing the workers to the privacy threats introduced in Sect. 3. By integrating FOUGERE, any mobile crowdsourcing app simply delegates the data dissemination to the library. FOUGERE enforces the worker's privacy settings and applies the appropriate LPPMs to the forwarded data. Such mechanisms include *privacy filters* (to discard the data), *privacy distortions* (to alter the data) and *privacy aggregation* (to group the data).

Enabling Crowdsourced Dissemination. If the crowdsourced data has not been discarded by one of the configured LPPMs, FOUGERE stores a message for dissemination that is composed of *(i)* a *payload*, *(ii)* a *configuration* of remote

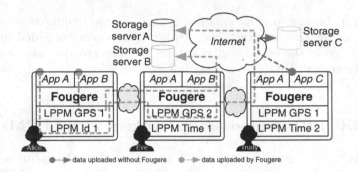

Fig. 2. Overview of FOUGERE

LPPMs, *(iii)* a *bloom filter* of forwarder devices, and *(iv)* a *time-to-live* (TTL) for the dissemination process. While the *payload* refers to the crowdsourced data, which has eventually been altered by the local LPPMs, the message also includes some *configuration* parameters for LPPMs that can be executed by remote instances of FOUGERE (*e.g.*, replacing the location of the source by the location of the forwarder). In order to avoid a given message to be forwarded by the same set of mobile devices, FOUGERE also includes a bloom filter that encodes the list of forwarder nodes, without discarding their identifier. The *bloom filter* is configured with a false positive probability of 0.1 and a number of expected elements equals to the TTL. Finally, the message encloses a *TTL* to define the numbers of workers hops requested by the worker to disseminate the message.

FOUGERE filters out the known workers by querying the bloom filter, and randomly picks and forwards the message to one the remaining nodes. Upon receiving such a message, a remote FOUGERE node eventually applies the LPPM listed in the configuration before checking the TTL. If the TTL equals 0, then FOUGERE stores the payload for being forwarded by the mobile crowdsourcing app to the remote storage server. Otherwise, FOUGERE decreases the TTL, adds its own identifier to the bloom filter, and stores the resulting message for further dissemination.

Mobile crowdsourcing apps share similarities with *Delay Tolerant Networks* (DTN) by considering that the crowdsourced data does not have to be immediately uploaded to the remote server and can tolerate delays ranging from minutes to hours. We exploit this property to adopt a multi-hop forwarding scheme in FOUGERE, which ensures that at least k neighboring devices with the same mobile app are also potentially collecting data in the same area, thus preventing the worker to be spotted as an outlier.

Furthermore, FOUGERE complements existing privacy-preserving mechanisms, like the TOR anonymity network, which can also be used by FOUGERE to upload the crowdsourced data to the remote server. Using TOR, therefore, hides workers from the remote server, but it loses the physical proximity information that is useful for local LPPMs. For example, when an isolated worker is contributing from within the countryside, she can still report data using TOR but she will remain exposed to location privacy attacks.

Controlling LPPMs from Devices. In order to give the worker more control over her own data, FOUGERE includes several LPPMs that can be configured by the worker to decide upon the quality and the volume of crowdsourced data to be obfuscated. In particular, we consider 3 classes of LPPMs: *filters*, *distortions*, and *aggregations*, which can be implemented within a mobile device and used to obfuscate one of the SPI of the user.

Privacy Filters are a group of LPPMs that can decide autonomously if a crowdsourced data can be shared with the crowdsourcing platform or not. For example, a LocationFilter applies to *points of interests* and can be configured by the worker to define *white areas* or *black areas* that delimit zones where the mobile crowdsourcing app can or cannot collect data, respectively. Similarly, a TimeFilter rather applies on *routines* and is used with configured periods along which a mobile crowdsourcing app can or cannot collect data. Finally, a QuotaFilter is a more generic filter that can accept a worker-defined quota of crowdsourced data to be uploaded before discarding once this quota is reached.

Privacy Distortions are another class of LPPMs that can modify the value of an enclosed SPI in the crowdsourced data to be shared. For example, a IdentifierDistortion will change the value of an identifier at a given frequency (every request, hour, day), while a location distortion adds a controlled random noise to the worker's location (depending on radius r with a level of privacy that depends on r) into the reported coordinates [15].

Privacy Aggregations reflect the last class of LPPMs that are supported by FOUGERE and propose to delay the dissemination of crowdsourced data by grouping them along a given criteria. For example, a TimeAggregation will group data per hour and apply an aggregation operator (like the average, the median, the min or the max) to the enclosed timestamp in order to report the same value for all the aggregated samples before reporting them. A MarkerAggregation is an example of remote LPPMs that will be encapsulated with the crowdsourced data and wait for a given marker (*e.g.*, the ISP name) to appear at least k times before being uploaded. This LPPM is an example of a distributed implementation of the k-anonymity algorithm [9,34] that we can apply on a wide diversity of SPI, including GPS coordinates.

Summary. By combining an opportunistic dissemination scheme with worker-defined LPPMs, FOUGERE aims at leveraging the privacy properties of legacy mobile crowdsourcing apps and platforms. Before assessing the efficiency of FOUGERE, we now report on the implementation of these principles on the Android platform.

5   Implementation Details on Android

On Android, FOUGERE is packaged as an open source library that deploys system service within the mobile device of a worker. This system service currently builds on the Wi-Fi Direct network interface to exchange crowdsourced data between nearby devices of workers. It can be shared by multiple crowdsourcing apps of a given device to centralize the control of privacy settings, which are exposed to the worker as a dedicated preference panel. Thanks to its modular architecture, FOUGERE can be further extended with additional LPPMs, which are not covered by this paper.

Application Programming Interface. Any mobile crowdsourcing app can integrate FOUGERE through a simple API that exposes the following operations:

`hasFields(...)` is called by the mobile crowdsourcing app to declare any SPI as a `PrivacyField`, that refers the classes `IDENTIFIER`, `POI`, `ROUTINE`, and `MARKER`;

`forward(...)` enlists a task in charge of uploading a crowdsourced data sample to the remote server when the TTL expires;

`send(...)` delegates the dissemination of a crowdsourced data to FOUGERE.

Opportunistic Dissemination. The current implementation of the FOUGERE dissemination module builds on the WiFi-Direct technology to discover nearby devices. When a mobile crowdsourcing app forwards a message, FOUGERE triggers the configured LPPMs and accumulates the data in the forwarding queue. For each data accumulated in the forwarding queue, FOUGERE picks a random peer that has never received this data and forwards it.

If the message reaches the configured number of device hops ($ttl = 0$), then the forwarded data is placed in an uploading queue, which will be emptied as soon as the remote mobile crowdsourcing app runs by invoking the upload handler registered by the app.

LPPM Integration. FOUGERE combines the implementation of a decentralized dissemination scheme with the integration of LPPMs that can filter out data or alter its content depending on the worker's privacy settings. More generally, FOUGERE intends to leverage the integration of additional LPPMs to better control the data uploaded by any compatible crowdsourcing app. FOUGERE organizes these LPPMs along the 4 categories of SPI it supports. An LPPM complies to am interface `Lppm<T extends PrivacyField>` that declares the category `T` of SPI it considers and implements a method to apply a privacy mechanism on the uploaded data, which eventually returns the anonymized data to be further processed by FOUGERE.

In order to effectively apply the worker's privacy settings, FOUGERE operates by first applying the privacy filters, before proceeding with privacy distortions and finally privacy aggregations. In addition to that, privacy distortions and aggregations can also be triggered remotely to implement decentralized algorithms that build on neighboring samples to increase the privacy of workers [1].

6   Evaluations of FOUGERE

6.1   Evaluation Protocol

Beyond the challenges related to the integration in legacy mobile crowdsourcing systems, FOUGERE intends to deliver an efficient adoption of LPPMs in a decentralized context. The validation of such a capability requires consideration of a realistic deployment of mobile devices in order to assess the benefits of FOUGERE. Given that we are interested in providing a proof of feasibility for FOUGERE, we are not interested in simulating the behaviour of LPPMs, but rather in assessing the reference implementation of FOUGERE. However, testing mobile applications that make use of opportunistic communications is hard to achieve and reproduce with real mobile devices. We propose to deploy a cluster of emulated devices to reproduce the behavior of a crowd of workers who contribute to a mobile crowdsourcing campaign. We use mobility datasets that are publicly available to control the emulated devices and we collect their interactions to trace their actions *a posteriori*. The crowdsourced dataset collected on the remote server are evaluated by the LPM^2 toolkit [32] to evaluate the preservation of workers' privacy. By adopting such an empirical validation, we can evaluate real applications integrating FOUGERE and we can observe the impact of changing the parameters of FOUGERE (number of hops, LPPMs' specific parameters).

In the remainder of this section, we select the legacy MOBIPERF [22] mobile app as the mobile crowdsourcing app that we considered to assess FOUGERE.

Emulating Crowds of Workers. The assessment of our opportunistic dissemination scheme and the associated LPPMs requires consideration of a crowd of workers who installed a mobile crowdsourcing app that integrates FOUGERE. While running an emulator on a single machine is rather resource-consuming and cannot scale, we propose to consider the deployment of a cluster of servers to host multiple Android emulators. As Android emulators do not provide any support for ad hoc communications, such as WiFi-Direct, we use ANDROFLEET [27] to control the discovery of nearby devices within a cluster of emulators.

Controlling Crowds of Workers. To assess the efficiency of FOUGERE in the ANDROFLEET cluster, the emulated devices are required to be controlled in order to update their location and eventually internal state, to reproduce the mobility of a crowd of workers. While the choice of such a mobility dataset might be challenging depending on the category of mobile crowdsourcing app, we use the `epfl/mobility` dataset that is publicly available from CRAWDAD [30] to emulate 15 workers who are performing network measurements with the MOBIPERF mobile app. The crowdsourced dataset contains network measurements reported every 5 min by the workers moving in the San Francisco bay area.

Attacking Crowdsourced Datasets. To evaluate the impact of FOUGERE on the privacy of workers, we use the LPM^2 toolkit [32], which is a state-of-the-art tool for measuring location privacy. In particular, LPM^2 covers the evaluation of the LPPMs that are supported by FOUGERE, like the obfuscation mechanisms including perturbations (adding noise), reducing precision, location hiding. To validate FOUGERE against privacy attacks, for each configuration, we run an experiment that follows these steps:

1. Run ANDROFLEET with MOBIPERF and FOUGERE (incl. privacy settings),
2. Assign tasks to workers during 3 days, and wait 4 more days for the data dissemination to complete,

3. Gather the logs of data exchanges between workers to evaluate the opportunistic dissemination scheme,
4. Retrieve all the raw crowdsourced data stored on the remote server,
5. Construct the adversary knowledge by tagging the crowdsourced data of one worker (as required by LPM^2),
6. Evaluate the privacy support of FOUGERE with the LPM^2 toolkit,
7. Report on performance, utility, robustness and uncertainty, which are the parameters proposed by Verykios *et al.* [36] to assess LPPMs.

6.2   Empirical Evaluation

In this section, we instantiate the above experimental protocol to assess FOUGERE as a practical support to improve the location privacy of workers.

Experimental Setup. In particular, thanks to the ANDROFLEET [27] emulation platform, we can reproduce the execution of a deployment of 15 mobile instances emulating a one-week crowdsourcing campaign, thus proposing a realistic input dataset to evaluate FOUGERE. Then, we compare the behaviors of 6 configurations of the MOBIPERF app:

1- VANILLA refers to the reference implementation of the MOBIPERF Android app, as it can be downloaded from http://www.mobiperf.com. This configuration is used to demonstrate the vulnerability of legacy mobile crowdsourcing apps with regards to potential privacy threats. It is also used as a witness to evaluate the benefits of the other configurations including FOUGERE;
2- FOUGERE *with no LPPM* refers to the extension of MOBIPERF with the FOUGERE library. This configuration is used to isolate the properties of our opportunistic dissemination schemes independently of the impact of LPPMs. In particular, we consider the following worker configurations for the number of required hops to disseminate the crowdsourced data and the WiFi-Direct discovery scans: (a) $\langle 1\,hop, 5\,min \rangle$, (b) $\langle 4\,hops, 5\,min \rangle$ (default configuration), and (c) $\langle 4\,hops, 10\,min \rangle$;
3- FOUGERE *with LPPMs* refers to the FOUGERE library with the default configuration 2-b selected with 2 privacy distortions—*location noise* and *time noise*—and 1 privacy aggregation—*k-anonymity*, which are representative LPPMs used by the state-of-the-art. To configure these LPPMs, we consider 2 worker profiles, which are mapped to the following values:
   (a) *weak privacy profile* where location noise is set to $\langle 1, 0.1, 0.05 \rangle$, thus reducing the location precision by 1 digit with a probability of 0.1 and possibly removing the location with a probability of 0.05. Time noise is set to $\langle 30, 0.1, 0.05 \rangle$, thus reducing the time precision to half an hour with a probability of 0.1 and possibly removing the timestamp with a probability of 0.5, and finally k-anonymity is set to $\langle 2 \rangle$, meaning that at least 2 samples should be produced in the same area to be forwarded;
   (b) *strong privacy profile* configured with location noise = $\langle 2, 0.2, 0.1 \rangle$, time noise = $\langle 60, 0.2, 0.1 \rangle$ and k-anonymity = $\langle 4 \rangle$ as privacy settings.

None of these configurations includes a privacy filter as these LPPMs are expected to be used to hide the living and working places of workers and the input dataset does not include this information. Furthermore, this paper does not aim at evaluating the efficiency of individual LPPMs, but rather demonstrating the benefit of combining them in an open framework like FOUGERE.

Performance Analysis. FOUGERE implements an opportunistic dissemination scheme to improve the privacy of workers. By doing so, FOUGERE exploits the physical proximity of workers to exchange crowdsourced data and to guarantee that the uploaded data has been forwarded along a number of hops requested by the worker. Figure 3 depicts the *time to converge* as a metrics to evaluate *(i)* the impact of integrating FOUGERE on a legacy mobile crowdsourcing app like MOBIPERF, and *(ii)* the effect of the number of hops and the WiFi-Direct discovery duration parameters. One can observe that, by using FOUGERE, not all the crowdsourced data is reported back to the remote storage server. This can be explained by the fact that some workers are contributing in sparsely populated areas, which prevents FOUGERE from disseminating the collected measurements. This result is actually a strength of FOUGERE as it automatically protects the workers from adversaries who would apply some location distribution attacks to identify them.

Regarding the parameters of FOUGERE, one can note that the delay to upload data and the volume of reported data is more affected by the discovery duration than the number of hops required to upload the crowdsourced data. By increasing the delay of peer discovery, mobile devices miss some other workers in their vicinity in order to improve the time to converge. Therefore, we privilege the configuration 2-b (4 hops and 5 min) as the default configuration for FOUGERE. However, the worker remains free to adjust each of these parameters.

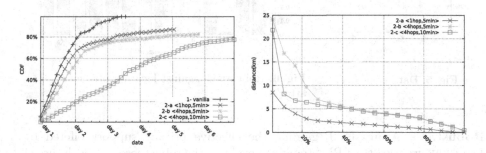

Fig. 3. Measurements' time to converge   **Fig. 4.** Distance traveled by measurements

The *traveling distance* is another interesting metrics to evaluate the efficiency of the dissemination process and the relevance of peer-to-peer communications. Increasing this data traveling distance with FOUGERE contributes to better shuffle crowdsourced data produced by a crowd of workers. Figure 4 reports on this distance traveled by the crowdsourced data before being uploaded back to the remote storage server. In particular, the default configuration of FOUGERE maximizes the traveled distance with 20% of data that traveled at least 10 km (6.2 *miles*), thus ensuring that the data was conveyed by FOUGERE as far as possible from the location where it has been produced.

Utility Analysis. While FOUGERE aims at improving the location privacy of workers, the utility of the resulting dataset should not be neglected. Figure 5 reports on the tradeoff between utility and anonymity of the configurations we considered. While the vanilla configuration (1) offers the highest utility with no anonymity, one can observe that the integration of FOUGERE seriously improves the anonymity of workers without seriously impacting the utility of the resulting dataset. As mentioned in Fig. 3, the loss of 20% utility is mainly due to crowdsourced data in sparsely populated areas that were retained by FOUGERE. Furthermore, adding some LPPMs (configurations 3-a and 3-b) strongly increase the anonymity of workers.

Interestingly, one can observe that the *weak privacy profile* offers a good privacy/anonymity tradeoff compared to the *strong privacy profile*, which seriously harms the dataset utility without bringing any further improvement over anonymity.

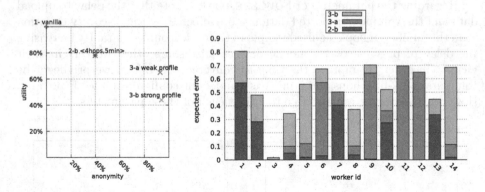

Fig. 5. Dataset utility   **Fig. 6.** Robustness against location privacy attacks

Robustness Analysis. Regarding the effective privacy support offered by FOUGERE, we used the LPM^2 toolkit to evaluate the robustness of crowdsourced datasets that are uploaded through FOUGERE. We randomly select the crowd-sourced data reported by one of the workers as the adversary knowledge required by LPM^2 to apply location privacy attacks and we depict in Fig. 6 the reported robustness for 14 workers. While LPM^2 successfully defeats worker 3 (used as the adversary knowledge), the other 14 workers clearly benefit from the integration of FOUGERE. In particular, we can observe that the integration of LPPMs complements efficiently our opportunistic dissemination scheme by supporting workers who are not located in a dense area and by offering similar privacy guarantees. Successfully location privacy attacks requires to combine different strategies to cope with the profile of workers.

While FOUGERE offers the worker the possibility to manually adjust her privacy settings, one of the perspectives of this work consists in leveraging this configuration process by delivering privacy risk feedback that would guide her settings accordingly. By recommending the privacy settings of FOUGERE, we aim at maximizing the individual privacy of workers, while preserving the overall utility of the crowdsourced dataset (cf. Fig. 5).

Uncertainty Analysis. Finally, we consider the view of an adversary to study the level of uncertainty that introduces FOUGERE into the crowdsourced dataset. Figure 7 reports on the uncertainty metrics computed by LPM^2. One can observe that FOUGERE succeeds to increase the uncertainty of adversaries when it combines the opportunistic dissemination scheme with LPPMs, which confirms our previous observation. Furthermore, it also assesses that adopting a *weak privacy profile* already brings a reasonable level of privacy that puts adversaries in difficulties.

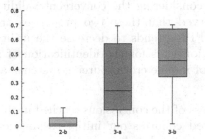

Indicator	Value
Crowdsourced dataset size	29,712
Exchanged messages	113,785
Contributions per user	59
Messages forwarded per user	227
Detected neighbors	1,730,827
Established connections	127,545
Isolated users	8

Fig. 7. Adversary uncertainty   **Fig. 8.** Overhead analysis for 500 workers

Overhead Analysis. To analyze the overhead induced by our data dissemination process, we report in Table 8 the statistics related to an experiment involving 500 emulated workers for 24 h. Along the experiment, the workers adopt the default configuration of FOUGERE $\langle 4\,hops, 5\,min \rangle$ (2-b). The overhead per user and at the scale of the crowd does not exceed 4 times the initial volume of contributions. FOUGERE also discards 8 users considered as isolated and thus identifiable by tools like LPM^2.

7   Threats to Validity

This section analyzes the factors that may threaten the validity of our results.

Internal validity concerns the relation between theory and observations. In this paper, they could be due to measurement errors reported during the experimentations. That is the reason why we did several experiments and we tried to reduce as much as possible external factors as explained in our experimental protocol in Sect. 6.2. We also performed our experiments on a crowd of emulated devices equipped with real mobile apps, instead of a simulation, to reduce the threats that could be due to an integration of the proposed approach in a real mobile crowdsourcing app or platform.

External validity relates to the possibility to generalize our findings. We believe that further validations should be done on different mobile crowdsourcing apps and with different configurations to broaden our understanding of the impact of LPPMs on the privacy of workers. Thus, we are not assuming that our results can be used to generalize the impact of a specific LPPM on privacy. However, we believe that this paper contributes to prove that there is a clear positive impact for the privacy threats we considered.

Reliability validity focuses on the possibility of replicating our experiments and results. We attempt to provide all the necessary details to replicate our study and our analysis. Furthermore, the reference implementation of FOUGERE, the input datasets, case studies and testing environment are made available online to leverage its reproduction by the research community.

Construct validity has been covered by considering the convergent validity of privacy and utility properties. We observed that these two properties are related in practice, as the application of LPPMs tends to decrease the utility of the crowdsourced dataset. This observation calls for the identification of a privacy and utility trade-off in the context of mobile crowdsourcing systems, as acknowledged by [5].

Conclusion validity refers to the correctness of the conclusions reached in this paper. The empirical evaluation we reported confirms our initial assumption that *a priori* anonymization techniques can be used to leverage the privacy of workers. We were also careful with our conclusion with regards to the impact on the utility of crowdsourced dataset.

8   Conclusion

Mobile crowdsourcing apps and platforms are more and more challenged to protect their workers' privacy. To address this challenge, we introduce FOUGERE to increase worker's privacy in mobile crowdsourcing systems. FOUGERE operates a system-level service that collaborates with a mobile crowdsourcing app to declare SPI and delegate the dissemination of crowdsourced data by leveraging the physical proximity of workers. This opportunistic dissemination scheme is complemented by the integration of LPPMs that can be configured by the workers, independently of the installed mobile crowdsourcing apps.

Finally, we consider the deployment of FOUGERE in a realistic Android environment by emulating a crowd of 15 mobile devices hosting different versions of MOBIPERF and FOUGERE to assess our contribution. We show that FOUGERE succeeds to improve the workers' privacy by defeating location privacy attacks implemented by the LPM^2 toolkit.

References

1. Andrés, M.E., Bordenabe, N.E., Chatzikokolakis, K., Palamidessi, C.: Geo-indistinguishability: differential privacy for location-based systems. In: Proceedings of CCS 2013, pp. 901–914 (2013)
2. Balan, R.K., Misra, A., Lee, Y.: LiveLabs: building an in-situ real-time mobile experimentation testbed. In: ACM HotMobile (2014)
3. Boutsis, I., Kalogeraki, V.: Location privacy for crowdsourcing applications. In: Proceedings of UbiComp 2016 (2016)
4. Brouwers, N., Langendoen, K.: Pogo, a middleware for mobile phone sensing. In: Proceedings of Middleware 2012 (2012)
5. Cerf, S., et al.: PULP: achieving privacy and utility trade-off in user mobility data. In: Proceedings of SRDS 2017, September 2017
6. Chatzimilioudis, G., Konstantinidis, A., Laoudias, C., Zeinalipour-Yazti, D.: Crowdsourcing with smartphones. IEEE Internet Comput. **16**(5), 36–44 (2012)
7. Chen, R., Fung, B.C.M., Mohammed, N., Desai, B.C., Wang, K.: Privacy-preserving trajectory data publishing by local suppression. Inf. Sci. **231**, 83–97 (2013)
8. Choi, H., Chakraborty, S., Charbiwala, Z.M., Srivastava, M.B.: SensorSafe: a framework for privacy-preserving management of personal sensory information. In: Jonker, W., Petković, M. (eds.) SDM 2011. LNCS, vol. 6933, pp. 85–100. Springer, Heidelberg (2011). https://doi.org/10.1007/978-3-642-23556-6_6
9. Chow, C.Y., Mokbel, M.F., Liu, X.: A peer-to-peer spatial cloaking algorithm for anonymous location-based service. In: Proceedings of ACM SIGSPATIAL (2006)
10. Chow, C.Y., Mokbel, M.F., Liu, X.: Spatial cloaking for anonymous location-based services in mobile peer-to-peer environments. GeoInformatica **15**(2), 351–380 (2011)
11. Christin, D., Bub, D.M., Moerov, A., Kasem-Madani, S.: A distributed privacy-preserving mechanism for mobile urban sensing applications. In: Proceedings of ISSNIP 2015 (2015)
12. Christin, D., Reinhardt, A., Kanhere, S.S., Hollick, M.: A survey on privacy in mobile participatory sensing applications. J. Syst. Softw. **84**(11), 1928–1946 (2011)
13. Cornelius, C., Kapadia, A., Kotz, D., Peebles, D., Shin, M., Triandopoulos, N.: Anonysense: privacy-aware people-centric sensing. In: Proceedings of Mobisys 2008 (2008)
14. Das, T., Mohan, P., Padmanabhan, V.N., Ramjee, R., Sharma, A.: PRISM: platform for remote sensing using smartphones. In: Proceedings of MobiSys 2010 (2010)
15. Fawaz, K., Shin, K.G.: Location privacy protection for smartphone users. In: Proceedings of CCS 2014. ACM (2014)
16. Gambs, S., Killijian, M.O., del Prado Cortez, M.N.: GEPETO: a geoprivacy-enhancing toolkit. In: Proceedings of AINA Workshops 2010 (2010)
17. Gambs, S., Killijian, M.O., Del Prado Cortez, M.N.: Next place prediction using mobility Markov chains. In: Proceedings of MPM 2012 (2012)
18. Gambs, S., Killijian, M.O., del Prado Cortez, M.N.: De-anonymization attack on geolocated data. J. Comput. Syst. Sci. **80**(8), 1597–1614 (2014)
19. Gao, S., Ma, J., Shi, W., Zhan, G., Sun, C.: TrPF: a trajectory privacy-preserving framework for participatory sensing. IEEE Trans. Inf. Forensics Secur. **8**(6), 874–887 (2013)
20. Haderer, N., Rouvoy, R., Seinturier, L.: A preliminary investigation of user incentives to leverage crowdsensing activities. In: Proceedings of PerCom 2013 (2013)

21. Hu, L., Shahabi, C.: Privacy assurance in mobile sensing networks: go beyond trusted servers. In: 2010 8th IEEE International Conference on Pervasive Computing and Communications Workshops (PERCOM Workshops), pp. 613–619. IEEE (2010)

22. Huang, J., et al.: MobiPerf: mobile network measurement system. Technical report, University of Michigan and Microsoft Research (2011)

23. Kifer, D.: l-diversity: privacy beyond k -anonymity. In: Proceedings of ICDE 2006, vol. 1, no. 1, March 2006

24. Krumm, J.: Inference attacks on location tracks. In: LaMarca, A., Langheinrich, M., Truong, K.N. (eds.) Pervasive 2007. LNCS, vol. 4480, pp. 127–143. Springer, Heidelberg (2007). https://doi.org/10.1007/978-3-540-72037-9_8

25. Lin, J., Sadeh, N., Amini, S., Lindqvist, J., Hong, J.I., Zhang, J.: Expectation and purpose: understanding users' mental models of mobile app privacy through crowdsourcing. In: Proceeding of UbiComp 2012 (2012)

26. Ma, C.Y., Yau, D.K., Yip, N.K., Rao, N.S.: Privacy vulnerability of published anonymous mobility traces. In: Proceedings of MobiCom 2010 (2010)

27. Meftah, L., Gomez, M., Rouvoy, R., Chrisment, I.: ANDROFLEET: testing WiFi peer-to-peer mobile apps in the large. In: Proceedings of ASE 2017 (2017)

28. Ninghui, L., Tiancheng, L., Venkatasubramanian, S.: t-closeness: privacy beyond k-anonymity and l-diversity. In: Proceedings of ICDE 2007 (2007)

29. Peng, T., Liu, Q., Meng, D., Wang, G.: Collaborative trajectory privacy preserving scheme in location-based services. Inf. Sci. **387**, 165–179 (2017)

30. Piorkowski, M., Sarafijanovic-Djukic, N., Grossglauser, M.: CRAWDAD dataset epfl/mobility, February 2009. https://crawdad.org/epfl/mobility/20090224. Accessed 24 Feb 2009. https://doi.org/10.15783/C7J010

31. Prandi, C., Salomoni, P., Mirri, S.: mPASS: integrating people sensing and crowdsourcing to map urban accessibility. In: Proceedings of CCNC 2014 (2014)

32. Shokri, R., Theodorakopoulos, G., Le Boudec, J.Y., Hubaux, J.P.: Quantifying location privacy. In: Proceedings of S&P 2011, May 2011

33. Shokri, R., Theodorakopoulos, G., Papadimitratos, P., Kazemi, E., Hubaux, J.P.: Hiding in the mobile crowd: location privacy through collaboration. IEEE Trans. Dependable Secur. Comput. **11**(3), 266–279 (2014)

34. Sweeney, L.: k-anonymity: a model for protecting privacy. Int. J. Uncertainty **10**(5), 557–570 (2002)

35. Terrovitis, M., Mamoulis, N.: Privacy preservation in the publication of trajectories. In: Proceedings of MDM 2008 (2008)

36. Verykios, V.S., Bertino, E., Fovino, I.N., Provenza, L.P., Saygin, Y., Theodoridis, Y.: State-of-the-art in privacy preserving data mining. ACM SIGMOD Rec. **33**(1), 50–57 (2004)

37. Wernke, M., Skvortsov, P., Dürr, F., Rothermel, K.: A classification of location privacy attacks and approaches. Pers. Ubiquit. Comput. **18**(1) (2014). https://doi.org/10.1007/s00779-012-0633-z

On the Performance of ARM TrustZone
(Practical Experience Report)

Julien Amacher and Valerio Schiavoni$^{(\boxtimes)}$ (iD)

Université de Neuchâtel, Neuchâtel, Switzerland
{julien.amacher,valerio.schiavoni}@unine.ch

Abstract. The TRUSTZONE technology, available in the vast majority of recent ARM processors, allows the execution of code inside a so-called *secure world*. It effectively provides hardware-isolated areas of the processor for sensitive data and code, *i.e.*, a trusted execution environment (*TEE*). The OP-TEE framework provides a collection of toolchain, open-source libraries and secure kernel specifically geared to develop applications for TRUSTZONE. This paper presents an in-depth performance- and energy-wise study of TRUSTZONE using the OP-TEE framework, including secure storage and the cost of switching between secure and unsecure worlds, using emulated and hardware measurements.

Keywords: Trusted Execution Environment · ARM · TrustZone · Benchmarks

1 Introduction

Internet of Things (IoT) devices are expected to offer the pervasive computing that was promised at its advent [47]. The economic impact of the IoT ecosystem has created many new business opportunities and is expected to continue growing rapidly. As a result, the number of devices owned per user is anticipated to increase up to 26 by 2020 [44]. ARM, expects 275bn active devices by 2025 - a 11× improvement over 2019 [6] - while already having sold 100bn processors. For instance, Fig. 1 reports the sales for ARM processors in the last 20 years.

These IoT devices gather, distribute and process information on their own, effectively pushing intelligence to edge devices. Due to their nature, these devices are mostly nomad: easy to relocate, designed as wearable, embedded in vehicles or left in remote locations. As such, assets need to be protected from attackers, in particular those easily subject to physical tampering. Hence, ensuring that confidential data is processed in a secure manner, even in hostile environments, remains a challenging prerequisite for such devices. Indeed, an attacker with physical access can relatively easily inspect and modify the execution workflow of any program. Nowadays, even more disturbing attacks not requiring physical access are surfacing [51], reinforcing the need to exploit hardware-based security mechanisms when available. Hardware-based protections offer an additional

© IFIP International Federation for Information Processing 2019
Published by Springer Nature Switzerland AG 2019
J. Pereira and L. Ricci (Eds.): DAIS 2019, LNCS 11534, pp. 133–151, 2019.
https://doi.org/10.1007/978-3-030-22496-7_9

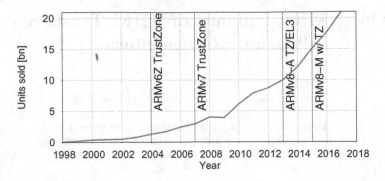

Fig. 1. Sales and popularity of ARM processors in the last 20 years [4,5]

security layer, by physically separating processing of secure and non-secure data components. These can be dedicated processing chips (hardware security modules –HSM–), or regular chips to which security extensions were added. Examples of the latter include Intel's *Software Guard Extensions* (*i.e.*, SGX [21]) since the Skylake architecture (2015), or ARM's TRUSTZONE [7] since ARMv6 (2008).

ARM devices are often battery-powered and must therefore make optimal use of their limited energy capacity. This is especially true nowadays, when battery capacity is becoming the limiting factor when deploying new functionalities. Despite the availability of such devices on the market, to the best of our knowledge we could not find a public study on the performance and energy-related consumption for these security extensions.

The contributions of this work are as follows. We begin by providing the first public experimental analysis of the performance and energy requirements of the TRUSTZONE security extensions based on hands-on metrics. Second, we report on the advantages and limitations of OP-TEE [26], an open-source framework that supports TRUSTZONE. Third, we provide a methodology to extend the kernel of OP-TEE in order to offer new syscalls inside TRUSTZONE. We leverage this methodology to implement two new additional syscalls, *e.g.*, to fetch thermal metrics and for secure time measurements in the TRUSTZONE. Finally, we report on our in-depth experimental analysis along several dimensions (including energy) of the current secure processing capabilities offered by some widely popular IoT devices (*i.e.*, Raspberry Pi) shipping TRUSTZONE processors. Our results are put into perspective by comparing them against an emulated environment aware of the TRUSTZONE extensions.

The paper is organized as follows. Sect. 2 describes the TRUSTZONE architecture and key concepts of world isolation. Sect. 3 explains how the kernel was extended to expose new syscalls within TRUSTZONE, how all the data was gathered, as well as the hardware and software tools that were developed. Sect. 4 presents our in-depth evaluation using real hardware and under emulation, for several hardware components (*e.g.* CPU, memory, secure storage) and metrics (*e.g.* performance, energy and power consumption). We discuss some lessons learned in Sect. 5, before concluding in Sect. 6.

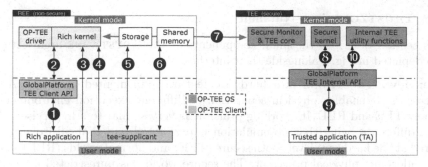

Fig. 2. TRUSTZONE components and interaction workflow.

2   Background

This section provides some background on TRUSTZONE. First we define a few terms used throughout this paper. Sect. 2.1 describes TRUSTZONE's main mechanisms and limitations, while Sect. 2.2 introduces OP-TEE.

Rich Execution Environment. The REE (or *normal world*) is the regular, non-secure operating system of a device. The memory, registers, and caches are not isolated or protected by any hardware mechanism. Typically, the REE is not focused on security and is difficult to review for security vulnerabilities, due to its large size and complexity.

Trusted Execution Environments. Also called TEE or *secure OS*, it is the so-called *secure world* operating system part of the TRUSTZONE specifications. It complies with the GlobalPlatform's TEE System Architecture specifications [57], a set of operations offered to secure applications. These include interactions with persistent (secure) storage [57, Chapter 5], memory [57, Chapter 4.11], and cryptographic operations [57, Chapter 6]. As such, a secure application can easily be ported to another platform, due to the standardized nature of available services. Similar to what a non-secure operating system offers to its running applications, the TEE offers access to special services only available to secure applications (such as the secure storage feature, which we evaluate). This environment has a small footprint, contrary to a full-fledged operating system, and only implements the very minimal set of features required to operate. Its small size makes it simpler to review for security vulnerabilities, as any could potentially compromise all secure applications.

Trusted Application. A trusted application (*TA*), also called secure application is designed to be run exclusively inside the secure world. It uses services provided by the TEE kernel to access resources, specifically: (1) disk via the secure storage subsystem exclusively, (2) TCP/IP sockets, (3) memory allocation, (4) other custom services. Trusted applications provide services to either standard userland programs or other TAs. OP-TEE expects TAs to be written in C.

2.1 TRUSTZONE in a Nutshell

This section describes the main components of the TRUSTZONE architecture, also depicted in Fig. 2 alongside their interfaces.

Overview. TRUSTZONE is a hardware feature implemented in recent ARM processors. It enables physical separation of different execution environments, namely TEE and REE. Its working principle is very similar to a hypervisor, the main difference being that no emulation is performed and that all isolation is offered at the hardware level. Both secure (TEE) and normal worlds (REE) share the underlying physical processor. The secure world has unrestricted access to memory regions, hardware and devices. This is realized by using an additional addressing line, the NS (Non Secure) bit. Hardware checks performed by the TZASC (TRUSTZONE Address Space Controller) [42,50] determines, if the access is authorized based on this NS-bit.

Memory. Parts of the memory can be isolated for exclusive use by the secure world by means of special hardware support. The memory management unit (MMU) is secure-world aware, and secure and non-secure descriptors are stored alongside each other. The differentiation is done by the *Non-secure TLB ID* (NSTID) [12], an extra bit of the TLB. The secure applications (TAs) must fit in the on-chip memory. Due to high costs of the secure memory, it is usually limited in size, in the order of 3–5 MB. Hence, TAs are expected to have small memory footprints and only contain the minimal subset of features required. Clearly, this reduces the attack surface exposed by TAs.

Interrupts. The *Fast Interrupt* (FIQ) secure interrupt mode is used exclusively by devices residing in a memory region allocated to the secure world. As such, regular interrupts (IRQ), which are of lower priority, cannot be used to prevent the secure world from executing, in particular if a physical secure clock (*i.e.*, RTC) is used. Secure clocks are crucial to ensure a TA is safely executed: an external clock is a common attack vector and can be easily tampered with [53]. Latest ARM processors include secure clocks.

World Switching. Switching between worlds requires the state of the processor to be saved and then restored, respectively when entering and exiting a new world. Processor registers are saved by the monitor when entering, and restored when leaving the secure world. The NS-bit is changed accordingly. Normal world applications use TRUSTZONE indirectly, by invoking functionalities implemented in a dedicated TA. When in PL-1 [1,43] privilege level, a special hardware instruction, *Secure Monitor Call* (SMC), allows switching between worlds. Recent Cortex-A processors [48] support SMC calls by the kernel in the normal world. Entry to a different world (from secure to unsecure and vice versa) is done on a core-basis, thus limiting the parallel execution of TAs to the number of available cores. To enter the secure world, a kernel thread executes the monitor, which in turn issues the SMC instruction to the CPU [8,29]. Calls to SMC by a processor not in kernel mode trigger an undefined exception trap. TAs can be called from userland programs residing in the REE or from other

Table 1. Existing frameworks for TEE-based applications.

Framework	License	Technology
OP-TEE [26]	BSD	TRUSTZONE
Trustonic TEE [38]	Commercial	TRUSTZONE
Open TEE [52]	Apache License 2.0	TRUSTZONE
OpenEnclaves [23]	MIT	SGX1 & TRUSTZONE
TLK [54]	BSD	NVIDIA Tegra
Android Trusty TEE [2]	Apache License 2.0	TRUSTZONE[1]

[1]: emulated under Intel's VT

TAs. The latter is particularly useful to reduce code duplication and to keep the TA's attack surface minimal. Data is passed back and forth between worlds by memory pointers or direct copies.

Secure Storage. TRUSTZONE supports persistent data storage for TAs using secure storage. Objects are stored encrypted on disk, and are signed for anti-tampering countermeasure. TAs access the files in cleartext: the TEE layer runs the cryptographic stack transparently. These files have a unique numeric name based on a counter. An encrypted index of files is maintained alongside the files. Operations on the index are atomic, ensuring integrity protection by means of a hash tree data structure that guards the index. To protect against storage replay attacks, an eMMC storage device (*embedded MultiMediaCard*, a type of non-volatile, non-removable solid-state storage device [22]) is required. This security feature is entirely implemented in the eMMC storage in the form of *Replay Protected Memory Block* (RPMB) [55].

Key Management. The key manager starts with a device-specific key, the *Secure Storage Key* (SSK). It is derived from two pieces of information unique to each device's processor: the chip identifier and the hardware key. The *TA Storage Key* (TSK) is a per-TA key, derived from the SSK and the TA's UUID identifier. The *File Encryption Key* (FEK) is a per-file key generated upon file creation. It is used to protect the file contents, including its metadata, and is encrypted using the TSK.

Resilience to Attacks. It is of paramount importance to ensure that only trustworthy applications are deployed to the secure world. Vulnerabilities in any TA, the TEE or a compromised secure kernel do compromise the security of the secure world. Prevention against buffer overflow attacks in the secure world are currently only provided using basic stack canaries [31]. Future support for ASLR (Address Space Layout Randomization) will improve resilience against those attacks. Finally, there exist mitigations against Meltdown and Spectre speculative execution attacks [13–16]. Covert data channels [45] can also be used when required.

2.2   The Op-Tee Trusted OS

While there are few options (Table 1) to develop applications for TEEs, we rely on Op-Tee, due to its fast development cycle and native support for the Trust-Zone.

Op-Tee is a security framework that includes several components: a minimal secure-world operating system (the Op-Tee Os [26]); the *tee-supplicant* [30], offering normal world services to the secure world; a complete build toolchain [24], the testing tool [28] (*OPTEE sanity testsuite*), a secure privileged layer enabling world switching, a basic REE image, and several utility functions for developers to implement TAs. Op-Tee is flexible and can be deployed to platforms for which there exists a manifest, that lists the dependencies required to build for the platform it describes, as well as its hardware characteristics. Additionally, the Qemu open source emulator [33] allows to deploy and evaluate Op-Tee in emulated mode on ubiquitous machines. The TEE interface implemented in Op-Tee is compliant with the GlobalPlatform's specifications.

Details. Op-Tee imposes a specific interface regarding TA interactions initiated from the REE. First, a request to load the desired TA is made by passing its UUID to *TEEC_InitializeContext* which returns a context object. The UUID is defined at compile-time and must be unique amongst all TAs. Next, this context is passed to *TEEC_OpenSession* which returns a session. This session is then used to invoke actual services in the TA using the *TEEC_InvokeCommand*, which takes as parameters the service identifier as well as any optional parameters. A single session can be used to call *TEEC_InvokeCommand* any number of times. Sessions are finally closed using *TEEC_CloseSession* and ultimately, the context is closed by calling *TEEC_FinalizeContext*. To support multiple sessions, the TA must be compiled with the *TA_FLAG_MULTI_SESSION* flag set. Op-Tee signs TAs with a private RSA key, but the toolchain does not allow a unique key per-TA (all TAs are signed with the same device key). Upon TA loading, the Op-Tee core checks the integrity of the TA by verifying its signature based on its signed header. The framework includes a minimal OS that offers services to TAs, and leverages the tee-supplicant application to access resources residing in user land.

3   Methodology

This section describes the tools and techniques used to carry out our evaluation. We focus on four metrics : (1) execution time for various types of benchmarks (CPU-bound, volatile and non-volatile memory), (2) power consumption under different CPU governors, (3) energy consumption, and (4) thermal behaviour of the CPU.

Hardware Measurement Tools. Energy and power measurements are carried out using a Power-Z KM001 unit [32], plugged in-between the USB power supply and the Raspberry Pi device. The variant used in our testbed features two main USB ports (to provide power and one from where the power is drawn) of the

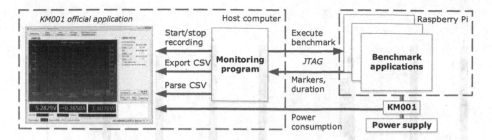

Fig. 3. Experimental setup and approach used to run our measurements

current mainstream USB types (type A, micro and type C). In our configuration, type A is used for both input and output of power delivery. An additional (micro) USB port is used to fetch power consumption measurements. The KM001 unit supports different USB protocols, including USB PD (Power Delivery) 2.0 and Qualcomm QC (QuickCharge) from version 2.0 up to 4.0. This configuration allows the power used by the Raspberry Pi to be measured directly as the losses of the power supply itself are not taken into account. We use this device to measure only power [W] and energy [Wh], for which it produces 1 record per second. Unfortunately, the software (Fig. 3, left) provided by the unit manufacturer is a closed-source 32-bit Windows binary, and the protocol used to exchange messages over USB is undocumented. To overcome these limitations, we used the following approach. Specific markers (*e.g. start recording* and *stop recording*) are generated during execution of benchmark applications, allowing for precise recording of areas of interest (Fig. 4). These markers are monitored by a custom program (on a separate node) that pilot the Windows binary (Fig. 5). The pilot sends automated messages to the binary instance using the Win32 API through P/Invoke (Platform Invokation Service) [11] issued by a monitoring program implemented in C#.

CPU Governors. The Linux kernel supports several CPU governors [46], used to adjust the frequency of each core depending on its load and temperature. Several options exist: `powersave` and `performance` for minimum and maximum operating frequency; `ondemand` toggles between the previous two, and a more `conservative` mode that operates less aggressively; `userspace`, to manually set the CPU frequency; and `schedutil`, where the frequency is set by the scheduler. The core frequency is increased during the execution of stressful workloads and reduced right after, for instance when the maximum temperature is reached in order to prevent overheating. This is different from a hardware thermal throttling, which tries to prevent damage caused by excessive heat. The OP-TEE kernel uses `powersave` governor by default. This reduces heat output by reducing the frequency of the core clocks, allowing passive cooling - even without heatsink - but also negatively impacts performance. In a compute-intensive datacenter, one would typically use the `performance` governor. Instead, if energy

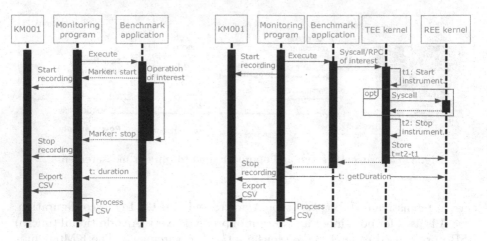

Fig. 4. Use of markers   **Fig. 5.** Microbenchmarking: workflow

constraints are important, the powersave mode is best suited. Our benchmarks consider both governors and compare them for REE and TEE executions.

Timing issues. Initially, we planned on porting STRESS-NG [36] to run inside TRUSTZONE. Unfortunately this proved to be not straightforward, given its reliance on system calls not available inside the TEE kernel. As such, we decided to implement custom ad-hoc benchmark applications. Execution time is measured using either the gettimeofday(2) [18] or the clock_gettime(3) [10] syscall, which support the following parameters:

1. CLOCK_REALTIME: the realtime clock of the system, can be adjusted by NTP and thus can go forward and backwards.
2. CLOCK_MONOTONIC: a monotonic time since an unspecified starting point (usually system startup, as is the case with our setup)
3. CLOCK_PROCESS_CPUTIME_ID: per-process timer
4. CLOCK_THREAD_CPUTIME_ID: thread-specific CPU-time clock

For our experiments we exclusively use CLOCK_MONOTONIC. Our benchmarks include the instrumentation delay, *e.g.*, the overhead introduced by the measurement itself. This is especially important from the TEE perspective (*i.e.*, inside a TA) where one syscall can lead to a second one if REE needs to be accessed (*e.g.*, Figs. 2-❾ and 2-❼).

Kernel and Op-Tee modifications. To access and store the monotonic time and temperature from within a TA using the secure kernel, and to retrieve it later on within the REE, we extended the kernel with four new system calls: TEE_GetCpuTemperature, sys_ktraceadd, sys_ktraceget and sys_ktracereset.

To gather the temperature measurements, we used two methods: (1) software, via thermal APIs[1] and (2) external hardware sensor. Originally, we planned on

---

[1] /sys/class/thermal/thermal_zone[0-9]+/temp.

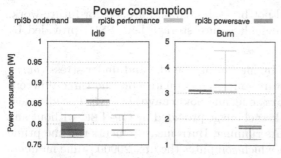

Fig. 6. Idle (left) and burn (right) power consumption.

Table 2. Average power consumptions for idle and burn experiments (see Fig. 6)

Governor	Idle		Burn	
	W	BTU/h	W	BTU/h
ondemand	0.78	2.66	3.08	10.51
performance	0.86	2.93	3.32	11.33
powersave	0.78	2.66	1.65	5.63

using a script to record the temperature at fixed intervals during the CPU stress tests executed by userland threads. However, since kernel threads executing the TAs have a higher priority, the userland threads were starved and thus did not produce enough data points. This is a typical scenario of normal world starvation occurring when TAs monopolize all cores. We overcome this problem by accessing the CPU temperature from inside the TA, and sending it periodically to the monitoring software for safekeeping. To use the temperature gathering syscall from within the TA, we additionally had to implement the corresponding TEE kernel syscall wrapper. An extensive walkthrough on this process is given at https://github.com/vschiavoni/on-the-performance-of-arm-trustzone.

4 Evaluation

This section presents our in-depth evaluation and performance analysis, the main contribution of this work. Energy results are always presented by systematically excluding idle energy consumption, *e.g.*, we only show the energy cost of the given operation. Energy requirements are shown on a per-operation fashion. To prevent thermal throttling, all tests run while the onboard chip is actively cooled.

Evaluation Settings. We use the Raspberry Pi 3B, a popular yet representative single-board device, equipped with Broadcom BCM2837 *System-On-Chip* (1 GB of RAM, ARM Cortex A53 quad core running at 1.2 GHz). For some of our measurements, we compared the hardware experiments against a modified version of the Qemu emulator provided by OP-TEE with support for TRUST-ZONE [34]. This mimics the scenario of an Infrastructure-as-a-Service provider offering access to ARM nodes (as virtual machines) to cloud tenants without having the corresponding hardware infrastructure and thus relying on TRUSTZONE virtualization [49]. Qemu uses the Cortex A53 emulation profile on an Ubuntu host residing on a VMWare ESXi [40] machine equipped with an i7 6820HQ running at 2.7 GHz. Note that the Raspberry Pi 3B lacks support for secure boot and hardware separation of memory and peripherals [27], hence these aspects of the TRUSTZONE ecosystem could not be evaluated and are left for future work. Finally, we do not override the default secure storage key (SSK) provided by OP-TEE.

Power consumption. We start by measuring the idle and under-stress (*burn*) power consumption of our hardware unit. We evaluate how the three different CPU governors (`ondemand`, `performance`, and `powersave`) behave. The idle measurements use the standard REE kernel image provided by OP-TEE, without any user-intensive applications nor TAs running. Burn measurements run the prime benchmark, a single-threaded TA which computes the first 20000 prime numbers before exiting. We run 8 instances in parallel, ensuring maximum heat output on the 4 cores. Measurements start 60 seconds after the benchmark instances. Figure 6 shows our results, respectively for idle (left) and burn (right) experiments. Table 2 shows the average W and BTU/h. We use a box-and-whiskers plot: the first and third quartile are shown as a colored box, the median as horizontal black bar. Min/max values are also included. Results for *ondemand* and *powersave* are on par with the *ondemand* governor, in particular when the CPU frequency is set at 600 MHz. As expected, we observe higher power consumption using the `performance` governor even in idle, as the cores are boosted up to 1.2 GHz. Overall, the board's power consumption is very low, in particular below 1 W in idle mode.

Load & unload TAs. Next, we measure the time required to load and unload a TA inside the TRUST-ZONE, respectively executing *TEEC_InitializeContext* [56, Chapter 4.5.2] and *TEEC_FinalizeContext* [56, Chapter 4.5.3] functions. We compare results obtained with a TA of size smaller and another one of size larger than the 512 kB L2 cache of the Broadcom BCM2837 processor, respectively 102 kB and 517 kB. Our experiments show no significant

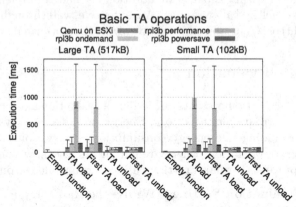

Fig. 7. Basic TA operations: loading, unloading and successive calls to load/unload the same TA.

difference between TAs of different sizes. For each configuration, Fig. 7 shows average and standard deviation over 10k executions. We include the time spent to execute an empty function inside the TA once it is loaded (1.31 ms), to give a baseline of comparison.

Surprisingly, our results do not show a significant differences on subsequent loadings compared to the first loading, despite the tee-supplicant is supposed to cache the TA code. We will investigate this aspect in future work.

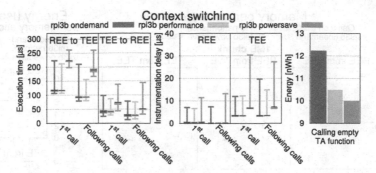

Fig. 8. World switching performance and energy requirements

Context (World) Switching. Switching between worlds is a key operation when deploying applications that execute inside and outside the TRUSTZONE. To measure the switching time, we implemented an ad-hoc benchmark made by a host application and a TA. Both programs record the monotonic time when entering and exiting the world in which they reside. The host issues a call to an almost empty function, which only contain time-measuring code. Two calls are made to the TA per session, recording the time taken to switch between TEE and REE, and vice versa. Figure 8 (left) shows these results. To evaluate possible caching effects, we also include the results obtained for all the calls following the first one. As expected, it is more time-consuming to switch from the REE to the TEE (110 μs with the performance-oriented governors) than the opposite (47 μs). The instrumentation delay (Fig. 8, center) is the difference between two consecutive calls to the time measurement function. An increased instrumentation delay is observed in the TEE compared to the REE, due to the additional world switch. Finally, we also evaluate the energy spent for calling an empty TA function from the REE (Fig. 8, right). The timer starts and stops when leaving and re-entering the REE, respectively. The *ondemand* governor is the most energy-eager (up to 12.1 nWh), while *powersave* is the most energy efficient.

Volatile Memory. Next, we consider simple in-memory operations (*e.g.*, read and write, sequential or at random), for two different sizes of volatile memory (1 MB and 100 KB) used by the REE and the TEE. We consider inter-(REE←TEE) and intra-world (*e.g.*, REE↔REE, TEE↔TEE) memory readings, as TRUSTZONE restrictions prevents reading TEE memory from the REE. We compute the average and standard deviation over 100 run, always using the high-resolution monotonic counter. Figure 9 shows our results, for the Raspberry Pi device with 3 CPU governors and using Qemu. Performance of accessing a single byte in TEE memory from the TEE is on par with accessing REE memory from the TEE, on average 0.01 μs, around 2× under emulation. Interestingly, using memory from within the TEE is also less energy eager (Fig. 10), also verified by the cost of the single operations in the various configurations. We observe how the operations in the TEE↔TEE case are on average 2× faster on bare metal and 1.2× under emulation than in the other cases.

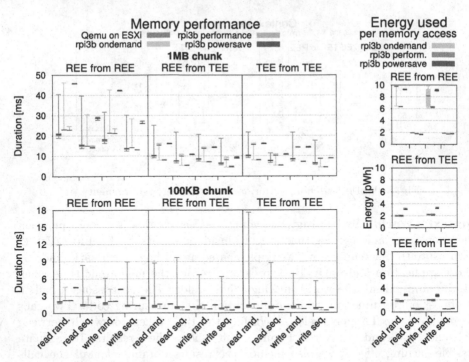

Fig. 9. Benchmark for memory ops

Fig. 10. Energy: memory accesses

Secure Storage: performance. We evaluate the performance of TRUSTZONE's secure storage via the corresponding GlobalPlatform's API implemented by OP-TEE. Specifically, we benchmark the cost of creating, writing, reading and closing objects inside the secure storage area, for two different object sizes (100 KB and 1 MB), although current memory allocator limitations prevented to cover some cases [19,20,35,39]. Figure 11 (left) shows that closing and deleting objects are fast operations, and opening and writing are the slowest ones. Iterating over objects in the secure storage (*e.g.*, the execution of a find operation) is slow, up to a few hours in the worst case (Fig. 11, right). Adding more objects in secure storage degrade the results even more (up to $2.01 \times object\_count\_ratio$).

Secure Storage: Cost Breakdown. To understand how each low-level syscall affects the performance of a file-system inside the secure storage, we implemented a simple microbenchmark, inside ree_fs_create and ree_fs_write. Specifically, these tests create and write data into a new object. Figure 14 shows a breakdown cost using stacked bars for writing and creating files. These two functions are atomic and thus are surrounded by a monitor (mutex) which adds a considerable delay (not shown) regarding the *write* operation. The impact is negligible on the *create* operation. We observe that opening the file and setting the filename accounts for the most time spent.

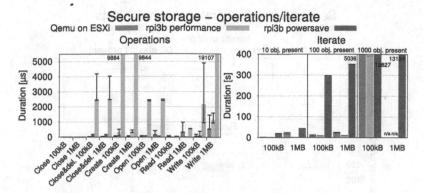

Fig. 11. Secure storage: basic operations (left) and iteration (right)

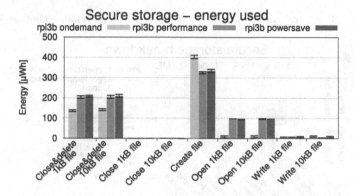

Fig. 12. Secure storage: energy measurements for basic operations

Secure Storage: Energy. Being a feature often used by nomad devices with low energy autonomy, we deeply investigate its energy impacts. Figure 12 shows that creating objects is the most energy-demanding (up to 403 μWh), irrelevant of the size. Power consumption of writing objects is dependent on their size. Interestingly, the *ondemand* governor achieves slightly worse results when creating a file, whereas for closing and deleting files it stands out. Figure 13 shows the energy requirements to iterate over a single stored object (top) [57, Chapter 5.8] during enumeration of all stored objects in secure storage or rename (bottom) a single object, when additional 10 or 100 objects (of the same size) are already in the secure storage. We execute this test for 2 different file sizes (1 kB and 10 kB). We observe that the energy required to iterate over a single object depends on the number of objects stored (in particular when using `performance` and `ondemand`), whereas the size of the object is irrelevant.

CPU Benchmarks. To benchmark the raw performance of the ARM processors of our units, we implemented and deployed a single-threaded TA that executes a CPU-bound task, *e.g.*, computes the first 20000 prime numbers. We run multiple

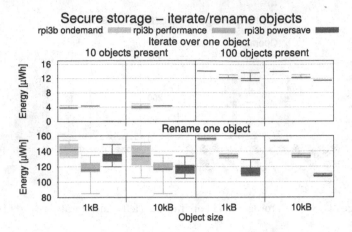

Fig. 13. Secure storage, energy to iterate (top) and rename (bottom)

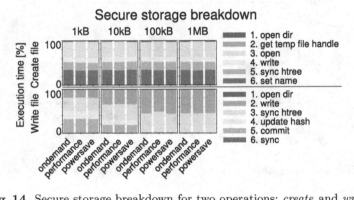

Fig. 14. Secure storage breakdown for two operations: *create* and *write*

instances concurrently, and while they execute we also gather energy measurements (for all cases minus the emulation mode). Figure 15 presents these results.

As expected, the `performance` governor ensures the fastest computing time. Due to emulation costs, the Qemu results are the worst ones. As the number of instances exceed the available hardware cores, we observe an increase of energy consumption. Overall, in this benchmark the `ondemand` governor is the most energy eager. This can be explained by the fact that adjusting the core frequencies (from 600 MHz and 1.2 GHz) seems to be a relatively costly operation [41].

Thermal Benchmarks. We conclude our evaluation by looking at the thermal envelope of the *SoC*. To do so, we execute 8 concurrent instances of the prime benchmark inside TRUSTZONE. Figure 16 presents the measurements fetched using the kernel's thermals API. Additionally, we monitor the surface temperature of the chip using a Texas Instruments LM35 precision linear sensor with the help of an external micro controller. Thermal conductivity between the *SoC* and the LM35 is ensured by using a thermal compound (Arctic MX-4 [3]). The

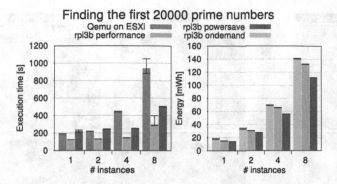

Fig. 15. CPU benchmark: processing delay and energy requirements.

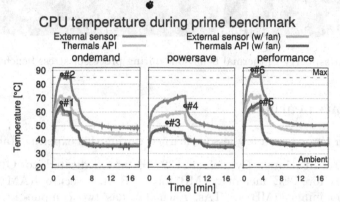

Fig. 16. Evolution of CPU temperature with different cooling modes and governors.

ambient temperature is of around 21.9 °C. Results returned by the LM35 are calibrated and checked at rest against a Fluke thermocouple, and against a Flir E4 [17] thermal camera (see pictures in Fig. 17). Marked points in Fig. 16 refer to measurements done using the thermal camera. We observe a small margin of error of 3 °C, and a discrepancy between the thermals API and the LM35 of over 15 °C at times. This could be problematic because the measured surface temperature exceeds the rated continuous temperature of 85 °C specified by the chip's manufacturer. In this situation, the thermals API returns an incorrect temperature that is well below the acceptable temperature. As a consequence measures which should be taken to reduce the temperature, such as software thermal throttling, are not undertaken. A passively cooled Raspberry Pi should therefore only operate in powersave mode or risk being hardware throttled or worse, suffer damage. An actively cooled system on the other hand can operate in any mode and stay well within acceptable conditions, even without additional heat sink. Once the maximal temperature is reached, recovery time is around 8 minutes when passively cooled and less than a minute with active cooling.

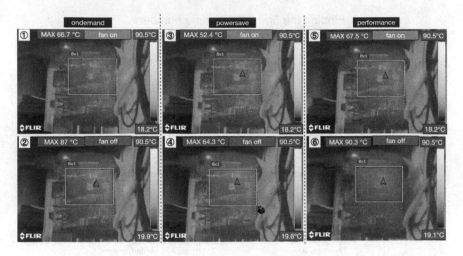

Fig. 17. Raspberry Pi thermal behaviour during processor stress benchmarks.

5 Lessons Learned

This section reports on a few lessons learned during this experimental work.

Memory Limitations. By default, 32 MB are dedicated to OP-TEE, of which: 1 MB for TEE memory, 1 MB for PUB (non-secure RAM) memory, and the remaining 30 MB for TAs. Each TA has two compile-time options, *TA_STACK_SIZE* and *TA_DATA_SIZE* (in *user_ta_header_defines.h*), defining the stack size and heap size that can be utilized by a TA. These values are set at very low values by default, 2 kB and 32 kB respectively [25]. For larger memory allocations, the TA's MMU L1 table must be set accordingly, as the default mapping is 1 MB. We were unable to allocate more than 3 MB for a single TA, even with shared memory enabled. Consequently, the OP-TEE benchmark framework [9] could not be used.

Compliance to Standards. The GlobalPlatform's implementation in OP-TEE is not error-free and some parts of the implementation do not comply fully with the specification. For instance, the *TEE_BigIntAdd* [57, p. 252] function, contrary to its definition, does not allow to use the same pointers for both input and output [37]. Being relatively new, OP-TEE is improving rapidly. While this offers great advantages, such as mitigations against the latest attacks, it also introduces incompatibilities by deprecating older APIs. However, the GlobalPlatform consortium offers strong incentives for TEE vendors to comply with their API, which is unlikely to introduce breaking changes. Establishing this level of compliance ensures interoperability of TAs between existing TEE solutions which is undeniably of great interest to secure application developers.

Developers Toolchain. The OP-TEE framework groups all required dependencies in a single project while also including several components of its own, such as the secure kernel. This greatly facilitates development of secure application by reducing setup and development efforts. The OP-TEE project includes a few TA examples and host applications, which are a good foundation to introduce the TEE paradigm.

6   Conclusion

TRUSTZONE is a widely available technology that offers Trusted Execution Environment guarantees to low-energy devices. The goal of this practical experience report was to uncover the performance of these systems. To perform our experiments, we extended[2] both secure and rich kernels so that secure timing measurements and thermal metrics could be fetched from within TRUSTZONE. Our work highlights several advantages as well as limitation of the currently available software platforms, such as the OP-TEE framework chosen in our case, to implement and deploy TAs. We would like to point out two major limitations. (1) the lack of several basic features inside the REE kernel for security reasons, which materialize in the lack of basic syscalls (*e.g.* fopen, msgget). For this reason, it is paramount to reduce syscall dependencies when developing TAs. (2), the current limitations regarding memory allocation and addressing, which could negatively affect the facility to deploy more complex TAs inside TRUSTZONE. We hope this work will provide useful insights to TRUSTZONE software developers.

Acknowledgments. The research leading to these results has received funding from the European Union's Horizon 2020 research and innovation programme under the LEGaTO Project (http://legato-project.eu), grant agreement No 780681.

References

1. AArch64 Exception Handling - System calls to EL2/EL3. http://infocenter.arm.com/help/index.jsp?topic=/com.arm.doc.den0024a/ch10s02s04.html
2. Android Trusty TEE. https://source.android.com/security/trusty
3. Arctic MX-4. https://www.arctic.ac/ch_en/mx-4.html
4. ARM Everywhere. https://hexus.net/static/arm-everywhere/
5. ARM Financial Results. https://www.arm.com/company/investors/financial-results
6. ARM Inside The Numbers - 100bn. https://community.arm.com/processors/b/blog/posts/inside-the-numbers-100-billion-arm-based-chips-1345571105
7. ARM TrustZone Developer. https://developer.arm.com/technologies/trustzone
8. ARM1176JZF-S Technical Reference Manual - 2.12.13. Secure Monitor Call (SMC). http://infocenter.arm.com/help/index.jsp?topic=/com.arm.doc.ddi0301h/ch02s12s13.html
9. Benchmark framework. https://github.com/OP-TEE/optee_os/blob/master/documentation/benchmark.md
10. clock_gettime(3) - Linux man page. https://linux.die.net/man/3/clock_gettime

---

[2] Details at https://github.com/vschiavoni/on-the-performance-of-arm-trustzone.

11. Consuming Unmanaged DLL Functions. https://docs.microsoft.com/en-us/dotnet/framework/interop/consuming-unmanaged-dll-functions
12. Cortex-A9 Technical Reference Manual - 6.3. Memory Access Sequence. http://infocenter.arm.com/help/index.jsp?topic=/com.arm.doc.ddi0388f/Ciheiecd.html. Accessed 12 Sept 2018
13. CVE-2017-5715. https://nvd.nist.gov/vuln/detail/CVE-2017-5715
14. CVE-2017-5753. https://nvd.nist.gov/vuln/detail/CVE-2017-5753
15. CVE-2017-5754. https://nvd.nist.gov/vuln/detail/CVE-2017-5754
16. CVE-2018-3639. https://nvd.nist.gov/vuln/detail/CVE-2018-3639
17. Flir E4. https://www.flir.com/products/e4/
18. gettimeofday(2) - Linux man page. https://linux.die.net/man/2/gettimeofday
19. Hikey: trying to allocate more physical memory to secure world. https://github.com/OP-TEE/optee_os/issues/1396
20. How to alloc 10M memory by TEE_Malloc(). https://github.com/OP-TEE/optee-os/issues/2090
21. Intel SGX. https://software.intel.com/en-us/sgx
22. Kingston Embedded Solutions. https://www.kingston.com/en/embedded/emmc
23. Microsoft OpenEnclave Framework. https://github.com/Microsoft/openenclave
24. OP-TEE Build on Github. https://github.com/OP-TEE/build. Accessed 12 Apr 2018
25. OP-TEE FAQ on Github. https://github.com/OP-TEE/OP-TEE-website/tree/master/faq. Accessed 12 Apr 2018
26. OP-TEE OS on Github. https://github.com/OP-TEE/optee_os. Accessed 12 Apr 2018
27. OP-TEE Raspberry 3B platform specific documentation. https://www.op-tee.org/docs/rpi3/
28. OP-TEE sanity testsuite on Github. https://github.com/OP-TEE/optee_test. Accessed 12 Apr 2018
29. OP-TEE source. https://github.com/OP-TEE/optee_os/blob/master/core/arch/arm/kernel/generic_entry_a64.S. Accessed 12 Sept 2018
30. OP-TEE Supplicant on Github. https://github.com/OP-TEE/optee_client/tree/master/tee-supplicant. Accessed 12 Apr 2018
31. OPTEE-OS kernel thread.c init_canaries. https://github.com/OP-TEE/optee_os/blob/master/core/arch/arm/kernel/thread.c#L150
32. POWER-Z KM001C. http://www.chargerlab.com/archives/536.html
33. Qemu. https://www.qemu.org. Accessed 12 Apr 2018
34. QEMU with WIP TrustZone Support. https://git.linaro.org/virtualization/qemu-tz.git
35. Shared memory size bigger than 1 MB. https://github.com/OP-TEE/optee_os/issues/1523
36. Stress-NG. https://kernel.ubuntu.com/~cking/stress-ng/. Accessed 20 Jan 2019
37. TEE_BigIntAdd fails when dest=op OP-TEE OS Issue #2577. https://github.com/OP-TEE/optee_os/issues/2577
38. TRUSTSONIC. https://www.trustonic.com/solutions/trustonic-solutions-iot
39. Using more than 1 Mb with TEE_Malloc. https://github.com/OP-TEE/optee_os/issues/2178
40. VMware ESXi. https://www.vmware.com/products/esxi-and-esx.html
41. Workloads and governor effects. https://www.ibm.com/developerworks/library/l-cpufreq-3/
42. ARM: ARM® CoreLink™ TZC-400 TrustZone®Address Space Controller (2014)

43. ARM Limited: SMC CALLING CONVENTION System Software on ARM® Platforms (2016)
44. Barbosa, M., et al.: SAFETHINGS: data security by design in the IoT. In: 2017 13th European Conference on Dependable Computing Conference (EDCC), pp. 117–120. IEEE (2017)
45. Cho, H., et al.: Prime+Count: novel cross-world covert channels on ARM trustzone. In: Proceedings of the 34th Annual Computer Security Applications Conference, ACSAC 2018, New York, NY, USA, pp. 441–452. ACM (2018)
46. Brodowski, D.: CPU frequency and voltage scaling code in the Linux(tm) kernel (2018)
47. Gartner: Leading the IoT Gartner Insights on How to Lead in a Connected World (2017)
48. Greenhalgh, P.: big.LITTLE processing with arm cortex-a15 & cortex-a7. ARM White paper 17 (2011)
49. Hua, Z., Gu, J., Xia, Y., Chen, H., Zang, B., Guan, H.: vTZ: virtualizing ARM trustzone. In: Proceedings of the 26th USENIX Security Symposium (2017)
50. Lentz, M., Sen, R., Druschel, P., Bhattacharjee, B.: SeCloak: ARM trustzone-based mobile peripheral control, pp. 1–13, June 2018
51. Lipp, M., et al.: Nethammer: Inducing Rowhammer Faults through Network Requests. arXiv preprint arXiv:1805.04956 (2018)
52. McGillion, B., Dettenborn, T., Nyman, T., Asokan, N.: Open-TEE-an open virtual trusted execution environment. In: Proceedings of the 2015 IEEE Trustcom/BigDataSE/ISPA, vol. 01, pp. 400–407. IEEE Computer Society (2015)
53. NCC Group: Implementing practical electrical glitching attacks (2015)
54. nVidia: Trusted Little Kernel (TLK) for Tegra, FOSS edn. (2015)
55. Reddy, A.K., Paramasivam, P., Vemula, P.B.: Mobile secure data protection using eMMC RPMB partition. In: 2015 International Conference on Computing and Network Communications (CoCoNet), pp. 946–950. IEEE (2015)
56. G-Technology: GlobalPlatform TEE Client API Specification v1.0 (2019)
57. G-Technology: TEE Internal Core API Specification Version 1.1.2.50 (2018)

CapBAC in Hyperledger Sawtooth

Stefano Bistarelli[1], Claudio Pannacci[2], and Francesco Santini[1(✉)]

[1] Department of Mathematics and Computer Science,
University of Perugia, Perugia, Italy
{stefano.bistarelli,francesco.santini}@unipg.it
[2] Faculty of Technology, Linnæus University, Växjö, Sweden
cp222kr@student.lnu.se

Abstract. In the *Internet of Things* (*IoT*) context, the number of connected devices can be too large for a centralised server. This paper focuses on how to enforce authorisation in such a distributed and dynamic environment. The key idea is to use a blockchain-based technology both as a way to maintain a common distributed ledger to store and use access control information, and as a way to enforce Access Control policies in the form of smart contracts. An implementation of an access-control system is presented as a proof of concept: it corresponds to an adaptation of the *Capability-based Access Control Model* (*CapBAC*) in the form of a transaction family in *Hyperledger Sawtooth*. The main claim is that the features and simplicity of CapBAC magnify the usefulness of a blockchain to control the access in the IoT.

1 Introduction

Regarding decentralised systems, recent years have seen the success of *Bitcoin* [13], based on the blockchain technology and the first crypto-currency that solved the double spending problem, which consequently granted trust in a trustless peer to peer network. Bitcoin opened the door for a new era of decentralisation touching every sector, not only the economical one, with improvements, variants and generalisations of the protocol enabling for a variety of services, like messaging platforms and distributed file storage, to be secure without a grantee.

Many researchers started to work on/with the blockchain, some of them seeing in this new technology also a solution for some problems related to the security in the *Internet of Things* (*IoT*). This paper follows in this belief: it is focused on the research of an *Access Control Model* (simply, *ACM*), among the ones already designed specifically for the IoT, which addresses all or most of the features required, such as *scalability*, *lightweightness*, and *privacy* [3], while being compatible with the blockchain architecture.

In this IoT scenario, the goal of this paper is "go back" and propose a "simple" ACM, as the *Capability-based Access Control Model* (*CapBAC*) [7], adapted to an underlying *Hyperledger Sawtooth* blockchain, with the purpose to manage capabilities. We implemented all the components of the proposed ACM in

© IFIP International Federation for Information Processing 2019
Published by Springer Nature Switzerland AG 2019
J. Pereira and L. Ricci (Eds.): DAIS 2019, LNCS 11534, pp. 152–169, 2019.
https://doi.org/10.1007/978-3-030-22496-7_10

Python (code released in a public repository, link in the following) and using Sawtooth. Sawtooth is also scalable and secure, two features needed by ACM for the IoT world (see Sect. 2.1). Among all Hyperledger blockchains, Sawtooth also comes with an SDK that allows its integration into Android applications. The "simplicity" of CapBAC and its focus on capability tokens lead to a high usability level in this kind of apps, particularly if compared to more complex ACMs (see Sect. 2.2).

However, we present this work as a proof-of-concept, mapping from the abstract model to the actual components, and paving the way to future ad-hoc blockchains. In fact, we believe (and explain why in the following of the paper) that CapBAC perfectly and easily integrates with the blockchain principles, but an ad-hoc blockchain developed to support CapBAC would overcome the limitations of Sawtooth and additional current ledgers. For instance, allowing untraceability and using "light" cryptography, in order to use constrained devices (even more constrained than mobile phones).

The paper is organised as follows: in Sect. 2 we introduce blockchains and ACMs. In Sect. 3 we describe CapBAC and we motivate why the use of a capability-based blockchain reinforces CapBAC as an ACM for the IoT. Section 4 describes our case-study by implementing such a model with Sawtooth. Section 5 reports related work, while Sect. 6 finally wraps up the paper with conclusive thoughts and future work.

2 Background

We divide background information into two different subsections, about blockchains (Sect. 2.1) and ACMs for the IoT (Sect. 2.2) respectively.

2.1 Blockchain

A *distributed ledger* (also *Distributed Ledger Technology* or *DLT*) is a consensus of replicated, shared, and synchronised digital data distributed across multiple sites. A peer-to-peer network and a consensus algorithms among such peers are required to ensure consistent replication across the nodes. One of the possible forms of DLT implementation is the blockchain system.

In 2009, Bitcoin [13] was proposed by Satoshi Nakamoto as a new crypto-currency: approximately every 10 minutes, the nodes on the network come to consensus on a set of unspent coins, and the conditions required to spend them. This data set, known as the "unspent transaction output" (*UTXO*), can be modified by submitting transactions to the network that replace one or more UTXOs with a new set of unspent transaction outputs. In order to ensure that all nodes come to consensus, the Bitcoin protocol leverages a set of transaction validation rules and a consensus mechanism known as *Proof-of-Work* (*PoW*) [13]; this allows a permissionless[1] and anonymous participation in the consensus protocol.

---

[1] In permissioned blockchains, the network owners decide who can join the network, and in general any action as block verification, transaction issuing, or just consulting the blockchain, can be allowed or not by some *administrator*.

After Bitcoin, many other blockchain systems with different characteristics have been proposed, mainly with the purpose to improve its limited scalability, limited scripting language, and intermediate-statelessness design. However, most of them share the following characteristics:

- *Distributed*: The blockchain database is shared among potentially untrusted participants and it is demonstrably identical on all nodes in the network (at least in case of permissionless blockchains).
- *Immutable*: The blockchain database is an unalterable history of all transactions that uses block hashes to make it easy to detect and prevent attempts to alter the history.
- *Secure*: All changes are performed by transactions that are signed by known identities. These features and agreed-upon consensus mechanisms work to provide "adversarial trust" among all participants in a blockchain network.

Hyperledger[2] is an umbrella project of open source blockchains and related tools. All the frameworks part of the project (as *Fabric*, *Sawtooth* and *Iroha*, *Burrow* and *Indy*) share the common goal of improving performance of blockchains with the purpose to support global business transactions by technological, financial, and supply chain companies. The code is open-source and the same standards are followed in order to achieve inter-operability.

To implement the access control scheme we propose in this paper, we took advantage of *Hyperledger Sawtooth* because of the following features.

Scalability: Sawtooth was originally designed to overcome scalability challenges of a typical blockchain, such as Bitcoin. For this reason, the lightweight consensus algorithm *PoET* (*Proof-of-Elapsed-Time*) is adopted. PoET is a form of random leader election, wherein each validator node waits a random amount of time before trying to claim a block. In other random leader election algorithms like PoW, that randomness is enforced by searching for partial hash collisions.[3] A benchmark that measures the scalability of different blockchains (Hyperledger included) is presented in [5].

Security: in order to narrow the attack surface, Sawtooth has a contract logic which is termed as transaction families (more details in the following).

There are five core components in Sawtooth:

- A peer-to-peer network for passing messages and transactions between nodes;
- A distributed log which contains an ordered list of transactions;
- A state machine/smart contract logic layer for processing the content of those transactions;
- A distributed state storage for storing the resulting state after processing transactions;
- A consensus algorithm for achieving consensus across the network on the ordering of transactions and the resulting state.

---

[2] Hyperledger project: https://www.hyperledger.org.
[3] PoET replaces that work (needed by PoW) with trusted computing.

In Sawtooth, the data model and transaction language are implemented in a *transaction family*. A transaction family is a group of operations or transaction types that a programmer allows on the ledger. The users are expected to build custom transaction families that reflect the unique requirements of their ledgers.

The Sawtooth framework elaborates on the concept of smart contracts by viewing them as a state machine, or *transaction processor*. After passing through a strictly-ordered distributed log (i.e., a blockchain), transactions are routed to the appropriate processor. These processors than ingest the payload of transactions, as well as any relevant state, before processing the transaction (updating the state). Sawtooth is capable of supporting both the stateless (UTXO) and stateful (Ethereum-style[4]) models. Smart contracts can be written in different languages (e.g., Python or Solidity). By creating a domain specific transaction processor, it is much easier to limit the types of actions that can be performed on a blockchain network, which can improve security and performance.

Sawtooth is a configurable blockchain with a focus on security and designed for IoT scenarios, however, as already stated in Sect. 1, the model we propose in this paper is not meant to be blockchain-specific. To develop an "ad hoc" blockchain could be the only way to include constraint devices in the secure peer-to-peer network.

2.2 IoT and ACMs

The term "Internet of Things" was used for the first time in 1999 to describe a scenario in which computers, and so the Internet as a whole, can gather real world data without human intervention [2]. In recent years the term became widespread under the acronym "IoT" and usually refers to a network of constrained devices, as embedded systems with sensors and actuators, connected to the Internet.

Concerning how the security of the IoT can be enforced, in this paper we focus our attention on *authorisation*. It refers to the specification of access rights or privileges to specific resources, which in our case is the information gathered and managed by IoT devices. The OM-AM[5] reference model proposed in [15] gives a better view of what authorisation means in the IoT world. Among its required objectives, authorisation has to be *decentralised, anonymous* or *pseudonymous* (*unlinkability* prevents from connecting pseudonyms to real ids), *scalable, lightweight* (low use of resources such power and memory), it needs to offer revocation and delegation of rights, the response time has to be low, and access information needs to last for a long time.

In the following, we will briefly discuss some ACMs frequently used in the IoT; for their connection to related work, see Sect. 5. CapBAC-based schemes, access rights are granted to subjects based on the concept of capability, which is a transferable and unforgeable token of authority (e.g, a key), and describes a set of access rights for each subject (in Sect. 3 we will provide more details).

---

[4] Sawtooth also supports Ethereum smart contracts via *Seth*, a Sawtooth transaction processor integrating the *Hyperledger Burrow Ethereum Virtual Machine*.

[5] Objective-Model Architecture-Mechanism layers (OM-AM).

DCapBAC [9] is a distributed version of CapBAC developed with the specific purpose to control the access in the IoT. The framework conceived in this paper moves the distribution-related features of DCapBAC to the blockchain level.

In the *RBAC*-based schemes [6], access control is based on the roles (e.g., administer or guest) of subjects (i.e., entities that access to resources) within an organisation. By associating roles with access rights (e.g., read, write, execute) and assigning roles to subjects, the RBAC-based schemes can establish a many-to-many relationship between access rights and subjects.

The *ABAC*-based schemes [10] exploit policies that combine various types of attributes, such as subject attributes, object (i.e., the entity that holds resources) attributes and environment attributes, in order to define a set of rules expressing under what conditions access rights can be granted to subjects.

OrBAC [11] focuses on the concept of organisation: a security policy that applies to a given organisation is defined as a collection of permissions, prohibitions, obligations, and recommendations.

Finally, the work in [3] proposes a Trust-based ACM (*TBAC*), which adds a trust evaluation on top of the decentralised architecture of DCapBAC.

3   CapBAC and Blockchains

In Sect. 3.1 we introduce the basic components of CapBAC and their interaction, while in Sect. 3.2 we suggest how it smoothly integrates with a blockchain system.

3.1   CapBAC

In a typical use-case of CapBAC, after the owner of a *resource*, hosted by a *device*, or someone delegated to do so, referred to as the *issuer*, issues a *capability token* in name of a *subject* for that particular resource, *subject* is then able to access to a resource by sending an *access request* to *device* in which the capability token is attached. The authorisation is granted if the token passes the *authorisation procedure*. We now briefly introduce all the main actors in such a scenario.

A **resource** is a univocally identifiable and actable-upon object (e.g. a REST-ful resource). A **capability token** is a communicable object (e.g. in *JSON*) digitally signed by the issuer, in which the subject is represented by its public key. It is unequivocally identifiable by its id, it has a time-stamp and a validity time interval. Moreover, it has a field to store the issuer's capability that is used to specify from which parent capability it is derived from, in case of delegation. A capability with no parent is said to be a *root capability*. In a delegation every token is chained to the one it is derived from up to the root. A **revocation token** contains the issuer's capability as authorisation. The revoked token is specified along with the revocation type. An **access request** for a service/operation on a resource also includes (or refer to) a capability token. A **policy decision-point** (*PDP*) is a resource-agnostic service in charge of managing the validation of the access rights granted in the received capabilities against local policies, and it updates the capability database. A **resource manager** manages the requests

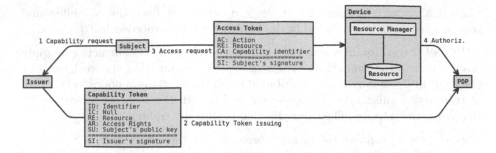

Fig. 1. Token issuing and the access request procedure in CapBAC.

for a resource. It checks the acceptability of the capability token shipped with the service request, as well as the validity and congruence of the requested service/operation against the presented capability, by taking also the validation outcome from the PDP into account. The **revocation service** validates incoming capability revocations and it updates the capability and revocation databases (storing the revocation tokens).

When an access request for a resource is received by a device, the **authorisation procedure** is executed: the resource manager first *(i)* checks the *formal validity* of all the capabilities in the authorisation chain, then *(ii)* it checks the *logical validity* of the request by evaluating the congruence of the operation granted by the capability with the operation reported in the initial request; finally, *(iii)* it forwards the request to the PDP. The PDP checks the applicability of the operation by *(i)* verifying the logical validity of each capability in the delegation chain, and *(ii)* inquiring the revocation service. The revocation service checks in the revocation database if the capability wasd. After this step succeeds, the authorisation is granted. Figures 1 and 2 summarise the issuing procedure of a token, the access request and revocation procedures in the CapBAC model.

3.2 Blockchains with CapBAC: Characteristics

In this section we survey the advantages in adopting CapBAC supported by a blockchain model, highlighting the compatibility between the two, and commenting about related work.

Capability and Revocation Database. The main advantage of a blockchain is that it offers a trusted distributed database, which can be used in an ACM to address revocation and delegation in an effective way. In DCapBAC [9], both revocation and delegation are abandoned in favour of pure distribution (we instead keep both these two phases in our proposal): the *PDP* is integrated into the device itself and the capability tokens, once issued, are stored by their subject, which attaches the whole token to its requests. On the other hand, a ledger can be used to store both the capability and revocation tokens granting revocation and delegation even in a distributed scenario: this feature is almost always required when dealing with IoT security. A single database for both the capability and revocation tokens was adopted in the implementation proposed in [7].

PDP and Revocation Service. A blockchain featuring smart contracts can apply any rule-set to the validation of transactions; this means that the work done by the PDP in [7] and [3] can be distributed to all the blockchain nodes in the form of transaction validation. The same also holds with the controls performed by the revocation service. Their computation is thus distributed.

Tokens. In our proposal, tokens are represented on the ledger state of Sawtooth. In this case, the CapBAC model has the great advantage, over other ACMs, of using tokens, i.e. the capability tokens, that behave in a similar way to transactions in a token-based crypto-currency. The authorisation/ownership is granted by the issuer/sender with the inclusion of the subject/receiver's public key in the token/transaction; the issuer/sender has to digitally sign the token/transaction; the whole delegation chain/transaction history is required in order to prove the validity/ownership of the capability/token. In such a CapBAC blockchain, a transaction is considered valid only if it contains all the fields of a capability token and the hash of the parent transaction (owned by the issuer), which has to allow the delegation on all the stated access-rights. The revocation concerns a different kind of transaction (without owners), also chained to a pre-existing capability transaction in order to spend/revoke it and/or its descendants. Once added to the ledger, a capability transaction is valid until it (or a capability in its chain of transactions) expires or it is revoked.

Privacy. Blockchain privacy is controversial. In our proposal, transparency is granted by default since anyone in the network can access to the ledger. The capability system is user-driven by design, since the owner of a resource is always in full control of the rights granted: owning the root capability, she can easily revoke any derived access right. The challenge is represented by anonymity: while *pseudonymity* is obtained by using signature validation as identification and authentication means, blockchains usually do not easily grant *unlinkability* or *untraceability*, e.g. the identity of the participants can be inferred by looking at the transaction history [16]. A capability token-based blockchain, however, could achieve the complete detachment between identities and capabilities by exploiting the delegation system as described in [7, Sect. 6].[6] Moreover, *unobservability* of accesses is granted, since the request validation can be performed without broadcasting any information, and *decentralisation* is the key feature offered by both capability-based models and blockchains.

Confidentiality and Integrity. As previously stated, the selling points of the proposed system are the *granularity* of access control rights and an effective *delegation* and *revocation* procedures.

---

[6] This issue in not addressed in this paper, but ad-hoc blockchains can be designed following the example of untraceable tokens as in *Monero* crypto-currency.

Reliability and Availability. The *offline mode* is not available with a blockchain: the communication among devices is required during the authentication procedure. The *short-term availability* of information depends on the implementation: e.g., Sawtooth provides a low latency [5]. Finally, *long-term availability* is a key feature of the blockchain, since all the stored information is unalterable.

Social and Economic Aspects. Given the diffusion of inter-operating private blockchains, such as the *Hyperledger* project, collaboration is to be expected between different implementations following the same standards: we propose CapBAC as an ACM to be supported by different blockchains. To achieve *context-awareness*, additional considerations need clarifications, as the use of a level of trust, either in access control rules or in underling consensus algorithm.

Technological Constraints. While the proposed system provides high *flexibility* and *scalability*, the main question is whether or not it would be able to run on constrained devices, i.e. if it provides the *lighweightness* required by IoT. At first the idea of having every device storing a copy of the whole ledger could seem too memory intensive for it to be deployed on low-hardware devices, and it certainly is at the current state of technology. However, as for the PDP in [3] and [7], it is not necessary for every device to be a blockchain node, i.e. storing the ledger and providing validation, but the ones without enough resources could rely on a validator network composed of more powerful devices. We can also refer to [1] as a proof of the feasibility of this approach. Finally, *heterogeneity* would require some standardisation efforts, but it is achievable because nothing about the proposed system is hardware-specific.

Usability. The presented capability system is "simple", as well as the development of highly accessible applications that can mange rights through tokens (as crypto-currency *wallets* for mobile devices already do); this makes the proposed solution *user-friendly*. A high-level interface could allow everyone to manage the access-control rules of her own device.

4   Implementation

We dedicate this section to the presentation of our proof-of-concept, by using Hyperledger Sawtooth as the blockchain where to implement a CapBAC ACM. Ad-hoc blockchains could be envisioned in the future, for instance achieving untraceability (see Sect. 3.2), or fully exploiting cryptographic primitives of resource-constrained devices, typical of the IoT. However, the following implementation paves the way to such solutions, proving their feasibility.

We use the ledger state to represent the issued capability tokens, while the policies are enforced during blocks validations. The implementation runs in a *Docker*[7] using *Ubuntu* images on a 64bit architecture, thus it is not directly meant for constrained devices, but it is anyhow useful for a proof-of-concept. All the developed source code was committed to a *GitHub* repository[8].

---

[7] Docker.com: https://www.docker.com/.

[8] Proof-of-concept project: https://github.com/kappanneo/sawtooth-capbac.

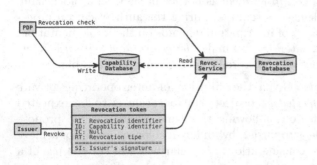

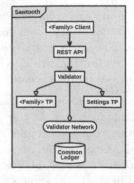

Fig. 2. CapBAC model: a visual description of the capability and revocation databases, and revocation service.

Fig. 3. A Sawtooth node with a custom transaction family.

Transaction Families. In Sawtooth it is possible to build a custom service on top of the pre-built blockchain architecture by defining a so called *Transaction Family (TF)*. This is possible because the core system is detached from the application layer. The main component of a TF is the *Transaction Processor (TP)* which, as the name suggests, is where the evaluation of incoming transactions is performed, according to the built-in rule-set (in a smart contract) written in one of the supported programming languages. More TPs can be attached to the same *validator*, which is a node in the peer-to-peer validator network responsible for maintaining the common ledger. For example, Sawtooth provides a TF for managing the settings saved in-state (including the ones used by the consensus module); its TP is always required on the side of all the others. Each TP has an addressing space in the ledger state for storing its information usually obtained from the family name itself. Between the validator and the client resides the *REST API*, also offered by Sawtooth, which manages the incoming requests. To be noted is the fact that Sawtooth allows the transmission of any kind of data format and encoding; the only requirement is that every participant to the network has to sign in with an *RSA* key pair in order to send transactions. Multiple transaction requests are encapsulated in a transaction batch (also signed), which is atomically validated (a single faulty transaction will cause the batch to be rejected). When a batch is accepted, the ledger state is modified accordingly to the transactions it contains. It is also possible to generate custom events that spread through the network and can be listened by any client aware of the specific transaction family from which they are generated. Figure 3 shows the relations between the various component: the validator is the main component, since it evaluates transaction requests forwarded from the REST API. It has a TP as additional module, and it behaves as a peer in the peer-to-peer validator network, which shares the same *Common Ledger*.

4.1 A New Transaction Family for CapBAC

We now describe the operations implemented by the new TF developed in Sawtooth. These operations can be performed by any client, where "client" is a software module that receives and executes commands in any peer of the network. The CapBAC transaction family allows users to issue and revoke capability tokens in which access rights for a particular resource are given to a specific subject. Since the tokens are stored in the ledger state, both issuing and revoking steps require a transaction request, sent to the validator and processed by the TP. A CapBAC client can also list the tokens stored in the current state for a specific device, sign an access token composed of a resource request and a capability id, and, finally, validate it over the ledger state. The client can be used from the command line with the following syntax:

```
list <device URI>
issue [--root] <not-signed capability token as JSON string>
revoke <not-signed revocation token as JSON string>
sign <not-signed access token as JSON string> .
validate <access token as JSON string>
```

State. Capability tokens are stored in-state in a *Concise Binary Object Representation* (*CBOR*) [4] encoded dictionary. The format in which they are stored is different from the one used for the issuing and as transaction payload, since the processor removes the fields that are not necessary anymore after validation, and it reformats the access rights to let the validation of access tokens be more efficient. In this scenario, the information contained in the ledger is already tamper-proof, thus there is no need for the token to be stored as it is: the state is obtained as a consequence of the whole transaction history and transactions are the ones to be stored as-they-are for validation purposes, so the signature for the capability tokens is no longer required; this is one of the main differences between an implementation of the model on top of the state of a new-generation blockchain, versus the use of ad-hoc blockchains where transactions themselves would represent capability tokens, hence without the need of a ledger state. For the same reason, the revocation tokens are not saved, but the state is changed according their content instead, just by removing revoked tokens. Since the global state is obtained as the result of the whole transaction history, it is always possible to inspect it in order to recover previously revoked tokens.

Addressing. CapBAC data is stored in the state dictionary using addresses that are generated from *(i)* the CapBAC name-space prefix, and *(ii)* the unique *URI* of the device. The latter is also the parameter passed to the list command, and one of the attributes of the JSON entry of the other commands ("DE" in the examples shown in Fig. 6), so that they all refer to the same address in the ledger state. The choice of a *per-device* addressing has many advantages: the whole capability token tree for a device is under the same address: neither a request has to include a reference to all the capabilities in the delegation chain, nor the validator has to search for them across the whole state. The address for the whole tree is the only input and output of the transaction, hence meaning that is by-design impossible to change access data for a device different from the one reported in a transaction. The URI of devices does not need to be explicitly saved in the state, thus it is removed to increase privacy. URIs are by definition unique: they will not cause name conflicts, while token identifiers can be reused for different devices. Addresses adhere to the following format:

- an address is a 70 character hexadecimal-string;
- the first 6 characters of the address are the first 6 characters of an *SHA512* hash of the CapBAC name-space prefix: `capbac`;
- the following 64 characters of the address are the last 64 characters of an `SHA512` hash of the device URI.

Transaction Payload. The payload is an object encoded in CBOR with two fields: the name of the action performed, and the corresponding token as object. As already said, the commands `capbac issue` and `capbac revoke` are the only ones that can be used to create and send transactions. Therefore, the object of the payload has only two possible formats: one for the capability, and one for the revocation token. The parameters of the transaction header are: the *inputs and outputs* (the address generated using the device URI), the *dependencies* (in our case `None` since our transaction family does not depend on any other transaction family), the *family name* (i.e., `capbac` version: 1.0), and the *encoding* (the encoding field needs to be set to `application/cbor`).

Execution. As shown in Fig. 4, when the TP receives a transaction it first checks the formal validity of the payload, including the specific token format in relation to the proposed action. In case of the `issue` command, also the logical validity of the time interval is checked. Finally, the signature is verified and the state is retrieved.

If the transaction is created for issuing a token, first the TP checks if a token with the same ID is not already in the state, and if the issuer is the owner of the parent capability; then, the token is reformatted to match the in-state representation and its validity is tested over the delegation chain, by checking at each step that all the access rights are included in the parent token, the delegation for each is allowed and the token is not expired. If all the delegation chain is valid up to the root capability, the token is added to the state.

If the transaction is due to the revocation of a token, then the authorisation of the requester is checked by also verifying that the revoker's capability is an ancestor of the revoked one. If the operation is valid, then the tokens are removed according to the revocation type. Finally, the signature of the token is verified against the requester public key, and the state is updated.

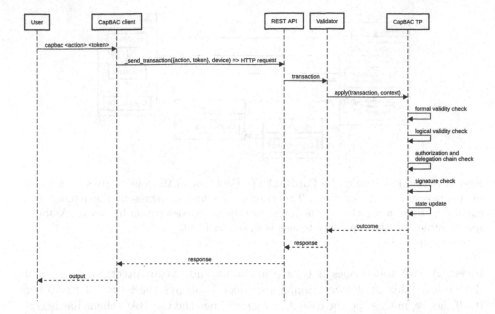

Fig. 4. The sequence diagram for the issuing or revocation of capabilities: the two possible values for *action* are `issue` and `revoke`, while *token* can respectively be a capability or a revocation token.

4.2 Testing Environment

Our implementation features a testing environment that can be assembled by using *Docker Compose*, a tool for defining and running multi-container Docker applications: we build a container for each actor in the scenario shown in Fig. 5. The REST API and validator both run in two separate containers assembled from the images offered by Sawtooth. This set-up can be used to test the functioning the introduced TF within a single node. Indeed, the same Docker images can be used to create a more complex network composed of multiple nodes. Scalability tests will be part of future work, also because we primarily believe in the development of an ad-hoc blockchain, and Sawtooth is used as a proof-of-concept towards this ultimate goal.

Issuing of a Capability Token. Tokens are issued using the `issue` command with an incomplete capability token (as the ones shown in Fig. 6) as parameter. An example of capability issuing is the one automatically performed by *device* before starting the *CoAP* server[9]. For testing purposes, the two resources *device* will open to requests are *(i)* `time` (the actual time on the machine) and *(ii)* `resource` (a re-writable string with no meaning). Since it is the first token to be issued under the address space for the URI `coap://device`, the token will be a root

---

[9] The *Constrained Application Protocol* [18], is the IoT standard transfer-protocol at the application layer, and it is based on the same RESTful principles as HTTP.

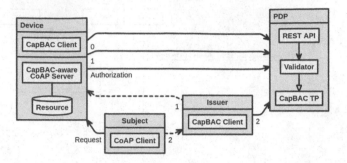

Fig. 5. A testing scenario of a CapBAC TF. Each one of the four entities is executed in a different Docker container. The numbered relations represent the issuing of a capability token and, when dashed, the corresponding delegation hierarchy. A JSON representation of the capability tokens is shown in Fig. 6.

token. A root token does not have a parent and, as architectural constraint desirable in this implementation, its subject is always the issuer of the token itself: hence, in this specific case it is *device*. Since the CapBAC client has access to the public key of the issuer of the token, the subject field is automatically filled in before signing the token, and the parent capability is set to `null`. The signing procedure also adds the TF version (1.0) and a timestamp, required for a signature to be unique. If a given token is not a root token, then also the parent capability needs to be specified. After a token is assembled, it is set as the object of a transaction payload, with action set to `issue`; then, it is sent to the validator through the REST API.

Delegation. The owner of a capability token can delegate to someone else any of the access rights it is granted, only if their *delegation depth* (DD) is greater than zero. This is done by issuing a new capability token for the same device that refers to her capability, also known as *issuer's capability* (IC) or *parent capability*, and listing a subset of those access rights. Moreover, in the access rights of the new token, the DD of each resource has to be strictly less than the one in the parent token. If this condition is not satisfied, then a token is invalidated by the TP, and the corresponding transaction is discarded by the validator. If the *device* now wants to delegate all its access rights to *issuer*, *device* can do so by using `issue` with a capability token formatted as the second one shown in Fig. 6. In the same way, if *issuer* wants to give to *subject* some access rights from the ones she also has, but without granting the possibility to delegate them any further, *issuer* can issue a capability token as the third one from the right in Fig. 6.

Accessing to a Resource. Once in possession of a capability token, *subject* can access to a resource on *device* by sending a CoAP request with an access token as a prefix to its payload. When *device* receives this request, first it checks that the access token matches the request itself, then it passes the token to `validate`. It searches for the referred capability in the ledger state, also *climbing* the delegation chain up to the root token. If the access token refers to a valid

```json
{
    "ID":"0000000000000000",
    "DE": "coap://device",
    "AR": [{
        "AC": "GET",
        "RE": "time",
        "DD": 100
    }, {
        "AC": "GET",
        "RE": "resource",
        "DD": 100
    }, {
        "AC": "PUT",
        "RE": "resource",
        "DD": 100
    }],
    "NB": str(int(time.time())),
    "NA": "2000000000"
}
```

```json
{
    "ID": "0000000000000001",
    "DE": "coap://device",
    "AR": [{
        "AC": "GET",
        "RE": "time",
        "DD": 99
    }, {
        "AC": "GET",
        "RE": "resource",
        "DD": 99
    }, {
        "AC": "PUT",
        "RE": "resource",
        "DD": 99
    }],
    "NB": "1525691114",
    "NA": "1540691114",
    "IC": "0000000000000000",
    "SU": <public key of issuer>
}
```

```json
{
    "ID": "0000000000000002",
    "DE": "coap://device",
    "AR": [{
        "AC": "GET",
        "RE": "resource",
        "DD": 0
    }, {
        "AC": "PUT",
        "RE": "resource",
        "DD": 0
    }],
    "NB": "1525691114",
    "NA": "1540691114",
    "IC": "0000000000000001",
    "SU": <public key of subject>
}
```

Fig. 6. An example of a delegation chain showing the JSONs used during the issuing of the respective capability tokens. The leftmost one is for a root capability. Following the same delegation relations shown in Fig. 1, both 1st and 2nd capabilities (from the right) are issued by the *device*, while the 3rd one by the *issuer*.

capability, then the operation requested by *subject* is performed. The whole access procedure is summarised in Fig. 7.

Revoking a Capability Token. At any time, an issued capability token can be revoked by its issuer or the issuer of an ancestor capability, i.e. a capability that is "higher" in the delegation chain of the revoked one. In our case this operation is performed via a **revoke** transaction including a revocation token in its payload. This transaction, as for the **issue** one, is built from an incomplete token, and it is completed by the CapBAC client. The revocation type (i.e., RT) field specifies the type of revocation, and it can be one of the following:

- **ICO** (Identified Capability Only): it revokes only the capability identified in the revocation;
- **DCO** (Descendant Capabilities Only): it revokes all the descendants of the identified capability;
- **ALL**: it revokes the identified capability and all its descendants.

5   Related Work

In order to overcome the problems related to ABAC and RBAC concerning scalability and flexibility, a CapBAC model is proposed in [7] with a focus on IoT. It offers revocation, delegation support, and granularity of the access rights. It is meant to be easy to understand and to use, removing the burden represented by the management of identities. Also, by design, it enforces the *Least Privilege* principle, i.e., only the rights strictly necessary are granted, so that abuses are not possible. However, it does not specify how the issuing of tokens could be

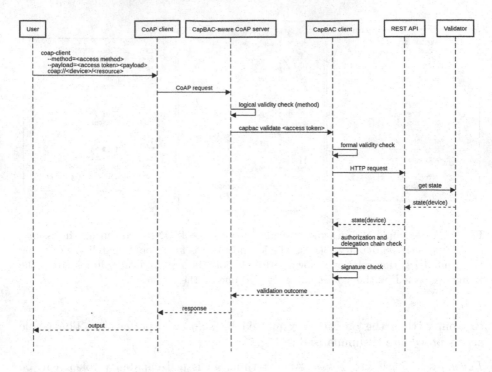

Fig. 7. A sequence diagram of scenario where a user want to access to a resource.

enforced and it is based on the *RSA* encryption scheme [17] for authentication, which is not supported by constrained devices, typical of the IoT world.

In [9], a distributed CapBAC is presented as DCapBAC. Compared to [7] it does not offer neither delegation nor revocation since the focus of the paper is the authentication through "Elliptic Curve Cryptography" (*ECC*), i.e. a public-key crypto-system compatible with constrained devices. Other improvements are the use of *JSON* as data format for the tokens, and the use of the *Constrained Application Protocol* (*CoAP*) [18], recently announced as the standard transfer protocol at the application layer for IoT, and based on the same RESTful principles as HTTP. As in [7], the generation of tokens is not discussed.

In [12] the authors propose a blockchain technology to publish the policies expressing the right to access a resource and to allow the distributed transfer of such rights among users. They take advantage of Attribute-Based Access Control (ABAC) policies. However, their proof-of-concept implementation is based on the Bitcoin blockchain (quite limited on the application side), which cannot handle smart contracts (as Sawtooth can instead do), and thus the actual authorisation system is external to the blockchain, which only stores tokens. Indeed, not having the authorisation logic on the blockchain is a critical point.

In [19] a blockchain access control ecosystem is implemented with *Hyperledger Fabric*; the Hyperledger composer modelling tool is used to implement the smart contracts or transaction processing functions that run on the blockchain network.

The authors adopt a RBAC-based scheme: users are assigned roles and roles are assigned privileges controlled by asset owners. A smart contract is triggered to pull the roles that have access to that asset. As advanced in Sect. 3, we believe that a simple scheme (as CapBAC) with no super-entity keeps the model more secure and scalable, particularly if the architecture is IoT-oriented.

In [1] an implementation of a token-based ACM on top of a private Ethereum blockchain network is showcased, featuring a *Proof of Possession* (*PoP*) consensus protocol, to bind the client's identity to an access token. The focus is on the feasibility of the blockchain architecture: neither the token format nor the access control model are described in details. However, this is not a limitation since the Ethereum's smart contract language allows for any access control rule to be described so that the proposed solution can potentially express any ACM.

Two other IoT-related ACMs are presented in [14] and [20]. The former proposes a private blockchain for managing *Identity and Access Management*, while the latter advances a proof-of-concept prototype implemented on both resources-constrained devices, tested on a local private blockchain network.

6   Conclusion and Future Work

The aim of this paper was to propose the use of CapBAC revitalised by managing capabilities for heterogeneous and light devices with a blockchain. The ultimate purpose is to secure the IoT with a scalable and decentralised implementation that takes advantage of an underlying blockchain-based architecture. Most features of CapBAC, as for instance its simplicity and fine-grainess, smoothly adapt to a distributed ledger, which on the other hand enforces trust in a naturally unsafe environment as the IoT. We have discussed the features of the proposed system along with its problems (and possible solutions to them). Finally, we showcased an implementation realised by exploiting the transaction families of Hyperledger Sawtooth, in order to show that the mapping from the proposed model to a real blockchain-based architecture is possible.

A possible continuation of this work could be the implementation of a capability-based access control solution using a new, memory-efficient and multipurpose private blockchain as proposed in [1], and featuring a lightweight public key encryption system (like what used also in [9]). Actually, different blockchains could implement this model, at different levels and for different scenarios, inter-operating to form a wide system in which authorisation decisions are taken thanks to a distributed effort. One of these technologies could even be a blockchain with the only purpose of managing accesses, in which the object of transactions are capability tokens and the validation operation is light enough to reach even the most constrained devices.

OAuth [8] is the standard currently proposed for authorisation frameworks, and it is also based on delegable tokens. However, it inherits the centralised approach from its previous version, and so it requires a trusted third-party in order to work. We leave a possible integration of OAuth with the model proposed in this paper as future work.

Acknowledgment. This research is supported by project "REMIX" (funded by Banca d'Italia and Fondazione Cassa di Risparmio di Perugia).

References

1. Alphand, O., et al.: IoTChain: a blockchain security architecture for the internet of things. In: IEEE Wireless Communications and Networking Conference, Murcia, 30100, Spain (2018). Technical report
2. Ashton, K., et al.: That 'internet of things' thing. RFID J. **22**(7), 97–114 (2009)
3. Bernabe, J., Ramos, J.H., Gomez, A.S.: TACIoT: multidimensional trust-aware access control system for the internet of things. Soft Comput. **20**, 1763–1779 (2015)
4. Bormann, C., Hoffman, P.: Concise binary object representation (CBOR). IETF RFC 7049 (2013)
5. Dinh, T.T.A., Liu, R., Zhang, M., Chen, G., Ooi, B.C., Wang, J.: Untangling blockchain: a data processing view of blockchain systems. IEEE Trans. Knowl. Data Eng. **30**(7), 1366–1385 (2018)
6. Ferraiolo, D., Kuhn, D.: Role-based access control. In: 15th National Computer Security Conference, pp. 554–563 (1992)
7. Gusmeroli, S., Piccione, S., Rotondi, D.: A capability-based security approach to manage access control in the internet of things. Math. Comput. Model. **58**, 1189–1205 (2013)
8. Hardt, D.: The oauth 2.0 authorization framework. RFC 6749, RFC Editor, October 2012. http://www.rfc-editor.org/rfc/rfc6749.txt
9. Hernàndez-Ramos, J., Jara, A., Marín, L., Gómez, A.S.: DCapBAC: embedding authorization logic into smart things through ECC optimizations (2016)
10. Hu, V.C., et al.: Guide to attribute based access control (ABAC) definition and considerations (draft). NIST special publication **800**(162) (2013)
11. Kalam, A.A.E., et al.: Organization based access control. In: 4th IEEE International Workshop on Policies for Distributed Systems and Networks (POLICY), p. 120. IEEE Computer Society (2003)
12. Di Francesco Maesa, D., Mori, P., Ricci, L.: Blockchain based access control. In: Chen, L.Y., Reiser, H.P. (eds.) DAIS 2017. LNCS, vol. 10320, pp. 206–220. Springer, Cham (2017). https://doi.org/10.1007/978-3-319-59665-5_15
13. Nakamoto, S.: Bitcoin: a peer-to-peer electronic cash system (2009)
14. Nuss, M., Puchta, A., Kunz, M.: Towards blockchain-based identity and access management for internet of things in enterprises. In: Furnell, S., Mouratidis, H., Pernul, G. (eds.) TrustBus 2018. LNCS, vol. 11033, pp. 167–181. Springer, Cham (2018). https://doi.org/10.1007/978-3-319-98385-1_12
15. Ouaddah, A., Mousannif, H., Elkalam, A., Ouahman, A.: Access control in the internet of things: big challenges and new opportunities. Comput. Netw. **112**, 237–262 (2016)
16. Pfitzmann, A., Köhntopp, M.: Anonymity, unobservability, and pseudonymity—a proposal for terminology. In: Federrath, H. (ed.) Designing Privacy Enhancing Technologies. LNCS, vol. 2009, pp. 1–9. Springer, Heidelberg (2001). https://doi.org/10.1007/3-540-44702-4_1
17. Rivest, R.L., Shamir, A., Adleman, L.M.: A method for obtaining digital signatures and public-key cryptosystems. Commun. ACM **21**(2), 120–126 (1978)

18. Shelby, Z., Hartke, K., Bormann, C.: The constrained application protocol (CoAP). IETF RFC 7252 10 (2014)
19. Uchibeke, U.U., Kassani, S.H., Schneider, K.A., Deters, R.: Blockchain access control ecosystem for big data security. CoRR abs/1810.04607 (2018)
20. Xu, R., Chen, Y., Blasch, E., Chen, G.: BlendCAC: a smart contract enabled decentralized capability-based access control mechanism for the IoT. Computers **7**(3), 39 (2018)

Developing Secure Services for IoT with OP-TEE: A First Look at Performance and Usability

Christian Göttel(✉) ⓘ, Pascal Felber ⓘ, and Valerio Schiavoni ⓘ

University of Neuchâtel, Neuchâtel, Switzerland
{christian.gottel,pascal.felber,valerio.schiavoni}@unine.ch

Abstract. The implementation, deployment and testing of secure services for Internet of Things devices is nowadays still at an early stage. Several frameworks have recently emerged to help developers realize such services, abstracting the complexity of the many types of underlying hardware platforms and software libraries. Assessing the performance and usability of a given framework remains challenging, as they are largely influenced by the application and workload considered, as well as the target hardware. Since 15 years, ARM processors are providing support for TRUSTZONE, a set of security instructions that realize a trusted execution environment inside the processor. OP-TEE is a free-software framework to implement trusted applications and services for TRUSTZONE. In this short paper we show how one can leverage OP-TEE for implementing a secure service (*i.e.*, a key-value store). We deploy and evaluate the performance of this trusted service on common Raspberry Pi hardware platforms.

We report our experimental results with the data store and also compare it against OP-TEE's built-in secure storage.

Keywords: OP-TEE · ARM TRUSTZONE · Secure storage · IoT

1 Introduction

Despite the availability of security-oriented instruction sets in consumer-grade processors, high-level frameworks that can help developers use such extensions are still at an early stage. Moreover, little has been said regarding the performance and usability of these frameworks. This is unfortunate given that the large majority of devices featuring ARM processors (mobile and not) feature the TRUSTZONE extensions, introduced since 15 years [12], and are constantly being improved with new processor revisions. For instance, ARM recently [4] updated its ARMv8.4 architecture of application processors enabling virtualization in the secure world. The introduction of virtualization in the secure world better improves the isolation of components and resources, and it is expected to

© IFIP International Federation for Information Processing 2019
Published by Springer Nature Switzerland AG 2019
J. Pereira and L. Ricci (Eds.): DAIS 2019, LNCS 11534, pp. 170–178, 2019.
https://doi.org/10.1007/978-3-030-22496-7_11

boost the trusted applications (TA) ecosystem in developing and using common standards and APIs.

It is only very recently that the first open-source tools aiming to exploit these capabilities have emerged. Notable examples include Linaro ARM Trusted Firmware [14], ARM GNU Toolchain [1], Android's Trusty [11], Trustonic's Kinibi [21], NVIDIA's TLK [18] and finally Linaro's OP-TEE [17].

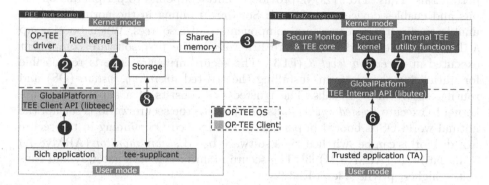

Fig. 1. Organization of components within TRUSTZONE and interaction with OP-TEE

A major challenge for developers of trusted applications resides in the complexity of the secure platforms themselves. Despite the existence of standards and APIs, trusted applications remain OS-specific because of the custom libraries provided by the different vendors. Theses libraries are specialized for the various processors and are required to access secure storage and processing elements. They rely on drivers shipped with the hardware by the silicon manufacturer. Furthermore, dispatching trusted OSs requires trusted OS-specific code in the firmware, which adds up to the issue. This greatly hinders the portability of trusted applications across different trusted OSs and, as consequence, forces TA developers toward implementing and supporting several versions of trusted OS-specific TAs.

In this paper, we focus on a specific framework, OP-TEE [17], which has gained much attention recently and is arguably the most mature open-source framework for developing trusted application with ARM's TRUSTZONE extensions. We describe its architecture and features, and we evaluate its usability and performance by developing a simple key-value store. Such a key-value store could be used to implement a secure password manager, or a secure session manager protecting session data. We also execute OP-TEE's secure storage benchmark and report our results. This preliminary study brings insights into the benefits of such framework, and in particular how it is able to hide the complexity of the underlying vendor-specific libraries and processor, as well as their performance and overhead.

2   Background

2.1   TrustZone in a Nutshell

The TRUSTZONE technology is available in ARM processors since 2003 [4]. It is a hardware-enforced mechanism isolating a *secure world* (trusted) from a *normal world* (untrusted), which includes all components within the SoC as well as peripherals. Thus, TRUSTZONE provides secure endpoints to peripherals on the bus and enables device root-of-trust. Software running in the normal world is unable to directly access secure components and resources. When booting up a TRUSTZONE-enabled SoC, secure firmware is the first software component executed at *exception level 3* (EL3). The secure firmware code is responsible for initializing the platform, installing the trusted *operating system* (OS) and routing secure monitor calls. The trusted OS consists of a small and secure kernel to execute *trusted applications* (TA). Once the secure world is set up, the normal world OS is booted in parallel to the trusted OS running in the secure world. Worlds can be switched via a software-based *secure monitor* (ARMv8-A) or in hardware (ARMv8-M) [3]. The secure monitor acts as a gateway and runs at the highest privilege level EL3 [2].

Table 1. Comparison of platforms

Device	QEMU	Raspberry
CPU	Intel Xeon E3-1270 v6	Broadcom BCM2837
CPU Frequency	3.8 GHz	1.2 GHz
Memory	63 GiB DDR4	944 MiB LPDDR2
Memory data rate	2400 MT/s	800 MT/s
Disk	Samsung MZ7KM480HMHQ0D3	Transcend micro SDHC UHI-I Premium
Disk Size	480 GB	16 GB
Disk Read Speed	528.33 MB/s	90 MB/s

2.2   The GlobalPlatform Specifications for TEEs

The main specifications for secure digital services and devices are published by industry associations [10,20]. In our study, we focus on the GLOBALPLATFORM specifications for TRUSTZONE. A *rich execution environment* (REE) is an execution environment that involves at least one device and all its components or an OS, excluding any trusted or secure component. In contrast, a *trusted execution environment* (TEE) provides a level of security to protect against attacks and secures data access. The TEE executes alongside the REE, but is shielded from it. A trusted application executes inside a TEE and exposes secure services to applications in the REE. *Trusted storage* is a hardware or cryptographically-protected device capable of storing data [9]. Data can be exchanged between an application in the REE and a TA by three types of shared memory: *whole* (an entire memory region and is allocated by the TEE), *partial* (only a subset of the *whole* with a specified offset), and *temporarily*, for which a memory buffer region allocate by the application in the REE temporarily shared with the TA for the duration of the API call [7].

2.3 The OP-TEE Framework

OP-TEE [17] is a TEE implementation of GLOBALPLATFORM specifications on top of TRUSTZONE. It can be used alongside a Linux-based distribution running in the REE. TAs are single-threaded executables stored inside the REE. Users develop TAs without having to recompile the entire framework. However, OP-TEE does not provide mechanisms to verify the integrity of a TA. TAs, that do not origin from a secure storage, can compromise the integrity or protection of the TEE upon modification. Alternatively, TAs can be directly integrated into OP-TEE as *pseudo TAs*. Pseudo TAs run inside OP-TEE OS' kernel (at secure EL1) as secure privileged-level services without access to GLOBALPLATFORM's Internal Core API. Thus, pseudo TAs can only use OP-TEE's core Internal API.

Secure storage allows applications to offload data from a TA to either the REE file system or a *replay protected memory block* (RPMB) partition of an *embedded multi-media controller* (eMMC) device using the Internal Core API. By default, the OP-TEE OS is configured to use the RPMB [16] if available. The secure storage is accessible and visible only to the TA that created it.

3 Usability

The communication between an application in the normal world and a TA evolves around functions handling the context, session, command and shared memory as shown in Fig. 1. This facilitates interoperability between different GLOBALPLATFORM API compatible TEE implementations and allows REE applications to set up multiple contexts. A context is initialized by referencing the device file Fig. 1-❶ connecting to the TEE driver Fig. 1-❷. TAs are identified by a *universally unique identifier* (UUID), which is referred to when setting up a session to a TA Fig. 1-❸. To set up a session, OP-TEE will load the TA from the normal world to the secure world with the help of `tee-supplicant` Fig. 1-❹. The `tee-supplicant` is a daemon running in the normal world used by OP-TEE to request services from the REE. These steps are skipped when a session to a pseudo TA is established. A TA can initialize and set up its environment upon TA creation and session establishment (Fig. 1-❺ and -❻). From this point on, the REE application can request services from the TA by invoking commands. These commands can pass up to four parameters, which are either values or references to shared memory regions. Values are pairs of unsigned 32 bit integers. Shared memory regions are allocated, registered and released through GLOBALPLATFORM API calls in `libteec`. Without the availability of `libteec`, developers would have to communicate directly with the kernel driver through `ioctl` system calls.

In OP-TEE, TAs can use services accessible through GLOBALPLATFORM Internal Core API Fig. 1-❻ implemented in `libutee`. TAs are statically linked against `libutee`, which wrapps the API functions around assembler macros to OP-TEE OS system calls. The library provides interfaces to secure storage Fig. 1-❽, time, arithmetic and cryptographic operations Fig. 1-❼. The secure storage API encrypts data objects by the use of a secure storage service. The encryption process involves three keys: *secure storage key* (SSK), *trusted application storage key* (TSK) and *file encryption key*. The SSK is generated from the *hardware unique key* and is used to derive TSKs. Each TA has a TSK that is generated from the SSK and the TA's UUID. Both SSK and TSK are generated using HMAC SHA256 algorithm [16]. Finally, for every created file, a *file encryption key* (FEK) is generated from the pseudo random number generator. The encrypted data objects are then transferred to the `tee-supplicant` by a series of remote procedure calls and stored in a special file. OP-TEE further provides TAs with libraries for TLS and SSL protocols (`libmbedtls` [5]), arithmetic (`libmpa`) and a subset of ISO C functions (`libutils`). These libraries are used in part by OP-TEE to implement GLOBALPLATFORM's Internal Core APIs, in particular the *Arithmetical API* and the *Cryptographic Operations API*. Without these libraries, TA developers would have to provide this code, and they would not be able to just simply link their TA's code against this set of initial libraries. Once the REE application has no further service requests, the session is terminated and the context is destroyed.

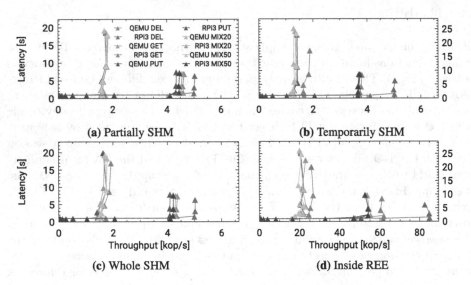

Fig. 2. Throughput-latency plots of shared memory types for key-value TA in TEE and REE

4 Performance Evaluation

4.1 Setup

The OP-TEE framework has built-in support for QEMU [6] deployments, which provides an easy to use and inexpensive way for developers to explore ARM TRUSTZONE, with little to no downsides compared to hardware deployments. For this reason, we decided to deploy the key-value store and OP-TEE's Sanity Testsuite v3.2.0 [15] on the following two platforms: Dell PowerEdge R330 Server and Raspberry Pi 3B v1.2. The Dell PowerEdge R330 is running Ubuntu 18.04.1 LTS with the 4.15.0-43-generic Linux kernel and is used to emulate the Raspberry Pi 3B platform with QEMU v2.12.0. A comparison of the two platforms can be found in Table 1. OP-TEE provides a build environment which, by default, deploys and emulates its OS on an ARM Virtual Machine `virt` using a Cortex-A57 with no more than two cores. The deployment was changed to match the specification of the Raspberry Pi 3B platform as close as possible.

4.2 Shared Memory

We have ported a simple key-value store to a TA, in order to evaluate the overhead and performance of different types of shared memory. As basis, we use a modified version of the hash table implementation of `kazlib` v1.20 [13], removing support for contexts and dynamic tables. The hash table is static, uses separate chaining to resolve collisions, applies a modular hashing and has 251 chains. We time every `DEL` (delete), `GET` and `PUT` operation for each benchmark by referring to `CLOCK_MONOTONIC` in the REE. Operations are uniformly distributed and issued 256 times at a rate of 1 to 32768 operations per second.

When using whole or partially shared memory introduced in Sect. 2.2, the REE application requests a shared memory region of 512 KiB and fills it with random data from `/dev/urandom`. Similarly, the REE application allocates and initializes a 512 KiB buffer used as temporarily shared memory. Before every invocation of a key-value operation, a random offset into the shared memory region is computed, which is also used as key. A chunk size of 1 KiB beginning at the random offset is used as data object. The `PUT` benchmark starts with an empty hash table. The `DEL` and `GET` benchmarks start with a pre-populated hash table of 256 data objects. Finally, the mixed benchmark (ratio of `GET` and `PUT` operations) begins with a pre-populated hash table relative to the percentage of `GET` operations.

Figure 2 shows throughput and latency for the different shared memory types and for running the key-value store entirely in the REE. On the QEMU platform, the operations do not separate as well as on the Raspberry platform; we assume due to reaching an I/O bound. The operations on the Raspberry platform separate as expected according to their throughput (lowest to highest): `PUT`, `MIX50`, `MIX20`, `GET`, and `DEL`. The overhead of the `PUT` operation is due to memory allocation, memory copy and object insertion. The `GET` operation looks up a data object and copies it to shared memory, resulting in a lower overhead.

The higher the portion of PUT operations in the MIX benchmarks is, the slower the average operation speed becomes. Thus, MIX50 (50% PUT operations) has a lower average throughput than MIX20. The DEL operation looks up a data object and frees its memory, avoiding time consuming memory operations. Comparing TEE throughput against REE throughput yields a 12 to 14 × overhead on the QEMU platform and a 12 to 17 × overhead on the Raspberry platform. A similar experiment was conducted in [19], where they compared the time spend in normal and secure world when invoking a noop operation.

4.3 Secure Storage

The secure storage benchmark is part of the OP-TEE sanity test suite adhering to the *Trusted Storage API for Data and Keys* described in [8]. Neither of the platforms is equipped with an eMMC, for which reason the secure storage has to be offloaded to the REE file system. The benchmark executes three commands WRITE, READ, and REWRITE, for data sizes in the range of 256 B to 1 MiB, that are accessed in chunks of at most 1 KiB. The REWRITE command first reads data from an object, resets the cursor and writes the data back to the same object. The data to be stored in the secure storage is allocated and filled with scrambled data within the TEE.

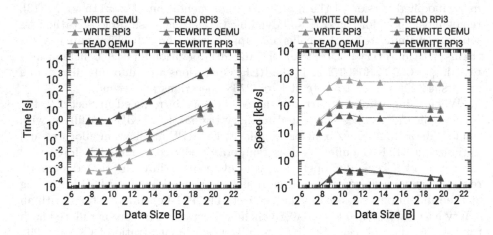

Fig. 3. Secure storage benchmark execution time and throughput

Figure 3 shows the overhead of accessing data in chunks of 1 KiB in the secure storage. In general, the overhead becomes more significant with increasing data sizes, more precisely once the data size exceeds the chunk size. Maximum speed is achieved when the data size equals the chunk size. Overall, the REWRITE command has the highest overhead, because it basically executes the READ and WRITE commands in one batch.

5   Concluding Remarks

Development of secure services benefits from well established APIs and standards. OP-TEE has implemented several of GLOBALPLATFORM's specifications and APIs and provides common interfaces for secure services. We have ported a simple key-value store to a TA and we have studied the performance and usability of secure storage and shared memory. The results of our benchmarks have shown that requesting services from TAs in TRUSTZONE on ARMv8-A using OP-TEE incurs a significant overhead compared to service execution in the normal world. Limiting the space available to a TA is sensible, in order to minimize the trusted computing base. However, the default memory limit of 1 MiB for TAs in OP-TEE becomes a major inconvenience with respect to secure storage and shared memory.

Generating the SSK in OP-TEE requires the HUK. However, most platforms lack of documentation to access or obtain the HUK. OP-TEE avoids this issue by considering a static string value instead of the HUK. This alternative can potentially weaken the cryptographic protection of the objects stored in the REE file system of the secure storage. TEEs would greatly benefit from unrestricted access to HUKs and could so improve the protection of trusted storage.

We expect the trusted application ecosystem to improve portability of TAs among TEEs. Furthermore, we hope that our evaluation of usability and performance of TAs provides deeper insight into future development of trusted services.

Acknowledgments. The research leading to these results has received funding from the European Union's Horizon 2020 research and innovation programme under the LEGaTO Project (legato-project.eu), grant agreement No. 780681.

References

1. Arm Limited: ARM GNU Toolchain. https://developer.arm.com/open-source/gnu-toolchain/gnu-a. Accessed 22 Feb 2019
2. Arm Limited: Fundamentals of ARMv8-A, March 2017. https://static.docs.arm.com/100878/0100/fundamentals_of_armv8_a_100878_0100_en.pdf. Accessed 22 Feb 2019
3. Arm Limited: Trustzone technology for the ARMv8-M architecture, March 2017. https://static.docs.arm.com/100690/0200/armv8m_trustzone_technology_100690_0200.pdf. Accessed 22 Feb 2019
4. Arm Limited: Isolation using virtualization in the secure world (2018). https://developer.arm.com/-/media/Files/pdf/Isolation_using_virtualization_in_the_Secure_World_Whitepaper.pdf?revision=c6050170-04b7-4727-8eb3-ee65dc52ded2. Accessed 22 Feb 2019
5. Arm Limited: mbed TLS, February 2019. https://tls.mbed.org. Accessed 22 Feb 2019
6. Bellard, F.: QEMU, January 2019. https://www.qemu.org. Accessed 22 Feb 2019
7. GlobalPlatform Inc.: TEE Client API Specification Version 1.0, July 2010, GPD_SPE_007

8. GlobalPlatform Inc.: TEE Internal Core API Specification Version 1.2, October 2018, GPD_SPE_010
9. GlobalPlatform Inc.: TEE System Architecture Version 1.2, November 2018, GPD_SPE_009
10. GlobalPlatform Inc.: GlobalPlatform Homepage, February 2019. https://globalplatform.org. Accessed 22 Feb 2019
11. Google LLC: Android Trusty, February 2019. https://source.android.com/security/trusty. Accessed 22 Feb 2019
12. HEXUS.net: ARM Everywhere. https://hexus.net/static/arm-everywhere/. Accessed 22 Feb 2019
13. Kylheku, K.: Kazlib, November 2000. http://www.kylheku.com/~kaz/kazlib.html. Accessed 22 Feb 2019
14. Linaro Limited: Linaro Trusted Firmware. https://www.linaro.org/engineering/projects/arm-trusted-firmware/. Accessed 22 Feb 2019
15. Linaro Limited: OP-TEE Sanity Testsuite, June 2018. https://github.com/OP-TEE/optee_test/tree/3.2.0. Accessed 22 Feb 2019
16. Linaro Limited: Secure Storage in OP-TEE, May 2018. https://github.com/OP-TEE/optee_os/blob/3.2.0/documentation/secure_storage.md. Accessed 22 Feb 2019
17. Linaro Limited: Open Portable Trusted Execution Environment, February 2019. https://www.op-tee.org. Accessed 22 Feb 2019
18. NVIDIA Corporation: TLK Repository, October 2015. http://nv-tegra.nvidia.com/gitweb/?p=3rdparty/ote_partner/tlk.git. Accessed 22 Feb 2019
19. Pettersen, R., Johansen, H.D., Johansen, D.: Secure edge computing with ARM TrustZone. In: Ramachandran, M., Muñoz, V.M., Kantere, V., Wills, G., Walters, R., Chang, V. (eds.) Proceedings of the 2nd International Conference on Internet of Things, Big Data and Security, vol. 1, pp. 102–109 (2017). https://doi.org/10.5220/0006308601020109
20. Trusted Computing Group, February 2019. https://trustedcomputinggroup.org. Accessed 22 Feb 2019
21. Trustonic: Trustonic Kinibi, February 2019. https://www.trustonic.com/markets/iot. Accessed 22 Feb 2019

Author Index

Printed in the United States
By Bookmasters